Victorian
Parlour Poetry

The boy stood on the burning deck
Whence all but he had fled.

—"Casabianca"

Victorian Parlour Poetry

An Annotated Anthology

EDITED BY
MICHAEL R. TURNER

DOVER PUBLICATIONS, INC., *New York*

PR
1223
.V5
1992

My thanks are due for permission to include copyright poems as follows:
to Mrs. George Bambridge and Macmillan & Co. Ltd. for "If—" by Rudyard Kipling from *Rewards and Fairies* and to Doubleday and Company,
Inc. (from *Rudyard Kipling's Verse*), Copyright 1910 by Rudyard Kipling; to Mr. Peter Newbolt for "Vitaï Lampada" and "Drake's Drum" by
Sir Henry Newbolt from *Poems New and Old*; to Routledge & Kegan
Paul Ltd. for "The Lifeboat," "In the Workhouse" and "Billy's Rose,"
all by George R. Sims; to A. & C. Black Ltd., Mrs. Frances L. Collins,
and Mrs. Ruth B. Sieley for "Solitude" and other excerpts from the poems
of Ella Wheeler Wilcox; to Methuen & Co. Ltd. for a stanza from "How
I Brought the Good News from Aix to Ghent (and Vice Versa)" by
R. J. Yeatman and W. C. Sellar from *Horse Nonsense*; to J. M. Dent &
Sons Ltd., and Little, Brown and Company for "The Calf" by Ogden
Nash from *Family Reunion*, Copyright 1935 by the Curtis Publishing Co.;
and to A. D. Peters & Co. for "A Lost Chord" by D. B. Wyndham Lewis.
Despite diligent inquiry I have not been able to trace the copyright holders
of one or two pieces by deceased authors, and to them I tender my apolo-
gies.

M.R.T.

Copyright © 1967, 1969 by Michael R. Turner.
All rights reserved under Pan American and International Copyright Conventions.

Published in Canada by General Publishing Company, Ltd., 30 Lesmill Road, Don
Mills, Toronto, Ontario.
Published in the United Kingdom by Constable and Company, Ltd., 3 The Lanches-
ters, 162–164 Fulham Palace Road, London W6 9ER.

This Dover edition, first published in 1992, is an unabridged and unaltered repub-
lication of the work originally published under the title *Parlour Poetry: A Casquet of
Gems,* The Viking Press, Inc., New York, 1969.

Manufactured in the United States of America
Dover Publications, Inc., 31 East 2nd Street, Mineola, N.Y. 11501

Library of Congress Cataloging-in-Publication Data

Victorian parlour poetry : an annotated anthology / edited by Michael R. Turner.
        p.   cm.
Originally published: Parlour poetry. New York : Viking Press, 1969.
Includes indexes.
ISBN 0-486-27044-0 (pbk.)
    1. English poetry—19th century. 2. American poetry—19th century. 3. Popu-
lar literature—Great Britain. 4. Popular literature—United States. I. Turner,
Michael R. II. Turner, Michael R. Parlour poetry.
PR1223.V5 1992
821'.808—dc20

                                                                    91-37613
                                                                    CIP

Preface

The gaslight hisses softly in a front parlour in late-nineteenth-century Brooklyn or the Bronx. Palm fronds sway gently to the strains of Schumann or Sullivan, tremble to the sonorous baritone rendition of "A Son of the Desert." A small boy, back as straight as a ramrod, buckled shoes together, pipes in an uncertain treble, "Casabianca by Mrs. Hemans the boy stood on the burning deck . . ." Around the corner on Main Street at the Majestic, Mr. DeWolf Hopper steps down to the footlights, glances up to the smoking loges, and begins, "The outlook wasn't brilliant for the Mudville nine that day. . . ."

Countless children committed poems of the highest moral rectitude to memory, poems with plain, easy rhythms, uncomplicated heroics, and unabashed pathos. Most people over the age of sixty can still recite chunks of them: these half-remembered scraps are the remnants of a curious verbal middle-class folk tradition. Today some are reduced to tags ('Tis Christmas Day in the workhouse . . .) or have a half life in parodies ('Tis the voice of the lobster . . .). Practically none of them, except a handful by the major nineteenth-century poets, are to be found in contemporary anthologies.

In these uneasy, cynical days we may look with nostalgia, with amusement not untinged, perhaps, with envy at the society that produced these verses. It appeared to have secure beliefs, even if the body was threatened by the most alarming ills. People, then as now, were cruel and selfish, poverty and misery were naggingly apparent, death was an obsession. Dying infants, starving paupers, wronged maidens, maimed soldiers, and sorrowing relatives are more numerous as dramatis personae of parlour poetry than requited lovers, bucolic rustics, and contented Christian households at family prayers. Typical victims

[v]

0

die for want of food ("In the Workhouse"), are frozen to death ("Excelsior," "The Mother in the Snow-Storm," "Billy's Rose"), freeze *and* drown ("The Wreck of the Hesperus"), are stabbed through the heart ("The Green Eye of the Yellow God"), are suffocated ("The Mistletoe Bough"), are eaten alive ("Bishop Hatto"), or are simply blown into tiny pieces ("Casabianca"). Disease, poverty, drink, senile decay, and heart-failure at the shock of being married to the wrong man account for a dozen more in this volume.*

The infant mortality, particularly, in any popular collection of verse published in the last century is startlingly high, even if one remembers that a child's life then was, in truth, precarious. The small protagonists of these poems toddle inevitably to the fate that awaits them in the final stanza; here is the conclusion of "Little Joe" by Peleg Arkwright:

> Here—wake up! Oh, don't look that way!
> Joe! My boy! Hold up yer head!
> Here's yer flowers—you dropped 'em, Joey!
> Oh, my God, can Joe be *dead?*

Indeed, he can. There seems to have been a minor but possibly quite lucrative poetic industry in the hymning of moribund babies. The tiny coffins of Little Billy, Little Willie, Little Bell and Little Nell, Little Jim and Little Joe, Little Wesley, Little Gottlieb, and Little Boy Blue are rivalled in number only by the frozen corpses of care-worn mothers who have perished in the snow. The summit of morbidity is reached with Felicia Hemans' lachrymose and all-embracing "The Graves of a Household":

> They grew in beauty, side by side,
> They filled one home with glee;—
> Their graves are severed, far and wide,
> By mount, and stream, and sea.

Disaster may lurk around every corner, but some things seem reassuringly safe; the ideals and framework of society are never questioned. God's in His Heaven, England and America in their rightful places—on top—simple moral values are universally accepted. Courage, honesty, tenderness, filial devotion, temperance, forbearance, endurance, charity, and, above all, hope: adhere to these touchstones of the Protestant ethic and, battered though you may be by the storms of this life, your reward awaits you in the Hereafter. It is this aura of

* The death-roll of *Parlour Poetry*, excluding the preface and notes, is thirty-nine men, women, and children, in addition to an unspecified number of soldiers, sailors, and German peasants, and two horses.

certainty and ultimate security of the spirit if not of the body that helps to give the lost world of late-nineteenth-century popular verse such nostalgic appeal today.

Extensive reading in this field produces, apart from a touch of literary indigestion, wonder at the persistence of certain themes. Again and again, the same situation is worked over with variations of setting and characters. The "Little Jim" syndrome has already been mentioned; let us examine another stock incident, the child saved from immolation beneath the hoofs of a horse or the wheels of some vehicle—the saviour often perishing in his noble act. In "Love, Sweet Love" (page 79) a father snatches his baby from the path of a runaway horse and dies in the attempt; in Eugene J. Hall's "The Engineer's Story" (page 104) the narrator finally marries the gritty lass who has saved a toddler from the wheels of his locomotive; in "A Fact," another father, another baby, and another railroad train—father and child survive; in "The Signal Box" by George R. Sims it is a mother who leaps to the rescue of her little son, Johnny, while her stationmaster husband naps in the signal box—all live to moralize upon the incident; in Frank L. Stanton's "The Printer's 'Devil,' Jim" the "devil," his editor's child, yet another train, and

> There in the dust and grime he lay—
> Jim! . . . he had given his life away!
> Not much need of their tears for him;
> "He was an angel—that boy, Jim!"

and, finally, in "The Coster's Kiddie," a Musical Monologue by W. Milton Thomson, the whole affair is brought right up to date with a speeding automobile robbed of its prey by a costermonger's daughter . . . at the cost of her life.

Other themes recur with some regularity: the lost seaman restored to his aged parents; the mother in the snow-storm; the gallant lad steadfast in perilous circumstances; the haughty but passionate Arab on his fiery stallion; the unprepossessing tough guy with a heart of gold; relics of mother such as Bibles, arm-chairs, and other domestic furniture; the messenger galloping urgent news from somewhere to somewhere else; moral exhortation of the "Never Give Up!" variety. These are a few examples from the pages of this collection. Some poems manage to combine several of them at once.

Most of the poems collected here belong to an oral tradition; they are remembered because they were recited or sung. Unlike true, anonymous folk poetry, however, nearly all of them appeared first in print with their authors' names or initials discreetly appended. Few of those names mean much to us today. Time has sifted the Tennysons from the Tuppers, but a literate middle-class family at the end of the nineteenth century knew and enjoyed the Honorable Mrs. Norton or George R. Sims as much as, if not more than, Keats or Swinburne. A Victorian anthologist, E. W. Cole, identified the "dozen grand and noble poets of humanity" as "Burns, Hood, Wordsworth, Mackay, Swain, Sims, Longfellow, Whittier, Lowell, Carleton, Felicia Hemans, and Letitia E. Landon." To illustrate this catholicity these pages bear some of the widely recited verses of Tennyson, Byron, Browning, Kipling, and other giants on the same terms as other, now forgotten poets. They also give, perhaps unkindly, a measure of comparison, and show that literary quality has a nodding acquaintance with popular taste. But after all, that enthusiastic bard Ella Wheeler Wilcox wrote, ". . . it is not Art, but Heart, which wins the wide world over."

The calling of poet was considered a noble one. Martin Tupper, in England, pointed with just pride to his social standing:

> Yea: how dignified and worthy, full of privilege and happiness,
> Standeth in majestic independence the self-ennobled author!
> —"Proverbial Philosophy"

and, on the other side of the Atlantic, the poetess Mary E. Lee sang, rather more lyrically:

> The poets—the poets—
> Those giants of the earth;
> In mighty strength they tower above
> The men of common birth:
> A noble race—they mingle not
> Among the motley throng,
> But move, with slow and measured steps,
> To music-notes along.
> —"The Poets"

Even the aberrations of Byron and Poe, bringing a whiff of brimstone into the halls of Parnassus, did not endanger public approbation of their verse, for, after all, were they not more to be pitied than condemned, the former a romantic English aristocrat and the latter a sad victim of intemperance?

Not a single one of these parlour poems was likely to bring the traditional blush to a maiden's cheek. They are eminently respectable and deal with the ruder elements of life with becoming restraint. The village-born beauty, thrown upon the streets, the haggard and obvious victim of venereal disease, is primly described as "quite impure." This careful and earnest popular art is of a variety that had not existed before, and probably never will again. It is the art of the emergent middle class, a class fearing and despising the blowsy Rabelaisian freedom of the poor and uneducated, shocked by the easy amorality of certain of the aristocracy, seeking to counter and reform both with its own stern but comforting ethic. The ideal pauper, to middle-class eyes, was the hero of "In the Workhouse," who, scornful to smug, condescending charity, will nevertheless let his wife starve to death rather than steal a loaf.

Is sentimental poetry bad verse? Only a literary snob would claim that the popular is automatically bad. Nevertheless, a few of the pieces in this volume are magnificently appalling, even by the high standards of *The Stuffed Owl,* the classic anthology compiled by D. B. Wyndham Lewis and Charles Lee. It is difficult to believe, for instance, that the muddle-headed Muse, Cacohymnia, was not sitting at J. G. Whittier's elbow when he was writing "Conductor Bradley":

> Lo! the ghastly lips of pain,
> Dead to all thought save duty's, moved again:
> "Put out the signals for the other train!"

> No nobler utterance, since the world began,
> From lips of saint or martyr ever ran,
> Electric, through the sympathies of man,

or inspired Clement Scott as he composed "The Story of a Stowaway":

> Pomps and pageants have their glory, in cathedral aisles are seen
> Marble effigies: but seldom of the mercantile marine.

Badness to this joyous degree is not uncommon; even so, only a handful of the poems in this collection also appear within the covers of *The Stuffed Owl.*

More seriously, Victorian popular verse can be indicted for being normally mawkish, pompous, bombastic, and mealy-mouthed. In their introduction to *The London Book of English Verse,* Herbert Read and Bonamy Dobrée comment distastefully on "what we are almost compelled to describe as the pathological condition of sentimentality which set in about 1810." One might query the force of "almost," but not dare to quarrel with their assessment. So an unpleasing poetic convention is banished to outer critical darkness. All the same, readers with grosser sensibilities are not prevented from finding it fascinating as a social and literary phenomenon, smiling wryly at the climate of moral certitude, enjoying the simple, often exciting rhythms, recognizing the half-forgotten, and, yes, discovering here and there nuggets of real gold. It is to be found in "The Private of the Buffs."

> Bright leagues of cherry-blossom gleam'd
> One sheet of living snow;

and, perhaps better known:

> All quiet along the Potomac tonight;
> No sound save the rush of the river;
> While soft falls the dew on the face of the dead—
> The picket's off duty forever!

Then, of course, there are the poems of twenty-four-carat quality, accepted in the critical pantheon, that were nonetheless popular currency and must therefore have a place in this volume, among them such magnificent pieces as "The Burial of Sir John Moore" and "Sennacherib."

Already critical favour has been extended to the metrical effusions of the tenements and the farms; enthusiastic scholars have been collecting the vigorous, often crude, often beautiful verse of ballad, folk-song, and broadsheet for many years. Indeed, the picture of respectable academics noting the precise regional variations of rural scatology is not without a piquant charm. So far, however, the strait-laced popular verse of the front-parlour has been ignored. Here is one humble attempt to show that it has a small but definite corner in literary history, and that it can still be enjoyed, if not always in the manner its authors intended.

It is the combination of instruction with entertainment that helped to give middle-class poetry its distinctive character. A typical musical evening of the eighties was varied with recitations, usually of an improving character, by the younger members of the family. Parish social gatherings, missionary and temperance meetings, too—all were likely to be enlivened in this way. In "The Dinglebury Testimonial," a story by Arthur F. Knight, just such an evening is graphically described. The climax is the recitation of "Little Jim" by Master Montague Memory:

> The cottage was a thatched one
> The outside old and mean
> But everything within that cot
> Was wondrous neat and clean
> He goes on Sunday to the church—
> John Gilpin was a citizen—a citizen—
> And sits among his boys
> He hears the parson pray and preach
> He hears his daughter's voice
> A train-band captain eke was he

Long years I've rung the curfew
Tried to do it just and right
Now I'm old I still must do it
Curfew it must ring tonight
Noah of old three babies had
Or grown-up children rather
Shem, Ham and Japhet they were called
Now who was Japhet's father
The boy stood on the burning deck
Up above the world so high
Whence all but he had fled
Like a diamond in the sky—
The light from off the battle's wreck
Shone round him o'er the dead
Oh stay my father shall I stay
Oh say my father shall I stay
Oh stay my say my father stay
My father say Oh shall I stay
etc., etc., etc., etc.

The poetry is gabbled through breathlessly, regardless of punctuation, and the reciter breaks down and sobs loudly at its close.

If the matter of the recitation was important, the manner of its performance was vital. This was the province of the elocutionist, and most juvenile reciters and other anthologies of verse and prose for parlour and platform give valuable advice on gesture as well as on voice production. Here are a few tips from *The Popular Elocutionist and Reciter* of 1902, edited by J. E. Carpenter, M.A., Ph.D.:

T R A N Q U I L L I T Y .—This may be expressed by the composure of the countenance and a general repose of the whole body, without the exertion of any one muscle. The countenance open, the forehead smooth, the eyebrow arched, the mouth nearly closed, and the eye passing with an easy motion from object to object, but not dwelling too long on one. Care must be taken to distinguish it from insensibility.

C H E E R F U L N E S S adds a smile to tranquillity, and opens the mouth a little more.

L O V E must be approached with the utmost delicacy; it is best expressed by a deep impassioned, fervent tone; the right hand may be pressed over the heart, but the "languishing eyes" recommended by some authors border too closely on burlesque. A steady, respectful gaze on the assumed object of affection may be permitted.

H A T R E D draws back the body as if to avoid the hated object; the hands at the same time spread out, as if to keep it off. The pitch of the voice is low, but harsh, chilling and vehement.

Rather surprisingly, among other useful hints from Dr. Carpenter about curing hoarseness by chewing a small piece of horse-radish, sucking a cayenned lozenge, or biting a lump out of the back of a red-herring, is the comforting suggestion that "Good bottled stout, which has been drawn sufficiently long for the froth to subside, is the best thing to sing or speak on." Sherry, spirits, and excessive water are to be avoided, although a glass or two of old, dry port wine is recommended.

Recitation was also a field for the professional. Poets such as Will Carleton and James Whitcomb Riley declaimed their dialect pieces on lucrative lecture tours, a mainly American activity that has hardly diminished in popularity over the last hundred years since Dickens and Little Nell conquered impressionable hearts on both sides of the Atlantic. In the music-hall and vaudeville, too, recitations with appropriate musical embellishments had a continuing vogue: a facet that has unaccountably been neglected in the recent spate of revivals.

Reciters' treasuries were still being sold in large numbers as late as the nineteen-twenties and -thirties, but they were used in a different way. Verse was still declaimed in school, rather less in the home, and with the arrival of radio and television, the old verbal tradition had become almost solely an educational activity. No longer informal, the art of reciting poetry entered the serious realm of "verse-speaking," of festivals and competitions. With the new century, the type of verse chosen for recitation altered, too. It was becoming more sophisticated, more "literary," more lyrical, and perhaps better as poetry. Uncomplicated narrative, moral exhortation, and patriotic feeling gradually disappeared and are now largely missing from modern anthologies. Generally, therefore, this collection ends with the death of Queen Victoria, although one or two later poetic Gems that belong in style and content to the nineteenth century are present.

In addition to verse written to be spoken as well as read in the closet, this anthology includes the lyrics of a few well-loved songs or "ballads." Naturally, many poems were later put to music—there is a particularly thrilling setting by M. W. Balfe of "Excelsior"—and they are often inseparable from their melodies: "A Lost Chord" is an example. Others, like "Come Home, Father," were songs right from the start: they are included here if they are remembered primarily for their words.

The earliest work in this volume is from the early eighteenth century, from the pious hymnodist Isaac Watts. "How Doth the Little Busy Bee" and " 'Tis the

Voice of the Sluggard," later parodied by Lewis Carroll, are perfect parlour poems: simple, moral, and recited by generations of well-brought-up children. The progression from Watts to Hemans, then by way of the upright poets of Queen Victoria's reign to Riley and Sims mirrors the rise and changing tastes of the bourgeoisie. The middle class entered the twentieth century triumphant, but its poetry was replaced by other, mechanical forms of entertainment.

These poems are mainly sentimental in the nonpejorative sense of the word: they express sentiments or fine thoughts. They should not mislead the reader into concluding that the public fancy was entirely serious. Comic verse had immense currency and a humorous section appeared in most reciters' anthologies. Modern collectors have frequently explored the purlieus of Victorian light verse, and the work of C. S. Calverley, W. S. Gilbert, Bret Harte, Charles G. Leland, and others is now far from neglected. Nevertheless, there are large tracts of Victorian comic writing (and, one might add, of serious poetry as well) that have not been penetrated by twentieth-century hunters, and for good reason: it is mostly long-winded and of an apparent dullness that can only be explained by a drastic change in our sense of humor over the past century. To add spice to this collection, however, examples from such volumes as *The Breitmann Ballads,* *The Ingoldsby Legends,* and *Bon Gaultier Ballads,* vastly popular in their time, have been included.

A hundred and seventeen poems can only represent the summit of a huge, forgotten mountain. The complete texts of several important specimens have so far eluded capture, so many readers may be disappointed that their favourite poem is missing. Some longer poems are omitted altogether, among them "Hiawatha," "The Pied Piper of Hamelin," and "The Rubáiyát" of Omar Khayyám, but these are easily to be found elsewhere. For the same reason, although Longfellow is strongly represented in these pages, many choice popular verses must be sought in his *Collected Works.*

A word on the texts of the poems is necessary. Some Victorian anthologists were no respecters of the purity of the original published versions: they chopped, changed, and even improved with no apology or indication to the reader of what they had done. Certain popular verses, such as "Home, Sweet Home" and "Curfew Must Not Ring Tonight," pose textual problems that may one day inspire doctoral theses at minor universities. If such a suggestion seems far-fetched, the reader should be reminded of the recent publication of *The Annotated Casey at the Bat.* Wherever possible, the earliest published texts are printed here and only amendments by the actual authors included, but it is quite likely that a number of versions are still corrupt.

Battered volumes from the shelves of second-hand bookshops have been the prime sources of this collection. They have charming titles, like *Favourite Poems by Gifted Bards* and *Golden Leaves from the American Poets*. One, above all, has provided the inspiration to explore the luxuriant byways of Victorian popular verse. It is entitled, with superb confidence, *The Thousand Best Poems in the World*, a volume in "The Federation of the World Library," published by Hutchinson. Well over a hundred thousand copies were sold in the 1890s. Its selector and arranger, E. W. Cole, of the Book Arcade, Melbourne, puts his finger unerringly on the qualities his readers required of their poetry. He can speak, too, for this present anthology:

> The pieces in this collection may not all be what a severe critic would call good poetry. I have selected them for their soul-stirring ideas rather than for their mere poetic embellishment. A grand idea which produces noble resolves, or a humane recital which brings tears of sympathy into the eyes, although given in simple, or even in ungrammatical language, is of far greater value to mankind than volumes, or dozens of volumes, of exquisite obscurities or "sublime nonsense." It is largely of these simple-touching poems dear to the heart of humanity rather than to the head that this book is composed. . . . I believe that hundreds of millions in the future will more frequently take up their favourite book of poetry to read to themselves, or say to some dear friends, in the spirit, if not in the words of one of the best poets of humanity.*

> Come, read to me some poem,
>   Some simple and heartfelt lay,
> That shall soothe this restless feeling,
> . And banish the thoughts of day.

> Then read from the treasured volume
>   The poem of thy choice,
> And lend to the rhyme of the poet
>   The beauty of thy voice.

> And the night shall be filled with music,
>   And the cares that infest the day
> Shall fold their tents, like the Arabs,
>   And as silently steal away.

M.R.T.

* Longfellow, in "The Day Is Done."

eAcknowledgments

Very many people have helped in the compilation of this anthology, and I should like to thank, in particular, Miss Tessa C. Harrow, Mr. Roy Giles, and Mr. Laurie Deval, who set me off collecting in the first place; Mr. Noel Morton; Mr. Laurence Cotterell; Mr. Eric Hiscock, who is still disappointed that I have not traced the source of the lines "Close the shutters, Willie's dead"; Mr. Granville Hicks, who introduced me to *McGuffey's Eclectic Readers*; Mr. John Willett; Mr. Edmund Vale; Mr. Desmond Elliott, who loaned me his remarkable collection of Wilcoxiana; Miss Ann Keep, who found the texts of two elusive Musical Monologues; and Miss Helen K. Taylor of The Viking Press, for much vital help in the selection and collection of native American Gems. Finally (and most of all) I must thank my wife for superhuman patience and understanding while the book was in the making.

M.R.T.

Contents

3. Love, Sweet Love

4. Strange Tales

5. *The Rolling Deep*

6. *Poor but Honest*

7. Tragic Ends

8. The Bivouac of Life

9. Heart of Oak

I

Little Jim and His Friends

Where did you come from, baby dear?
Out of the everywhere into here.

—Song from "At the Back of the North Wind"

Little Jim

EDWARD FARMER

The cottage was a thatch'd one,
  The outside old and mean,
Yet everything within that cot
  Was wondrous neat and clean.

The night was dark and stormy,
  The wind was howling wild;
A patient mother knelt beside
  The death bed of her child.

A little worn-out creature—
  His once bright eyes grown dim;
It was a collier's only child—
  They called him Little Jim.

And, oh! to see the briny tears
  Fast hurrying down her cheeks,
As she offer'd up a prayer in
      thought—
  She was afraid to speak,

Lest she might waken one she loved
  Far better than her life;
For there was all a mother's love
  In that poor collier's wife.

With hands uplifted, see, she kneels
  Beside the sufferer's bed;
And prays that He will spare her
      boy,
  And take herself instead.

She gets her answer from the child,
  Soft fell these words from him—

"Mother, the angels do so smile,
  And beckon Little Jim.

"I have no pain, dear mother, now,
  But oh! I am so dry;
Just moisten poor Jim's lips again,
  And, mother, don't you cry."

With gentle, trembling haste she
      held
  The tea-cup to his lips;
He smiled to thank her, as he took
  Three tiny little sips.

"Tell father when he comes from
      work,
  I said 'goodnight' to him;
And, mother, now I'll go to
      sleep,"—
  Alas, poor Little Jim.

She saw that he was dying—
  The child she loved so dear
Had uttered the last words that she
  Might ever hope to hear.

The cottage door was opened,
  The collier's step is heard,—
The father and the mother meet,
  Yet neither speak a word.

He knew that all was over,
  He knew his child was dead;
He took the candle in his hand,
  And walked towards the bed.

[3]

His quivering lips gave token
  Of the grief he'd fain conceal,
And, see, his wife has joined him—
  The stricken couple kneel.

With hearts bowed down with
    sadness
They humbly ask of Him,
In heaven, once more to meet again,
  Their own poor Little Jim.

This very typical ballad of a young life cut short in tragic circumstances shows the genre in full flower. Note that although Little Jim's humble father is a coalminer he lives in the archetypal thatched cottage, which is, of course, kept neat and spotless. The forces of pathetic fallacy are recruited for the inclement weather necessary for a death scene, and naturally father returns from work just too late for his son's last moments. "Jim," in popular verse, is usually a member of the lower—and sometimes unwashed—classes: Jane and Ann Taylor (see page 97) wrote of "Dirty Jim":

> There was one little Jim,
> 'Tis reported of him,
>   And must be to his lasting disgrace,
> That he never was seen
> With hands at all clean,
>   Nor yet ever clean was his face. . . .
>
> The idle and bad,
> Like this little lad,
>   May love dirty ways to be sure;
> But good boys are seen
> To be decent and clean,
>   Although they are ever so poor.

Many irreverent parodies commemorate "Little Jim," perhaps the best known being a version of the affecting eighth stanza:

> "I have no pain, dear mother, now,
>   But, oh, I am so dry;
> Connect me to a brewery
>   And leave me there to die."

Only a Baby Small

MATTHIAS BARR

Only a baby small,
　Dropped from the skies;
Only a laughing face,
　Two sunny eyes.

Only two cherry lips,
　One chubby nose;
Only two little hands,
　Ten little toes.

Only a golden head,
　Curly and soft;
Only a tongue that wags
　Loudly and oft.

Only a little brain,
　Empty of thought;
Only a little heart,
　Troubled with naught.

Only a tender flower
　Sent us to rear;
Only a life to love
　While we are here.

Only a baby small,
　Never at rest;
Small, but how dear to us,
　God knoweth best.

This charming lyric was composed about 1870.

Song

from "At the Back of the North Wind"

GEORGE MACDONALD

Where did you come from, baby dear?
Out of the everywhere into here.

Where did you get those eyes so blue?
Out of the sky as I came through.

What makes the light in them sparkle and spin?
Some of the starry spikes left in.

Where did you get that little tear?
I found it waiting when I got here.

What makes your forehead so smooth and high?
A soft hand stroked it as I went by.

What makes your cheek like a warm white rose?
I saw something better than anyone knows.

Whence that three-cornered smile of bliss?
Three angels gave me at once a kiss.

Where did you get this pearly ear?
God spoke, and it came out to hear.

Where did you get those arms and hands?
Love made itself into bonds and bands.

Feet, whence did you come, you darling things?
From the same box as the cherubs' wings.

How did they all just come to be you?
God thought about me, and so I grew.

But how did you come to us, you dear?
God thought about you, and so I am here.

G E O R G E   M A C D O N A L D (1824–1905) was known as a visionary
even while at College in Aberdeen. He was ordained as a Congregationalist, but,
after disputes with his congregation about the content of his sermons, determined
on a literary career, gaining a considerable reputation as a spiritual poet and a
novelist whose work was devoted by turns to the psychic and mystical and to
humble Scottish life. He preached, lectured (taking in the inevitable American
tour), wrote fairy stories, edited *Good Words for the Young,* and made friends
with notabilities as diverse as Browning, Carlyle, Morris, Tennyson, Arnold,
Octavia Hill, Dean Stanley, and the eighth Duke of Argyll.

Little Willie

GERALD MASSEY

Poor little Willie,
  With his many pretty wiles;
Worlds of wisdom in his look,
  And quaint, quiet smiles;
Hair of amber, touched with
  Gold of Heaven so brave;
All lying darkly hid
  In a workhouse grave.

You remember little Willie,
  Fair and funny fellow! he
Sprang like a lily
  From the dirt of poverty.
Poor little Willie!
  Not a friend was nigh,
When from the cold world
  He crouch'd down to die.

In the day we wander'd foodless
  Little Willie cried for "bread";
In the night we wander'd homeless,
  Little Willie cried for "bed."
Parted at the workhouse door,
  Not a word we said;
Ah! so tired was poor Willie!
  And so sweetly sleep the dead.

'Twas in the dead of winter
  We laid him in the earth;
The world brought in the new year
  On a tide of mirth.
But for the lost little Willie
  Not a tear we crave;
Cold and hunger cannot wake him
  In his workhouse grave.

We thought him beautiful,
  Felt it hard to part;
We loved him dutiful:
  Down, down, poor heart!
The storms they may beat,
  The winter winds may rave;
Little Willie feels not
  In his workhouse grave.

No room for little Willie
  In the world he had no part;
On him stared the Gorgon-eye
  Through which looks no heart.
"Come to me," said Heaven;
  And if Heaven will save,
Little matters though the door
  Be a workhouse grave.

The character of Little Willie is international. According to *The Reader's Encyclopedia of American Literature* he was "the most frequently epitaphed person in literary history," and his birth is credited to Julia Moore, "The Sweet Singer of Michigan," in 1876. Britain can confidently challenge that claim with the work printed here. In the present volume Little Willie appears under sundry aliases.

GERALD MASSEY (1828–1907) was a self-made man and was so admired by Samuel Smiles that the latter included him in *Self-help* and wrote a memoir for Massey's *Poetical Works*. The son of an English canal boatman, he was put to work at the age of eight in a silk mill, afterwards working as a straw-plaiter. Reading became a passion, and he developed ambitions as a poet, publishing a book of verse in Tring when he was twenty. His life was devoted to Christian Socialism, and he achieved fame as the "poet of liberty, labour, and the people." Later, Massey turned to journalism, then to spiritualism, on which he lectured during three tours of the United States.

Little Boy Blue

EUGENE FIELD

The little toy dog is covered with dust,
But sturdy and stanch he stands;
And the little toy soldier is red with rust,
And his musket moulds in his hands.
Time was when the little toy dog was new,
And the soldier was passing fair;
And that was the time when our Little Boy Blue
Kissed them and put them there.

"Now, don't you go till I come," he said,
"And don't you make any noise!"
So, toddling off to his trundle-bed,
He dreamt of the pretty toys;
And, as he was dreaming, an angel song
Awakened our Little Boy Blue—
Oh! the years are many, the years are long,
But the little toy friends are true!

Ay, faithful to the Little Boy Blue they stand,
Each in the same old place,
Awaiting the touch of a little hand,
The smile of a little face;
And they wonder, as waiting the long years through
In the dust of that little chair,
What has become of our Little Boy Blue,
Since he kissed them and put them there.

EUGENE FIELD (1850–1895), born in St. Louis, Missouri, was a journalist, one of the first of the regular newspaper columnists, a bibliomaniac, and a man with a penchant for practical jokes. Oddly enough, a biographer records that "he seems to have had no real enemies." It is perhaps in character that he became "the Yorick of American poetry, childhood's born laureate," the author of many verses for young people, including "Wynken, Blynken, and Nod." "Little Boy Blue" was set to a much-loved tune by Ethelbert Nevin.

Little Breeches

COLONEL JOHN HAY

I don't go much on religion,
    I never ain't had no show;
But I've got a middlin' tight grip, sir,
    On the handful o' things I know.
I don't pan out on the prophets
    And free-will and that sort of thing,—
But I b'lieve in God and the angels,
    Ever sence one night last spring.

I come into town with some turnips,
    And my little Gabe come along,—
No four-year-old in the county
    Could beat him for pretty and strong,
Peart and chipper and sassy,
    Always ready to swear and fight,—
And I'd larnt him to chaw terbacker
    Jest to keep his milk-teeth white.

The snow come down like a blanket
    As I passed by Taggart's store;
I went in for a jug of molasses
    And left the team at the door.
They scared at something, and started,—
    I heard one little squall,
And hell-to-split over the prairie
    Went team, Little Breeches, and all.

Hell-to-split over the prairie!
    I was almost froze with skeer;
But we rousted up some torches,
    And sarched for 'em far and near.
At last we struck hosses and wagon,
    Snowed under a soft white mound,
Upsot, dead beat,—but of little Gabe
    No hide nor hair was found.

And here all hope soured on me
Of my fellow-critter's aid;—
I jest flopped down on my marrow-bones,
Crotch-deep in the snow, and prayed.

. . . . . .

By this, the torches was played out,
And me and Isrul Parr
Went off for some wood to a sheepfold
That he said was somewhar thar.

We found it at last, and a little shed
Where they shut up the lambs at night.
We looked in and seen them huddled thar,
So warm and sleepy and white;
And thar sot Little Breeches and chirped,
As peart as ever you see,
"I want a chaw of terbacker,
And that's what the matter of me."

How did he git thar? Angels.
He could never have walked in that storm:
They jest scooped down and toted him
To whar it was safe and warm.
And I think that saving a little child,
And fotching him to his own,
Is a derned sight better business
Than loafing around The Throne.

"Little Breeches" is one of the Pike County Ballads of 1871, in the Western
dialect that was being popularized by Bret Harte and Mark Twain. The language, setting, and manners bring a bracing, fresh breeze into the parlour, a
corrective to "Little Boy Blue." Note, however, that rough and unpolished as
the narrator may appear, the sentiments of this touching story, with its note of
divine intervention at the denouement, are unexceptionable. There is another
Pike County Ballad, "Jim Bludso of the Prairie Belle," on page 167.

COLONEL JOHN HAY (1838–1905) came from Salem, Indiana. He was a lawyer who became Secretary and Aide-de-Camp to President Lincoln, Ambassador to England, and Secretary of State. His literary talent was exhibited in a book on Spain, leaders for the New York *Tribune*, poetry, a novel, a biography of Lincoln, and the (unearned) reputation of having composed a number of Lincoln's famous pieces.

Come Home, Father

HENRY CLAY WORK

Father, dear father, come home with me now!
   The clock in the steeple strikes one;
You promis'd, dear father, that you would come home,
   As soon as your day's work was done.
Our fire has gone out, our house is all dark,
   And mother's been watching since tea,
With poor brother Benny so sick in her arms,
   And no one to help her but me.
Come home, come home, come home,
Please father, dear father, come home.

   Hear the sweet voice of the child,
   Which the night-winds repeat as they roam!
   Oh! who could resist this most plaintive of pray'rs,
   "Please father, dear father, come home."

Father, dear father, come home with me now!
   The clock in the steeple strikes two;
The night has grown colder, and Benny is worse,
   But he has been calling for you.
Indeed he is worse—Ma says he will die
   Perhaps before morning shall dawn,
And this is the message she sent me to bring,
   "Come quickly or he will be gone."
Come home, come home, come home,
Please father, dear father, come home.

   Hear the sweet voice of the child, etc.

Father, dear father, come home with me now!
   The clock in the steeple strikes three;
The house is so lonely, the hours are so long
   For poor weeping mother and me.
Yes, we are alone—poor Benny is dead,

And gone with the angels of light,
And these were the very last words that he said,
"I want to kiss Papa goodnight."
Come home, come home, come home,
Please father, dear father, come home.

Hear the sweet voice of the child, etc.

Little Mary's Song is the traditional climax of the temperance melodrama *Ten Nights in a Bar-Room.* The vigil of the drunkard's wife and children (at least one of the family is invariably ailing) is a frequent theme in popular Victorian literature. Here are the last two verses of "The Gambler and Drunkard's Wife," by a poet called Coats:

"Nestle more closely, dear one, to my heart!
Thou'rt cold! thou'rt freezing! But we will not part.
Husband!—I die!—Father!—It is not he!
Oh Heaven! protect my child!"—The clock strikes "Three!"

They're gone! They're gone! The glimmering spark hath fled,
The wife and child are numbered with the dead!
On the cold hearth, outstretched in solemn rest,
The child lies frozen on it's [*sic*] mother's breast!
—The gambler came at last—but all was o'er—
Dead silence reigned around—he groaned—he spoke no more!

In *The Drunkard,* a Moral Domestic Drama by W. H. Smith (an American actor) and A Gentleman, there is a pathetic scene in which the prodigal's daughter prattles innocently:

"Yes; poor father! I cried last night when father came home and was so ill. Oh! he looked so pale; and when I kissed him for good night, his face was as hot as fire. This morning he could not eat his breakfast, could he? What makes him ill so often, mother? . . . Dear grandma so sick, too. Doctor and nurse both looked so sorry. Grandma won't die tonight, will she, mother?"

And, finally, what of the drunkard himself? Here he is, family waiting without fire or food, of course, in "Out in the Cold" by the Reverend Dwight Williamson:

Out of the bar-room into the cold,
Money all gone and manhood sold,

The poor man, weary from hunger and sin,
Breasted the storm with quivering chin;
Only the storm with its spectres was out,
And the eddying snow went whirling about;
Thousands were happy in the home-fold,
Nor thought of the drunkard out in the cold,
                    OUT IN THE COLD.

In this poem, for a change, it is the drunkard who is frozen to death. See also
"The Mother in the Snow-Storm" on page 227.

HENRY CLAY WORK (1832–1884), the American song-writer,
was a printer by trade but with leanings towards abolitionism and prohibition. He
also wrote the words and music for such musical Gems as "Grandfather's
Clock," "Watching for Pa," and "Marching through Georgia."

The Orphan Boy's Tale

MRS. OPIE

"Stay, lady, stay, for mercy's sake,
    And hear a helpless orphan's tale;
Ah! sure my looks must pity wake;
    'Tis want that makes my cheek so pale.
Yet I was once a mother's pride,
    And my brave father's hope and joy;
But in the Nile's proud fight he died,
    And now I am an orphan boy.

"Poor foolish child, how pleased was I,
    When news of Nelson's victory came,
Along the crowded streets to fly,
    And see the lighted windows flame!
To force me home my mother sought;
    She could not bear to see my joy;
For with my father's life 'twas bought,
    And made me a poor orphan boy.

"The people's shouts were long and loud,
    My mother, shuddering, closed her ears;
'Rejoice! rejoice!' still cried the crowd;
    My mother answered with her tears.
'Why are you crying thus,' said I,
    'While others laugh and shout with joy?'
She kissed me—and with such a sigh!
    She called me her poor orphan boy.

" 'What is an orphan boy?' I cried,
    As in her face I looked and smiled;
My mother through her tears replied,
    'You'll know too soon, ill-fated child!'
And now they've tolled my mother's knell,
    And I'm no more a parent's joy;
O lady, I have learned too well
    What 'tis to be an orphan boy!

"Oh, were I by your bounty fed!
Nay, gentle lady, do not chide—
Trust me, I mean to earn my bread;
The sailor's orphan boy has pride.
Lady, you weep!—ha!—this to me?
You'll give me clothing, food, employ?
Look down, dear parents! look, and see
Your happy, happy, orphan boy!"

Oh, men of dark and dismal fate,

sings Major-General Stanley to the desperadoes who seek to marry his daughters in *The Pirates of Penzance,*

Forgo your cruel employ,
Have pity on my lonely state,
I am an orphan boy!

and the opposition is totally disarmed. By W. S. Gilbert's time, Mrs. Opie's famous English poem had inspired on both sides of the ocean numerous pathetic ballads in which disclosure of the hero's parentless state acts as powerful emotional blackmail on all auditors. As the Major-General notes, when he is elected honorary member of the pirate band,

And it sometimes is a useful thing
To be an orphan boy.

MRS. AMELIA OPIE, *née* ALDERSON (1769–1853), was a high-spirited girl, a doctor's daughter in Norwich, who published poems in her teens and played the heroine in a tragedy which she wrote herself. Numerous admirers pursued her in vain, for she married John Opie, the celebrated painter, and, to keep her at home, he encouraged her to write the lachrymose poems and novels that reduced even Sir Walter Scott to tears. As Harriet Martineau observed, Mrs. Opie wrote "slowly and amidst a strenuous excitement of her sensibilities." As indefatigable in charitable works as she was in literary composition, she became a Quaker, her conversion hardly reducing her proclivities towards social gaiety and fashionable dress. In later years she was a portly, jolly old lady, who, when visiting the Great Exhibition of 1851 in a wheel-chair, challenged another octogenarian to a chair race.

Little Orphant Annie

JAMES WHITCOMB RILEY

Little Orphant Annie's come to our house to stay,
An' wash the cups an' saucers up, an' brush the crumbs away,
An' shoo the chickens off the porch, an' dust the hearth an' sweep,
An' make the fire, an' bake the bread, an' earn her board an' keep:
An' all us other children, when the supper things is done,
We set around the kitchen fire an' has the mostest fun
A-list'nin' to the witch tales 'at Annie tells about,
An' the Gobble-uns 'at gits you
                    Ef you
                         Don't
                              Watch
                                   Out!

Onc't they was a little boy wouldn't say his pray'rs—
An' when he went to bed 'at night, away up-stairs,
His mammy heerd him holler, an' his daddy heerd him bawl,
An' when they turn't the kivvers down, he wasn't there at all!
An' they seeked him in the rafter-room, an' cubby-hole an' press.
An' seeked him up the chimbly-flue, and every wheres, I guess,
But all they ever found was thist his pants an' roundabout!
An' the Gobble-uns'll git you
                    Ef you
                         Don't
                              Watch
                                   Out!

An' one time a little girl 'ud allus laugh an' grin,
An' make fun of ever' one an' all her blood an' kin,
An' onc't when they was "company," an' ol' folks was there,
She mocked 'em an' shocked 'em, an' said she didn't care!
An' thist as she kicked her heels, an' turn't to run an' hide,
They was two great big Black Things a-standin' by her side,

An' they snatched her through the ceilin' 'fore she knowed what she's
    about!
An' the Gobble-uns'll git you
             Ef you
               Don't
                  Watch
                     Out!

An' Little Orphant Annie says, when the blaze is blue,
An' the lampwick splutters, an' the wind goes woo-oo!
An' you hear the crickets quit, an' the moon is gray,
An' the lightnin'-bugs in dew is all squenched away,—
You better mind yer parents, and yer teachers fond and dear,
An' churish them 'at loves you, an' dry the orphant's tear,
An' he'p the pore and needy ones 'at clusters all about,
Er the Gobble-uns'll git you
             Ef you
               Don't
                  Watch
                     Out!

JAMES WHITCOMB RILEY (1849–1916), an Indiana news-
paperman, wrote many poems, like "Little Orphant Annie," in the Hoosier dialect
of his native state. It was Riley who was really responsible for the great burst of
sentimental dialect verse about childhood—and especially boyhood—that followed
the publication in 1883 of his book of poems, *The Old Swimmin' Hole and
'Leven More*. The author achieved great popular and financial success, and combined many talents as writer, musician, actor, reciter, artist, and, on at least one
occasion, practical joker. He composed a poem, "Leonainie," and published it
under the name of Edgar Allan Poe, a jape that caused him great notoriety. Annie
still lives on, somewhat metamorphosed, in the person of Little Orphan Annie in
Harold Gray's comic strip.

Song
from "The Water Babies"

REVEREND CHARLES KINGSLEY

I once had a sweet little doll, dears,
    The prettiest doll in the world;
Her cheeks were so red and so white, dears,
    And her hair was so charmingly curled.
But I lost my poor little doll, dears,
    As I played in the heath one day;
And I cried for her more than a week, dears,
    But I never could find where she lay.

I found my poor little doll, dears,
    As I played in the heath one day;
Folks say she is terribly changed, dears,
    For her paint is all washed away,
And her arm trodden off by the cows, dears,
    And her hair not the least bit curled:
Yet for old sakes' sake she is still, dears,
    The prettiest doll in the world.

REVEREND CHARLES KINGSLEY (1819–1875), born in Devon, was a precocious and pious child who produced sermons at the age of four. At school his poetical leanings and interests in natural history did not lead to popularity. He made up for this at Cambridge, where he threw himself into all manner of sports to distract his mind from the religious doubts fashionable at the time. Nevertheless, he took orders and within a few years was enormously active as a writer and Christian Socialist (although in later life he turned to toryism). As might, perhaps, be guessed from his story of a sweep-boy transformed by the pure, clear, sparkling river in *The Water Babies*, sanitary reform was a great passion, almost as much as the muscular Christianity with which he is associated.

Against Idleness and Mischief

DR. ISAAC WATTS

How doth the little busy bee
Improve each shining hour,
And gather honey all the day
From every opening flower!

In works of labour or of skill,
I would be busy too;
For Satan finds some mischief still
For idle hands to do.

How skilfully she builds her cell!
How neat she spreads the wax!
And labours hard to store it well
With the sweet food she makes.

In books, or work, or healthful play,
Let my first years be passed,
That I may give for every day
Some good account at last.

The moral backbone of the Anglo-Saxon nations was stiffened throughout the eighteenth and nineteenth centuries by volumes of improving verse for the young; one can imagine the delight and gratitude with which children greeted the task of committing these moral Gems to memory during the long hours of a Protestant Sunday. Isaac Watts began the good work with *Divine Songs for Children* in 1715, and so integral a part of a child's life were the hymns a century and a half later that Lewis Carroll was able to parody them in *Alice's Adventures in Wonderland*, knowing that his joke would be immediately appreciated. Now, of course, his parody is known to millions while the original is almost forgotten:

How doth the little crocodile
Improve his shining tail,
And pour the waters of the Nile
On every golden scale!

How cheerfully he seems to grin,
How neatly spreads his claws,
And welcomes little fishes in
With gently smiling jaws!

ISAAC WATTS (1674–1748), son of a Southampton clothier who composed sacred verses, showed such talents that a subscription was proposed to send him to university, but he preferred an education at a dissenters' academy. Illness deprived him of an active pastoral life, but as the protégé of Sir Thomas Abney he led a pious, sheltered, luxurious existence devoted to the production of divine and philosophical works, religious poetry, and his immensely popular songs for children. His famous hymns, among them "O God, Our Help in Ages Past" and "When I Survey the Wondrous Cross," took the dissenting church by storm in defiance of Calvin, becoming what can only be described as best-sellers.

The Little Shroud

LETITIA E. LANDON

She put him on a snow-white shroud,
    A chaplet on his head;
And gathered early primroses
    To scatter o'er the dead.

She laid him in his little grave,
    'Twas hard to lay him there
When spring was putting forth its flowers,
    And everything was fair.

She had lost many children—now
    The last of them was gone,
And day and night she sat and wept
    Beside the funeral stone.

One midnight, while her constant tears
    Were falling with the dew,
She heard a voice, and lo! her child
    Stood by her, weeping too!

His shroud was damp, his face was white,
    He said, "I cannot sleep,
Your tears have made my shroud so wet,
    Oh, mother, do not weep!"

Oh, love is strong!—the mother's heart
    Was filled with tender fears;
Oh, love is strong!—and for her child,
    Her grief restrained its tears.

One eve a light shone round her bed,
    And there she saw him stand
Her infant in his little shroud,
    A taper in his hand.

"Lo! mother, see my shroud is dry,
And I can sleep once more!"
And beautiful the parting smile
The little infant wore!

And down within the silent grave
He laid his weary head,
And soon the early violets,
Grew o'er his grassy bed.

The mother went her household ways
Again she knelt in prayer,
And only asked of heaven its aid
Her heavy lot to bear.

The sombre and pathetic visitant of this work may be compared to the rather more august presence who disturbs the slumbers of another unfortunate lady in "The Mother's Sacrifice," by Lydia H. Sigourney, on page 271. During the last century, both Miss Landon in England and Mrs. Sigourney in America were justly renowed for their tear-stained poems.

LETITIA ELIZABETH MACLEAN, *née* LANDON (1802–1838), published fluent and somewhat undisciplined poetry under the initials "L.E.L." A plump and precocious child, she was once observed reading a book while bowling a hoop. She contributed verse and reviews to the *Literary Gazette*, and, adept at hitting the taste of the day, was soon earning large sums to support her impoverished family (her father was a clergyman), and also provoking malicious gossip from less successful literati. Scandal, probably unfounded, caused her to break off an engagement and, on the rebound, she married George Maclean, governor of the English settlements in the Gold Coast. The newlywed couple arrived in West Africa, and only two months later L.E.L. was found dead, in her hand an empty bottle that had contained prussic acid. Speculation on the cause of the tragedy ranged from accident and suicide to vengeance by one of her husband's discarded mistresses.

Billy's Rose

GEORGE R. SIMS

Billy's dead, and gone to glory—so is Billy's sister Nell:
There's a tale I know about them were I poet I would tell;
Soft it comes, with perfume laden, like a breath of country air
Wafted down the filthy alley, bringing fragrant odours there.

In that vile and filthy alley, long ago, one winter's day,
Dying quick of want and fever, hapless, patient, Billy lay;
While beside him sat his sister, in the garret's dismal gloom,
Cheering with her gentle presence, Billy's pathway to the tomb.

Many a tale of elf and fairy did she tell the dying child,
Till his eyes lost half their anguish, and his worn, wan features smiled:
Tales herself had heard haphazard, caught amid the Babel roar,
Lisped about by tiny gossips playing round their mother's door.

Then she felt his wasted fingers tighten feebly as she told
How beyond this dismal alley lay a land of shining gold,
Where, when all the pain was over—where, when all the tears were shed—
He would be a white-frocked angel, with a gold thing on his head.

Then she told some garbled story of a kind-eyed Saviour's love,
How He'd built for little children great big playgrounds up above,
Where they sang and played at hop-scotch and at horses all the day,
And where beadles and policemen never frightened them away.

This was Nell's idea of heaven—just a bit of what she'd heard,
With a little bit invented and a little bit inferred.
But her brother lay and listened, and he seemed to understand,
For he closed his eyes and murmured he could see the Promised Land.

"Yes," he whispered, "I can see it—I can see it, sister Nell;
Oh, the children look so happy, and they're all so strong and well;
I can see them there with Jesus—He is playing with them too!
Let us run away and join them, if there's room for me and you."

She was eight, this little maiden, and her life had all been spent
In the garret and the alley, where they starved to pay the rent;
Where a drunken father's curses and a drunken mother's blows
Drove her forth into the gutter from the day's dawn to its close.

But she knew enough, this outcast, just to tell the sinking boy,
"You must die before you're able all these blessings to enjoy.
You must die," she whispered, "Billy, and I am not even ill;
But I'll come to you, dear brother,—yes, I promise that I will.

"You are dying, little brother,—you are dying, oh, so fast;
I heard father say to mother that he knew you couldn't last.
They will put you in a coffin, then you'll wake up and be there,
While I'm left alone to suffer in this garret bleak and bare."

"Yes, I know it," answered Billy. "Ah, but, sister, I don't mind,
Gentle Jesus will not beat me; He's not cruel or unkind.
But I can't help thinking, Nelly, I should like to take away
Something, sister, that you gave me, I might look at every day.

"In the summer you remember how the Mission took us out
To a great green lovely meadow, where we played and ran about,
And the van that took us halted by a sweet, bright patch of land,
Where the fine red blossoms grew, dear, half as big as mother's hand.

"Nell, I asked the good, kind teacher what they called such flowers as
        those,
And he told me, I remember, that the pretty name was rose.
I have never seen them since, dear—how I wish that I had one!
Just to keep and think of you, Nell, when I'm up beyond the sun."

Not a word said little Nelly; but at night, when Billy slept,
On she flung her scanty garments, and then down the stairs she crept.
Through the silent streets of London she ran nimbly as a fawn,
Running on and running ever till the night had changed to dawn.

When the foggy sun had risen, and the mist had cleared away
All around her, wrapped in snowdrift, there the open country lay.

She was tired, her limbs were frozen, and the roads had cut her feet,
But there came no flowery gardens her poor tearful eyes to greet.

She had traced the road by asking—she had learnt the way to go;
She had found the famous meadow—it was wrapped in cruel snow;
Not a buttercup or daisy, not a single verdant blade
Showed its head above its prison. Then she knelt her down and prayed.

With her eyes upcast to heaven, down she sank upon the ground,
And she prayed to God to tell her where the roses might be found.
Then the cold blast numbed her senses, and her sight grew strangely dim;
And a sudden, awful tremor seemed to seize her every limb.

"Oh, a rose!" she moaned, "good Jesus—just a rose to take to Bill!"
And as she prayed a chariot came thundering down the hill;
And a lady sat there, toying with a red rose, rare and sweet;
As she passed she flung it from her, and it fell at Nelly's feet.

Just a word her lord had spoken caused her ladyship to fret,
And his rose had been his present, so she flung it in a pet;
But the poor, half-blinded Nelly thought it fallen from the skies,
And she murmured, "Thank you, Jesus!" as she clasped the dainty prize.

· · · · · ·

Lo! that night from out the alley did a child's soul pass away,
From dirt and sin and misery to where God's children play.
Lo! that night a wild, fierce snowstorm burst in fury o'er the land,
And that morn they found Nell frozen, with the red rose in her hand.

Billy's dead, and gone to glory—so is Billy's sister Nell,
Am I bold to say this happened in the land where angels dwell—
That the children met in heaven, after all their earthly woes,
And that Nelly kissed her brother, and said "Billy, here's your rose"?

GEORGE ROBERT SIMS (1847–1922) was, until Arthur Calder Marshall presented a new edition of his verse, *Prepare to Shed Them Now,* in danger of being forgotten; his name does not even appear in the multitudinous pages of the British *Dictionary of National Biography.* At the end of the last century, however, he was placed by some enthusiasts in the English poetical pantheon (see page viii), and, under the pseudonym of "Dagonet," he published such vastly popular ballads as "In the Workhouse: Christmas Day" and "The Lifeboat," both of which appear in this anthology. One recitation, "Ostler Joe," written for the actor Edmund Yates, swept America and, Calder Marshall calculates, was read by about four-fifths of the adult population of the United States. A melodramatic piece about a hostler's errant wife who leaves him for a gay seducer ("Annie listened and was tempted—she was tempted and she fell/ As the angel fell from heaven to the blackest depths of hell"), it follows the harlot's progress to the poignant moment when Joe finds her again at last:

In his arms death found her lying, in his arms her spirit fled;
And his tears came down in torrents as he knelt beside her dead.
Never once his love had faltered through her base unhallowed life;
And the stone above her ashes bears the honoured name of wife.

Sims was principally a journalist, and his column "Mustard and Cress," imitative of Ambrose Bierce, ran for forty-five years. He was also famous as a dedicated and vigorous agitator for social reform, dramatist, novelist, short-story writer, *bon vivant,* breeder of bulldogs, and inventor of a hair restorer called Tatcho, after his publisher, Chatto of Chatto and Windus.

Yawcob Strauss

CHARLES F. ADAMS

I haf von funny leedle poy,
    Vot gomes schust to mine knee;
Der queerest schap, der createst rogue,
    As efer you dit see.
He runs, und schumps, and schmashes dings
    In all barts of der house;
But vot off dat? he vas mine son,
    Mine leedle Yawcob Strauss.

He get der measles und der mumbs,
    Und eferyding dot's oudt;
He sbills mine glass of lager bier,
    Poots schnuff indo mine kraut.
He fills mine pipe mit Limburg cheese,—
    Dot vas der roughest chouse;
I'd dake dot vrom no oder poy
    But leedle Yawcob Strauss.

He dakes der milk-ban for a dhrum,
    Und cuts mine cane in dwo,
To make der schticks to beat it mit,—
    Mine gracious, dot vos drue!
I dinks mine hed vas schplit abart,
    He kicks oup sooch a touse:
But never mind; der poys vas few
    Like dot young Yawcob Strauss.

He asks me questions, sooch as dese:
    Who baints mine nose so red?
Who vas it cuts dot schmoodth blace oudt
    Vrom der hair ubon mine hed?
Und vhere der blaze goes vrom der lamp
    Vene'er der glim I douse.
How gan I all dose dings eggsblain
    To dot schmall Yawcob Strauss?

I somedimes dink I schall go vild
  Mit sooch a grazy poy,
Und vish vonce more I gould haf rest
Und beaceful dimes enshoy;
But ven he vash asleep in ped,
  So guiet as a mouse,
I prays der Lord, "Dake anyding,
  But leaf dot Yawcob Strauss."

Leedle Yawcob's literary father was the Pennsylvania Dutch gentleman Hans
Breitmann, and a note on their German-American provenance may be found
on page 139. He has origins, too, in the exasperated-but-doting genre of verse
about children, of which Thomas Hood (1799–1845) was an early exponent:

Thou happy, happy elf!
(But stop—first let me kiss away that tear.)
Thou tiny image of myself!
(My love, he's poking peas into his ear!)
Thou merry, laughing sprite!
With spirits feather-light,
Untouched by sorrow, and unsoiled by sin,
(Good heavens! the child is swallowing a pin!)
—"A Parental Ode to My Infant Son"

CHARLES FOLLEN ADAMS (1842–1918), although from
Massachusetts, became fascinated by the German immigrants he met while a
soldier in the Civil War. He is now remembered for the single volume of
Yawcob Strauss verses.

A Child's Thought

BERTHA MOORE

If I were God, up in the sky,
   I'll tell you all vat I would do,
I would not let the babies cry
   Because veir tooths was coming froo.
I'd make them born wif tooths all white,
   And curly hair upon veir heads,
And so vat vey could sit upright
   Not always lie down in veir beds.

If I were God, up in the sky,
   I'd make the sweet primroses talk,
And tell me why vey sometimes sigh,
   When nurse and I close to them walk.
I 'spects it is 'cos vey do fear
   We'll tread upon vem when we run,
But we would not go *quite* so near,
   To kill a primrose is not fun.

If I were God, up in the sky,
   And mummie's head was *bery* bad,
I'd send an angel from on high
   And vat would make her, oh! so glad,
She'd beg God let him stay a while,
   And soon forget the horrid pain,
Talk to the angel, laugh and smile,
   And ven be quite herself again.

If I were God, up in the sky,
   I'd take all nasty little boys
Who play so rough and noisily
   And break veir sister's fav'rite toys.
I'd turn vem into tiny crabs,
   And make vem run around in sand,
And play wif fishes and wif dabs
   P'raps ven vey wouldn't be so grand.

If I were God, up in the sky,
  I'd have so many fings to do,
'Twould be a 'sponsibility.
  I really fink, 'tween me and you,
I'd raver be a little girl,
  Whom Daddy calls his "Precious Pearl."
It's *bery* difficult to try
  To be like God, up in the sky!

No sample of poems about children would be complete without a specimen from the great lava-flow of verse in baby talk that erupted towards the end of the last century, the literary counterpart of the talented drawings of Miss Mabel Lucie Attwell. To gain the full flavour of "A Child's Thought," it should be met with unawares in its place in Ernest Pertwee's *The Reciter's Second Treasury of Verse*, where it follows directly upon Adam's morning hymn from Milton's *Paradise Lost*.

2

Ballads
of the Brave

A youth, who bore, 'mid snow and ice,
A banner with the strange device.

—"Excelsior"

Excelsior

HENRY WADSWORTH LONGFELLOW

The shades of night were falling fast,
As through an Alpine village passed
A youth, who bore, 'mid snow and ice,
A banner with the strange device,
      Excelsior!

His brow was sad; his eye beneath
Flashed like a falchion from its sheath,
And like a silver clarion rung
The accents of that unknown tongue,
      Excelsior!

In happy homes he saw the light
Of household fires gleam warm and bright;
Above, the spectral glaciers shone,
And from his lips escaped a groan,
      Excelsior!

"Try not the Pass!" the old man said;
"Dark lowers the tempest overhead,
The roaring torrent is deep and wide!"
And loud that clarion voice replied,
      Excelsior!

"O stay," the maiden said, "and rest
Thy weary head upon this breast!"
A tear stood in his bright blue eye,
But still he answered, with a sigh,
      Excelsior!

"Beware the pine-tree's withered branch!
Beware the awful avalanche!"
This was the peasant's last Good-night;
A voice replied, far up the height,
      Excelsior!

At break of day, as heavenward
The pious monks of Saint Bernard
Uttered the oft-repeated prayer,
A voice cried through the startled air,
Excelsior!

A traveller, by the faithful hound,
Half-buried in the snow was found,
Still grasping in his hands of ice
That banner with the strange device,
Excelsior!

There in the twilight cold and grey,
Lifeless, but beautiful, he lay,
And from the sky, serene and far,
A voice fell, like a falling star,
Excelsior!

The galvanic call of *Excelsior!* has exercised the talents of various theorists. D. B. Wyndham Lewis and Charles Lee remark in *The Stuffed Owl* that it is possible that the youth intended to cry *Excelsius!*, the comparative of the adverb *excelse*, but confused it with the comparative of the adjective or past participle *excelsus*. Another conjecture has it that the poet was inspired by the ungrammatical motto on the State shield of New York. Be that as it may, the word is now firmly part of the English language and is laconically defined in the *Pocket Oxford Dictionary* as: "int. (esp. as trade mark or motto). Higher! (L)." The irreverent have gone so far as to replace the exhortation with another, as in the student song "Upidee!" and schoolboys are known to favour "Bottom uppermost." Needless to say, there are many parodies, ranging from "Paddy's Excelsior," in which the young protagonist gets no further than the arms of the maiden:

"Faith, I meant to kape on till I got to the top,
But as yer shwate self has axed me, I may as well shtop.
    Be jabbers!"

to a splendid version in pidgin English, ending thus:

That young man die: one large dog see
Too muchee bobbly findee he,

[*38*]

He hand b'long coldee, all same like ice,
He holdee flag, wit'h chop so nice—
Top-side Galah!

The most affecting and exciting use of the poem occurs in M. W. Balfe's setting
for vocal duet, in which the stirring effect of the cry echoing from Alp to Alp
is rivalled only by the imitation plainsong of the pious monks of Saint Bernard.

HENRY WADSWORTH LONGFELLOW (1807–1882),
America's most popular poet both during his lifetime and afterwards, has now
fallen from critical favour, possibly because he was so in harmony with the
literary tastes of his period. His life was as full of incidents, both lively and sad,
as his poetry. He travelled, held professorships, and married twice, both his wives
dying in tragic circumstances. He was so beloved by his English admirers that
they placed his bust in marble in the Poets' Corner of Westminster Abbey.

Sennacherib

LORD BYRON

The Assyrian came down like a wolf on the fold,
And his cohorts were gleaming in purple and gold;
And the sheen of their spears was like stars on the sea,
When the blue wave rolls nightly on deep Galilee.

Like the leaves of the forest when Summer is green,
That host with their banners at sunset were seen;
Like the leaves of the forest when Autumn hath blown,
That host on the morrow lay withered and strown.

For the Angel of Death spread his wings on the blast,
And breathed in the face of the foe as he pass'd;
And the eyes of the sleepers wax'd deadly and chill,
And their hearts but once heaved, and for ever grew still!

And there lay the steed with his nostril all wide;
But through it there roll'd not the breath of his pride:
And the foam of his gasping lay white on the turf,
And cold as the spray of the rock-beating surf.

And there lay the rider, distorted and pale,
With the dew on his brow and the rust on his mail;
And the tents were all silent, the banners alone,
The lances uplifted, the trumpet unblown.

And the widows of Ashur are loud in their wail;
And the idols are broke in the temple of Baal;
And the might of the Gentile, unsmote by the sword,
Hath melted like snow in the glance of the Lord!

The story of Sennacherib, king of Assyria, and his temerity in besieging Jerusalem is told in II Chronicles 32 and II Kings 19. Hezekiah the king and Isaiah the prophet combined in a powerful prayer for deliverance, and "it came to pass that night, that the angel of the Lord went out, and smote in the camp of the Assyrians an hundred fourscore and five thousand: and when they arose early in the morning, behold, they were all dead corpses." So Sennacherib returned "with shame of face to his own land," and, incidentally, to a nasty end.

GEORGE GORDON BYRON, LORD BYRON (1788–1824) thrilled the world with the braggadocio of his verse, and also gave it a delicious frisson of horror with his reprehensible private life. The editor of *The Popular Elocutionist and Reciter*, for instance, extolled Byron for the "new, more lofty, and more finished style of poetry than any that had preceded his, that of Shakespeare and Milton excepted." It was also necessary to add: "Of Byron's ill-starred marriage and subsequent excesses, something too much has already been written. His whole life reads like a romance of the most startling kind; his death . . . almost an inevitable consequence." As late as 1871, S. C. Hall, the editor of *The Book of Gems*, felt constrained to "warn the reader of his exquisite poetry, that danger lurks under the leaves." Byron redeemed himself in middle-class eyes, however, in the Greek War of Independence, and, as *Gleanings from the English Poets* has it, "the world saw with joy the poet forsake his life of indolent vice, and join in a noble struggle." He died of a fever, "weakened . . . by long habits of vice, and a wetting he got while out riding."

The Battle of Blenheim

ROBERT SOUTHEY

It was a summer evening,
  Old Kaspar's work was done,
And he before his cottage door
  Was sitting in the sun;
And by him sported on the green
His little grandchild Wilhelmine.

She saw her brother Peterkin
  Roll something large and round,
Which he beside the rivulet
  In playing there had found:
He came to ask what he had found,
That was so large, and smooth, and round.

Old Kaspar took it from the boy,
  Who stood expectant by;
And then the old man shook his head,
  And, with a natural sigh,
" 'Tis some poor fellow's skull," said he,
"Who fell in the great victory!

"I find them in the garden,
  For there's many here about;
And often when I go to plough,
  The ploughshare turns them out;
For many thousand men," said he,
"Were slain in that great victory!"

"Now, tell us what 'twas all about,"
  Young Peterkin he cries;
And little Wilhelmine looks up
  With wonder-waiting eyes;
"Now tell us all about the war,
And what they fought each other for."

"It was the English," Kaspar cried,
  "Who put the French to rout;
But what they fought each other for
  I could not well make out.
But everybody said," quoth he,
"That 'twas a famous victory!

"My father lived at Blenheim then,
  Yon little stream hard by;
They burn'd his dwelling to the ground,
  And he was forced to fly:
So with his wife and child he fled,
Nor had he where to rest his head.

"With fire and sword the country round
  Was wasted far and wide:
And many a childing mother then
  And new-born baby died.
But things like that, you know, must be
At every famous victory.

"They say it was a shocking sight
  After the field was won;
For many thousand bodies here
  Lay rotting in the sun.
But things like that, you know, must be
After a famous victory.

"Great praise the Duke of Marlb'ro' won,
  And our good Prince Eugene."
"Why, 'twas a very wicked thing!"
  Said little Wilhelmine.
"Nay, nay, my little girl," quoth he,
"It was a famous victory!

"And everybody praised the Duke
Who such a fight did win."
"But what good came of it at last?"
Quoth little Peterkin.
"Why, that I cannot tell," said he,
"But 'twas a famous victory!"

ROBERT SOUTHEY (1774–1843) is little read now, although he was one of the most voluminous writers of his own or any other age. Expelled from Westminster School for protesting against flogging, he went up to Balliol, where he met Coleridge, who converted him to Pantisocracy, which advocated an ideal life on the banks of the Susquehanna. These castles in the air were dissipated and, in the words of Robert Inglis in *Gleanings from the English Poets,* he "applied himself to the stern realities of life. In 1794 he married a Miss Fricker." Her sister married Coleridge, and for some years Southey supported not only his own family but Coleridge's as well on a small pension and by the labours of his pen. An opinionated if generous man who quarrelled with all who disagreed with him, he devoted himself to writing long poems and even lengthier historical works, collecting as he went along a government pension and the post of Poet Laureate. His wife died and, his mind already softening, he married again. His second wife was the poetess Caroline Bowles, now better known as Mrs. Southey. At his death, which followed shortly after, he left the considerable sum of £12,000, a figure that no Victorian biographer fails to note with approval.

The Battle of Hohenlinden

THOMAS CAMPBELL

On Linden, when the sun was low,
All bloodless lay the untrodden snow;
And dark as winter was the flow
    Of Iser, rolling rapidly.

But Linden saw another sight,
When the drum beat at dead of night,
Commanding fires of death to light
    The darkness of her scenery.

By torch and trumpet fast array'd,
Each horseman drew his battle-blade,
And furious every charger neigh'd,
    To join the dreadful revelry.

Then shook the hills with thunder riven;
Then rushed the steed to battle driven;
And louder than the bolts of heaven,
    Far flash'd the red artillery.

But redder yet that light shall glow,
On Linden's hills of stainèd snow;
And bloodier yet the torrent flow
    Of Iser, rolling rapidly.

'Tis morn; but scarce yon level sun,
Can pierce the war-clouds, rolling dun,
Where furious Frank and fiery Hun
    Shout in their sulph'rous canopy.

The combat deepens: On, ye brave!
Who rush to glory, or the grave!
Wave, Munich! all thy banners wave!
    And charge with all thy chivalry!

Few, few shall part where many meet!
The snow shall be their winding sheet,
And every turf beneath their feet
Shall be a soldier's sepulchre!

T H O M A S   C A M P B E L L (1777–1844) is now chiefly remembered as a battle-poet *par excellence*, composer of "Hohenlinden," "Ye Mariners of England," and "The Battle of the Baltic," but he left a considerable corpus of verse, including "Gertrude of Wyoming" in Spenserian stanzas, a tale of the destruction of a settlement by Indians, expressed with elegance and gentle pathos. His career was varied, successful, and comfortable, receiving from a grateful government a pension of £200 per annum and being appointed Rector of Glasgow University. Fame came to him in curious fashion: on returning to Leith after a tour of the Continent in 1803, he was taken for a spy and his box of papers was searched for evidence of treason. It is said that the first paper examined was the manuscript of "Ye Mariners of England," which was quickly published and gave Campbell immediate and immense acclaim.

The Burial of Sir John Moore

REVEREND CHARLES WOLFE

Not a drum was heard, not a funeral note,
  As his corse to the ramparts we hurried;
Not a soldier discharged his farewell shot
  O'er the grave where our hero we buried.

We buried him darkly, at dead of night,
  The sods with our bayonets turning,
By the struggling moonbeam's misty light,
  And the lantern dimly burning.

No useless coffin enclosed his breast,
  Not in sheet nor in shroud we wound him;
But he lay like a warrior taking his rest,
  With his martial cloak around him.

Few and short were the prayers we said,
  And we spoke not a word of sorrow;
But we steadfastly gazed on the face that was dead,
  And we bitterly thought of the morrow.

We thought as we hollow'd his narrow bed,
  And smoothed down his lonely pillow,
That the foe and the stranger would tread o'er his head,
  And we far away on the billow!

Lightly they'll talk of the spirit that's gone,
  And o'er his cold ashes upbraid him;
But little he'll reck if they let him sleep on,
  In the grave where a Briton has laid him.

But half of our heavy task was done,
  When the clock struck the hour for retiring,
And we heard the distant and random gun
  That the foe was sullenly firing.

Slowly and sadly we laid him down,
From the field of his fame fresh and gory;
We carved not a line, and we raised not a stone,
But we left him alone in his glory.

This perfect short elegy, which has a place in *The Oxford Book of English Verse* and many other anthologies, shows how verse can upon occasion be universally popular and also rank as poetry of the highest order. Inspired by Southey's account of Sir John Moore's death at Corunna, it originally appeared in the *Newry Telegraph* in 1817 and was discovered by Byron five years later, whereupon numerous would-be authors claimed it for their own. Wolfe himself wrote a scattered handful of poems: this is the only one to catch the public's eye.

REVEREND CHARLES WOLFE (1791–1823), born in County Kildare, entered the church after refusing to read for a fellowship at Trinity College, Dublin, because he did not relish the prospect of celibacy. Unfortunately, the object of his passions refused him, and, never robust, he fell victim to consumption.

The Blue and the Gray

By the flow of the inland river,
  Whence the fleets of iron have fled,
Where the blades of the grave-grass quiver,
  Asleep are the ranks of the dead:
    Under the sod and the dew,
      Waiting the judgment-day;
    Under the one, the Blue,
      Under the other, the Gray.

These in the robings of glory,
  Those in the gloom of defeat,
All with the battle-blood gory,
  In the dusk of eternity meet:
    Under the sod and the dew,
      Waiting the judgment-day;
    Under the laurel, the Blue,
      Under the willow, the Gray.

From the silence of sorrowful hours
  The desolate mourners go,
Lovingly laden with flowers
  Alike for the friend and the foe:
    Under the sod and the dew,
      Waiting the judgment-day;
    Under the roses, the Blue,
      Under the lilies, the Gray.

So with an equal splendor,
  The morning sun-rays fall,
With a touch impartially tender,
  On the blossoms blooming for all:
    Under the sod and the dew,
      Waiting the judgment-day;
    Broidered with gold, the Blue,
      Mellowed with gold, the Gray.

So, when the summer calleth,
On forest and field of grain,
With an equal murmur falleth
The cooling drip of the rain:
Under the sod and the dew,
Waiting the judgment-day;
Wet with the rain, the Blue,
Wet with the rain, the Gray.

Sadly, but not with upbraiding,
The generous deed was done,
In the storm of the years that are fading
No braver battle was won:
Under the sod and the dew,
Waiting the judgment-day;
Under the blossoms, the Blue,
Under the garlands, the Gray.

No more shall the war cry sever,
Or the winding rivers be red;
They banish our anger forever
When they laurel the graves of our dead!
Under the sod and the dew,
Waiting the judgment-day;
Love and tears for the Blue,
Tears and love for the Gray.

It is a commonplace that most sea-songs have been composed by landlubbers; one might also hazard that the vast majority of war poetry has been written by non-combatants. This is certainly the case where the American Civil War is concerned. Even more so, in fact, for some of the most popular has come from pens wielded by the gentle sex, as witness Julia Ward Howe's "Battle Hymn of the Republic" and "All Quiet Along the Potomac" by Ethel Lynn Beers, printed on page 244. Curiously, the great poets of America produced little of real note; perhaps only Whitman's "O Captain! My Captain!" occasioned by the death of President Lincoln, would be regarded today as a literary work of the first rank.

What did come from the Civil War, however, were a rich harvest of songs and a number of remarkably effective occasional verses by relatively unknown bards. If not exactly a one-poem poet, Francis Miles Finch is known for only one piece—the patriotic "Nathan Hale"—other than "The Blue and the Gray." This, it is believed, was composed after the poet had seen, in Friendship Cemetery, Columbus, Mississippi, ladies scattering flowers over the graves of fallen soldiers, Union and Confederate alike.

FRANCIS MILES FINCH (1827–1907), born at Ithaca, New York, seemed chosen as a follower of the Muses for he was the Class Poet at Yale. He evidently decided, however, that the law offered a more secure livelihood and eventually became a justice of the New York Court of Appeals, crowning his career as Dean of the Law School at Cornell.

The High Tide at Gettysburg
WILL HENRY THOMPSON

A cloud possessed the hollow field,
The gathering battle's smoky shield.
Athwart the gloom the lightning flashed,
And through the cloud some horsemen dashed,
And from the heights the thunder pealed.

Then at the brief command of Lee
Moved out that matchless infantry,
With Pickett leading grandly down,
To rush against the roaring crown
Of those dread heights of destiny.

Far heard above the angry guns
A cry across the tumult runs,—
The voice that rang through Shiloh's woods,
And Chickamauga's solitudes,
The fierce South cheering on her sons!

Ah, how the withering tempest blew
Against the front of Pettigrew!
A Khamsin wind that scorched and singed
Like that infernal flame that fringed
The British squares at Waterloo!

A thousand fell where Kemper led;
A thousand died where Garnett bled:
In blinding flame and strangling smoke
The remnant through the batteries broke
And crossed the works with Armistead.

"Once more in Glory's van with me!"
Virginia cried to Tennessee;
"We two together, come what may,
Shall stand upon these works today!"
(The reddest day in history.)

Brave Tennessee! In reckless way
Virginia heard her comrade say:
"Close round this rent and riddled rag!"
What time she set her battle-flag
Amid the guns of Doubleday.

But who shall break the guards that wait
Before the awful face of Fate?
The tattered standards of the South
Were shriveled at the cannon's mouth,
And all her hopes were desolate.

In vain the Tennesseean set
His breast against the bayonet!
In vain Virginia charged and raged,
A tigress in her wrath uncaged,
Till all the hill was red and wet!

Above the bayonets, mixed and crossed,
Men saw a gray, gigantic ghost
Receding through the battle-cloud,
And heard across the tempest loud
The death-cry of a nation lost!

The brave went down! Without disgrace
They leaped to Ruin's red embrace.
They only heard Fame's thunder's wake,
And saw the dazzling sun-burst break
In smiles on Glory's bloody face!

They fell, who lifted up a hand
And bade the sun in heaven to stand!
They smote and fell, who set the bars
Against the progress of the stars,
And stayed the march of Motherland!

They stood, who saw the future come
On through the fight's delirium!

They smote and stood, who held the hope
Of nations on that slippery slope
Amid the cheers of Christendom.

God lives! He forged the iron will
That clutched and held that trembling hill.
God lives and reigns! He built and lent
The heights for freedom's battlement
Where floats her flag in triumph still!

Fold up the banners! Smelt the guns!
Love rules. Her gentler purpose runs.
A mighty mother turns in tears
The pages of her battle years,
Lamenting all her fallen sons!

This full-blooded and uncomplicated piece is something of a poetical throwback. American verse of the War of Independence and the War of 1812 was, almost without exception, unashamedly heroic. The Civil War, however, awakened a new elegiac strain, to be observed in "The Blue and the Gray" and "All Quiet Along the Potomac" on page 244, very much in tune with the mid-nineteenth-century preoccupation with mortality and morality. It occurs even in such overtly popular verse as the anonymous "Me an' Jim":

'Twas the day that we fit at Seven Oaks
    Death came to Jim;
An', excuse me, please, but I sorter chokes
    Talkin' o' him.
Fer his rugged brown hand I held in mine
Till his soul passed out through the picket-line,
Whar an angel waited the countersign
    To git from Jim.

But then the poet of "The High Tide" was very young, and, unlike most contemporary bards, a soldier.

WILL HENRY THOMPSON (1848–1918) was born in Calhoun, Georgia, and after serving throughout the Civil War in the Confederate Army set up a law partnership with his brother Maurice, also known as a writer. The brothers were passionately devoted to outdoor sports, especially archery, and can be adjudged the poets laureate of the toxophilitic art. Will was, in addition, a noted orator.

The Charge of the Light Brigade

LORD TENNYSON

Half a league, half a league,
  Half a league onward,
All in the valley of Death
  Rode the six hundred.
"Forward the Light Brigade!
Charge for the guns!" he said:
Into the valley of Death
  Rode the six hundred.

"Forward the Light Brigade!"
Was there a man dismay'd?
Not tho' the soldier knew
  Some one had blunder'd:
Their's not to make reply,
Their's not to reason why,
Their's but to do and die:
Into the valley of Death
  Rode the six hundred.

Cannon to right of them,
Cannon to left of them,
Cannon in front of them
  Volley'd and thunder'd;
Storm'd at with shot and shell,
Boldly they rode and well,
Into the jaws of Death,
Into the mouth of Hell,
  Rode the six hundred.

Flash'd all their sabres bare,
Flash'd as they turn'd in air,

Sabring the gunners there,
Charging an army, while
  All the world wonder'd:
Plunged in the battery-smoke
Right thro' the line they broke;
Cossack and Russian
Reel'd from the sabre-stroke
  Shatter'd and sunder'd.
Then they rode back, but not,
  Not the six hundred.

Cannon to right of them,
Cannon to left of them,
Cannon behind them
  Volley'd and thunder'd;
Storm'd at with shot and shell,
While horse and hero fell,
They that had fought so well
Came thro' the jaws of Death
Back from the mouth of Hell,
All that was left of them,
  Left of six hundred.

When can their glory fade?
O the wild charge they made!
  All the world wonder'd.
Honour the charge they made!
Honour the Light Brigade,
  Noble six hundred!

The folly of Lord Lucan at Balaclava in ordering the Light Brigade to charge 12,000 Russians, who were fully prepared with artillery to receive them, produced not only the loss of 247 out of 673 officers and men but inspiration for the grandest of all poetical warhorses. Written at one sitting, it was based on *The Times* report of the tragic affair, a report which included the words, "some one had blundered." Sensitive friends of the poet urged him to omit that line, and when "The Charge" was published in the same volume as "Maud" it was indeed missing, to be replaced in the second edition.

ALFRED TENNYSON, FIRST BARON TENNY-SON (1809–1892), was recognized in his early teens as a future immortal: "If Alfred die," observed his admiring father, "one of our greatest poets will have gone." When, at the end of the century, Tennyson was laid to rest in Westminster Abbey, his pall-bearers were drawn from the aristocracy, politics, the universities, and the church, with not one poet or creative writer among them. As well as taking the role of national monument, he was an assiduous national servant, fulfilling his routine duties as Poet Laureate admirably by producing odes and elegies to order. His hymns to the triumphs of British arms and British pluck met with great public approval: besides "The Charge of the Light Brigade," he wrote "The Charge of the Heavy Brigade," "Riflemen, Form!" "The Defence of Lucknow," and, to maintain a balance between the services, "Jack Tar" and "The Revenge." It may be relevant to note that a reviewer of *In Memoriam*, published anonymously, hazarded that the author was "the widow of a military man."

The Song of the Western Men

REVEREND R. S. HAWKER

A good sword and a trusty hand!
A merry heart and true!
King James's men shall understand
What Cornish lads can do.

And have they fixed the where and when?
And shall Trelawney die?
Here's twenty thousand Cornish men
Will know the reason why!

Out spake their captain brave and bold,
A merry wight was he:
"If London Tower were Michael's hold
We'll set Trelawney free!

"We'll cross the Tamar, land to land,
The Severn is no stay,—
With one and all, and hand in hand,
And who shall bid us nay?

"And when we come to London Wall,
A pleasant sight to view,
Come forth! come forth, ye cowards all!
Here's men as good as you.

"Trelawney he's in keep and hold,
Trelawney he may die;
But here's twenty thousand Cornish bold
Will know the reason why!"

Trelawney of Bristol was one of the seven Bishops committed to the Tower by
James II for refusing to read the Declaration of Indulgence, whereby all the dis-
qualifications of Roman Catholics were removed. As the head of an ancient
house, Trelawney was held in respect by the men of Cornwall, who rose, as

related in the Ballad, with the determination of setting him free. The Bishops were acquitted by the jury, June 30, 1688.

REVEREND ROBERT STEPHEN HAWKER (1803–1875) was a Cornish parson with a consuming interest in the history, poetry, and people of Old Cornwall. He claimed "Trelawney" to be based on three traditional lines in the second stanza, but nobody else has found evidence of their antiquity. As an undergraduate of nineteen, Hawker married a wife of forty-one, and as vicar of Morwenstow was beset by money troubles, although as part of his assiduous parochial activities he instituted a weekly offertory. On his deathbed he was received into the Roman faith, an event that caused hot controversy in the religious press.

How They Brought the Good News from Ghent to Aix

ROBERT BROWNING

I sprang to the stirrup, and Joris, and he;
I galloped, Dirck galloped, we galloped all three;
"Good speed!" cried the watch, as the gate-bolts undrew;
"Speed!" echoed the wall to us galloping through;
Behind shut the postern, the lights sank to rest,
And into the midnight we galloped abreast.

Not a word to each other; we kept the great pace
Neck by neck, stride by stride, never changing our place;
I turned in my saddle and made its girths tight,
Then shortened each stirrup, and set the pique right,
Rebuckled the cheek-strap, chained slacker the bit,
Nor galloped less steadily Roland a whit.

'Twas moonset at starting; but while we drew near
Lokeren, the cocks crew and twilight dawned clear;
At Boom, a great yellow star came out to see;
At Düffeld, 'twas morning as plain as could be;
And from Mechlen church-steeple we heard the half-chime,
So Joris broke silence with, "Yet there is time!"

At Aerschot, up leaped of a sudden the sun,
And against him the cattle stood black every one,
To stare thro' the mist at us galloping past,
And I saw my stout galloper Roland at last,
With resolute shoulders, each butting away
The haze, as some bluff river headland its spray,

And his low head and crest, just one sharp ear bent back
For my voice, and the other pricked out on his track;
And one eye's black intelligence,—ever that glance
O'er its white edge at me, his own master, askance!
And the thick heavy spume-flakes which aye and anon
His fierce lips shook upwards in galloping on.

By Hasselt, Dirck groaned; and cried Joris, "Stay spur!
Your Roos galloped bravely, the fault's not in her,
We'll remember at Aix"—for one heard the quick wheeze
Of her chest, saw the stretched neck and staggering knees,
And sunk tail, and horrible heave of the flank,
As down on her haunches she shuddered and sank.

So we were left galloping, Joris and I,
Past Looz and past Tongres, no cloud in the sky;
The broad sun above laughed a pitiless laugh,
'Neath our feet broke the brittle bright stubble like chaff;
Till over by Dalhem a dome-spire sprang white,
And "Gallop," gasped Joris, "for Aix is in sight!
"How they'll greet us!" and all in a moment his roan
Rolled neck and croup over, lay dead as a stone;
And there was my Roland to bear the whole weight
Of the news which alone could save Aix from her fate,
With his nostrils like pits full of blood to the brim,
And with circles of red for his eye-socket's rim.

Then I cast loose my buffcoat, each holster let fall,
Shook off both my jack-boots, let go belt and all,
Stood up in the stirrup, leaned, patted his ear,
Called my Roland his pet-name, my horse without peer;
Clapped my hands, laughed and sang, any noise, bad or good,
Till at length into Aix Roland galloped and stood.

And all I remember is, friends flocking round
As I sate with his head 'twixt my knees on the ground,
And no voice but was praising this Roland of mine,
As I poured down his throat our last measure of wine,
Which (the burgesses voted by common consent)
Was no more than his due who brought good news from Ghent.

Of all the works in that heart-stirring art-form, the galloping poem, this must
take the palm. But there are strong competitors in Cowper's "John Gilpin" and

Longfellow's "The Midnight Ride of Paul Revere," not to mention Joaquin Miller's "Kit Carson's Ride," Thomas Buchanan Read's "Sheridan's Ride," "D'Artagnan's Ride" by Gouverneur Morris the younger, "The Arab's Ride to Cairo" by G. J. Whyte-Melville, and sundry others. There are many parodies: the most brilliant without any doubt whatever is that by R. J. Yeatman and W. C. Sellar, authors of *1066 and All That*. Entitled "How I Brought the Good News from Aix to Ghent (or Vice Versa)," it opens as follows:

> I sprang to the rollocks and Jorrocks and me,
> And I galloped, you galloped, he galloped, we galloped all three . . .
> Not a word to each other; we kept changing place,
> Neck to neck, back to front, ear to ear, face to face;
> And we yelled once or twice, when we heard a clock chime,
> "Would you kindly oblige us, *Is that the right time?*"
> As I galloped, you galloped, he galloped, we galloped, ye galloped, they two
> shall have galloped; *let us trot.*

Browning's story is imaginary and is not based on any historical event; so far no commentator has provided a satisfactory explanation of exactly what the good news was.

R O B E R T   B R O W N I N G   (1812–1889) did not merit much public notice until he was nearly sixty; for many years his work was overshadowed by that of his wife, Elizabeth Barrett Browning. Until later years his most popular poem seems to have been "Evelyn Hope," an elegy very much in tune with middle-class sentiment on the death of a sixteen-year-old girl. When success eventually came, he was naturally gratified but a little suspicious, refusing to have anything to do with the well-meant Browning Society for fear of ridicule. Maybe he still remembered what Miss Barrett once wrote about him in a fit of enthusiasm, describing him as a "pomegranate which, if cut deep down the middle, shows a heart within blood-tinctured, of a veined humanity."

The Midnight Ride of Paul Revere

HENRY WADSWORTH LONGFELLOW

Listen, my children, and you shall hear
Of the midnight ride of Paul Revere,
On the eighteenth of April, in Seventy-five;
Hardly a man is now alive
Who remembers that famous day and year.

He said to his friend, "If the British march
By land or sea from the town tonight,
Hang a lantern aloft in the belfry-arch
Of the North Church tower as a signal light,—
One if by land, and two if by sea;
And I on the opposite shore will be,
Ready to ride and spread the alarm
Through every Middlesex village and farm,
For the country-folk to be up and to arm."

Then he said, "Goodnight!" and with muffled oar
Silently rowed to the Charlestown shore,
Just as the moon rose over the bay,
Where swinging wide at her moorings lay
The *Somerset*, British man-of-war;
A phantom-ship, with each mast and spar,
And a huge black hulk, that was magnified
By its own reflection in the tide.

Meanwhile, his friend through alley and street,
Wanders and watches with eager ears,
Till in the silence around him he hears
The muster of men at the barrack-door,
The sound of arms, and the tramp of feet,
And the measured tread of the grenadiers,
Marching down to their boats on the shore.
Then he climbed to the tower of the Old North Church,
Up the wooden stairs, with stealthy tread,

To the belfry-chamber overhead,
And startled the pigeons from their perch
On the sombre rafters, that round him made
Masses and moving shapes of shade,—
Up the trembling ladder, steep and tall,
To the highest window in the wall,
Where he paused to listen and look down
A moment on the roofs of the town
And the moonlight flowing over all.

Beneath, in the churchyard, lay the dead,
In their night-encampment on the hill,
Wrapped in silence so deep and still
That he could hear, like a sentinel's tread,
The watchful night wind, as it went
Creeping along from tent to tent,
And seeming to whisper, "All is well!"
A moment only he feels the spell
Of the place and the hour, and the secret dread
Of the lonely belfry and the dead:
For suddenly all his thoughts are bent
On a shadowy something far away,
Where the river widens to meet the bay,—
A line of black that bends and floats
On the rising tide, like a bridge of boats.

Meanwhile, impatient to mount and ride,
Booted and spurred, with a heavy stride
On the opposite shore walked Paul Revere.
Now he patted his horse's side,
Now gazed at the landscape far and near,
Then, impetuous, stamped the earth,
And turned and tightened his saddle-girth;
But mostly he watched with eager search
The belfry tower of the Old North Church,
As it rose above the graves on the hill,
Lonely and spectral and sombre and still.
And lo! as he looks, on the belfry's height

A glimmer, and then a gleam of light!
He springs to the saddle, the bridle he turns,
But lingers and gazes, till full on his sight
A second lamp in the belfry burns!

A hurry of hoofs in the village street,
A shape in the moonlight, a bulk in the dark,
And beneath, from the pebbles, in passing, a spark
Struck out by a steed flying fearless and fleet;
That was all! And yet, through the gloom and the light,
The fate of a nation was riding that night;
And the spark struck out by that steed in its flight
Kindled the land into flame with its heat.
He has left the village and mounted the steep
And beneath him, tranquil and broad and deep,
Is the Mystic, meeting the ocean tides;
And under the alders that skirt its edge,
Now soft on the sand, now loud on the ledge,
Is heard the tramp of his steed as he rides.

It was *twelve* by the village clock
When he crossed the bridge into Midford town.
He heard the crowing of the cock
And the barking of the farmer's dog,
And felt the damp of the river fog,
That rises after the sun goes down.
It was *one* by the village clock
When he galloped into Lexington.
He saw the gilded weather-cock
Swim in the moonlight as he passed,
And the meeting-house windows blank and bare,
Gaze at him with a spectral glare,
As if they already stood aghast
At the bloody work they would look upon.

It was *two* by the village clock
When he came to the bridge in Concord town.
He heard the bleating of the flock,

And the twitter of birds among the trees,
And felt the breath of the morning breeze
Blowing over the meadows brown.
And one was safe and asleep in his bed
Who at the bridge would be first to fall,
Who that day would be lying dead,
Pierced by a British musket-ball.

You know the rest. In the books you have read,
How the British regulars fired and fled,—
How the farmers gave them ball for ball,
From behind each fence and farmyard wall,
Chasing the red-coats down the lane,
Then crossing the fields to emerge again
Under the trees at the turn of the road,
And only pausing to fire and load.

So through the night rode Paul Revere;
And so through the night went his cry of alarm
To every Middlesex village and farm,—
A cry of defiance, and not of fear,
A voice in the darkness, a knock at the door,
And a word that shall echo for evermore!
For, borne on the night-wind of the Past,
Through all our history, to the last,
In the hour of darkness and peril and need,
The people will waken and listen to hear
The hurrying hoof-beats of that steed,
And the midnight message of Paul Revere.

Silversmith, engraver, portrait painter, cartoonist, courier, picture-frame carver,
false-teeth maker, cannon manufacturer, church-bell founder, bank-note printer,
discoverer of how to roll sheet copper, politician, and patriot, Paul Revere (1735–
1818) is a figure not overemphasized by English history textbooks. It is rather
a shame to have to record that not only was he rather unsuccessful as a soldier
but that he was far from alone in carrying word from Boston to Lexington and
Concord that the British were on the move.

There is a note on Longfellow on page 39.

The Arab's Farewell to His Steed

HON. MRS. NORTON

My beautiful, my beautiful! that standest meekly by,
With thy proudly-arched and glossy neck, and dark and fiery eye!
Fret not to roam the desert now with all thy wingèd speed:
I may not mount on thee again!—thou'rt sold, my Arab steed!

Fret not with that impatient hoof, snuff not the breezy wind;
The farther that thou fliest now, so far am I behind!
The stranger hath thy bridle-rein, thy master hath his gold;—
Fleet-limbed and beautiful, farewell; thou'rt sold, my steed, thou'rt sold.

Farewell!—Those free untired limbs full many a mile must roam,
To reach the chill and wintry clime that clouds the stranger's home;
Some other hand, less kind, must now thy corn and bed prepare;
That silky mane I braided once must be another's care.

The morning sun shall dawn again—but never more with thee
Shall I gallop o'er the desert paths where we were wont to be—
Evening shall darken on the earth: and o'er the sandy plain,
Some other steed, with slower pace, shall bear me home again.

Only in sleep shall I behold that dark eye glancing bright—
Only in sleep shall hear again that step so firm and light;
And when I raise my dreamy arms to check or cheer thy speed,
Then must I startling wake, to feel thou'rt sold! my Arab steed.

Ah, rudely then, unseen by me, some cruel hand may chide,
Till foam-wreaths lie, like crested waves, along thy panting side,
And the rich blood that in thee swells, in thy indignant pain,
Till careless eyes that on thee gaze may count each starting vein!

Will they ill-use thee;—If I thought—but no,—it cannot be;
Thou art too swift, yet easy curbed, so gentle, yet so free;—
And yet, if haply when thou'rt gone, this lonely heart should yearn,
Can the hand that casts thee from it now, command thee to return?

"Return!"—alas! my Arab steed! what will thy master do,
When thou that wast his all of joy, hast vanished from his view?
When the dim distance greets mine eyes, and through the gathering tears
Thy bright form for a moment, like the false mirage, appears?

Slow and unmounted will I roam, with wearied foot, alone,
Where with fleet step, and joyous bound, thou oft hast borne me on;
And sitting down by the green well, I'll pause and sadly think—
" 'Twas here he bowed his glossy neck when last I saw him drink."

When *last* I saw thee drink!—Away! the fevered dream is o'er!
I could not live a day, and know that we should meet no more;
They tempted me, my beautiful! for hunger's power is strong—
They tempted me, my beautiful! but I have loved too long.

Who said, that I had given thee up? Who said that thou wert sold?
'Tis false! 'tis false, my Arab steed! I fling them back their gold!
Thus—thus, I leap upon thy back, and scour the distant plains!
Away! who overtakes us now shall claim thee for his pains.

The burning desert sands engaged the romantic imagination long before
Rudolf Valentino galloped away on his white stallion, Miss Agnes Ayres a not
too unwilling passenger. William Beckford, builder of the vast Gothick folly of
Fonthill, helped nurture the legend when he published his Arabian Tale, *Vathek*,
in 1786, but it bloomed prodigiously in the next century. The American
journalist and poet, Bayard Taylor made a bid to corner the Orient in the
1850s: his "Bedouin Song" (see page 99) is still famous in its musical setting.
One recalls many other works in the same genre, typical being the song "A
Son of the Desert," in which the Arabian aristocrat avers:

> And I know that Zuleika awaits in her tent,
> The fairest in all the sun-kiss'd Orient,
> Whose form has the grace of a palm heaven-sent,
> She will welcome her love, when the storm-cloud is spent.
> For a Son of the Desert am I, etc.

CAROLINE ELIZABETH SARAH NORTON, *née* SHERIDAN (1808–1877), was the granddaughter of Richard Brinsley Sheridan. She was a woman of striking beauty; her portrait by William Etty indicates a proud, fiery, and somewhat overwhelming personality completely in tune with the Byronic style of her verse. Like many another nineteenth-century poetess, she offered her first works to an indulgent public in her early teens. Her life was stormy. She married, disastrously, the Hon. George Norton, a commissioner of bankruptcy, whom she was forced to support by her pen, and, it seems highly likely, by the grant of her favours to Lord Melbourne, obtaining a metropolitan police magistracy for her husband in the process. She separated from the Hon. George, and fought him in the courts for many years afterwards. On his death, she married Sir William Stirling Maxwell, bart., but lived only a few months longer.

The Leak in the Dyke

PHOEBE CARY

The good dame looked from her cottage
  At the close of the pleasant day,
And cheerily called to her little son
  Outside the door at play;
"Come, Peter, come! I want you to go,
  While there is light to see,
To the hut of the blind old man who lives
  Across the dyke, for me;
And take these cakes I made for him,—
  They are hot and smoking yet;
You have time enough to go and come
  Before the sun is set."

Then the good wife turned to her labour,
  Humming a simple song,
And thought of her husband, working hard
  At the sluices all day long;
And set the turf a-blazing,
  And brought the coarse, black bread;
That he might find a fire at night,
  And find the table spread.

And Peter left the brother,
  With whom all day he had played,
And the sister who had watched their sports
  In the willow's tender shade;
And told them they'd see him back before
  They saw a star in sight,
Though he wouldn't be afraid to go
  In the very darkest night!

For he was a brave, bright fellow,
  With eye and conscience clear;
He could do whatever a boy might do,

And he had not learned to fear.
Why, he wouldn't have robbed a bird's nest,
Nor brought a stork to harm,
Though never a law in Holland
Had stood to stay his arm!

And now, with his face all glowing,
And eyes as bright as the day,
With the thoughts of his pleasant errand,
He trudged along the way;
And soon his joyous prattle
Made glad a lonesome place—
Alas! if only the blind old man
Could have seen that happy face!
Yet he somehow caught the brightness
Which his voice and presence lent;
And he felt the sunshine come and go
As Peter came and went.

And now, as the day was sinking,
And the winds began to rise,
The mother looked from her door again,
Shading her anxious eyes;
And saw the shadows deepen,
And birds to their homes come back,
But never a sign of Peter
Along the level track.
But she said: "He will come at morning,
So I need not fret nor grieve,—
Though it isn't like my boy at all
To stay without my leave."

But where was the child delaying?
On the homeward way was he,
And across the dyke while the sun was up
An hour above the sea.
He was stooping now to gather flowers,
Now listening to the sound,

As the angry waters dashed themselves
    Against their narrow bound.

"Ah! well for us," said Peter,
    "That the gates are good and strong,
And my father tends them carefully,
    Or they would not hold you long!
You're a wicked sea!" said Peter:
    "I know why you fret and chafe;
You would like to spoil our lands and homes,
    But our sluices keep you safe!"

But hark! through the noise of waters
    Comes a low, clear, trickling sound;
And the child's face pales with terror,
    And his blossoms drop to the ground.
He is up the bank in a moment,
    And, stealing through the sand,
He sees a stream not yet so large
    As his slender, childish hand,
'Tis a leak in the dyke! He is but a boy,
    Unused to fearful scenes;
But young as he is, he has learned to know
    The dreadful thing that means.
A leak in the dyke! The stoutest heart
    Grows faint that cry to hear,
And the bravest man in all the land
    Turns white with mortal fear.
For he knows the smallest leak may grow
    To flood in a single night;
And he knows the strength of the cruel sea
    When loosed in its angry might.

And the boy! he has seen the danger,
    And, shouting a wild alarm,
He forces back the weight of the sea
    With strength of his single arm;
He listens for the joyful sound

Of a footstep passing nigh;
And lays his ear to the ground to catch
    The answer to his cry.
And he hears the rough wind blowing,
    And the waters rise and fall,
But never an answer comes to him
    Save the echo of his call.
He sees no hope, no succour—
    His feeble voice is lost;
Yet what shall he do but watch and wait,
    Though he perish at his post!

So, faintly calling and crying
    Till the sun is under the sea!
Crying and moaning till the stars
    Come out for company;
He thinks of his brother and sister,
    Asleep in their safe warm bed;
He thinks of his father and mother,
    Of himself as dying—and dead;
And of how, when the night is over,
    They must come and find him at last;
But he never thinks he can leave the place
    Where duty holds him fast.

The good dame in the cottage
    Is up and astir with the light,
For the thought of little Peter
    Has been with her all night.
And now she watches the pathway,
    As yester eve she had done;
But what does she see so strange and black
    Against the rising sun?
Her neighbours are bearing between them
    Something straight to her door—
The child is coming home, but not
    As he ever came before!

"He is dead!" she cries; "my darling!"
And the startled father hears,
And comes and looks the way she looks,
And fears the thing she fears;
Till a glad shout from the bearers
Thrills the stricken man and wife,—
"Give thanks, your son has saved our land,
And God has saved his life!"
So, there in the morning sunshine,
They knelt about the boy;
And every head was bared and bent
In tearful, reverent joy.

'Tis many a year since then; but still,
When the sea roars like a flood,
Their boys are taught what a boy can do
Who is brave and true and good.
For every man in that country
Takes his son by the hand,
And tells him of little Peter,
Whose courage saved the land.
They have many a valiant hero,
Remembered through the years;
But never one whose name so oft
Is named with loving tears.
And his deed shall be sung by the cradle,
And told to the child on the knee,
So long as the dykes of Holland
Divide the land from the sea.

PHOEBE CARY (1824–1871) and Alice Cary (1820–1871) were
born near Cincinnati, Ohio. These poetical sisters, having published a book of
verse together, migrated to New York, where their weekly receptions were
celebrated as a centre of literary life. Their combined talent for moral but
melancholy verse afforded them a modest competence, and Phoebe was lively
enough to write parodies as well as more conventional effusions on faith, hope,
and love. Her sister's pathetic verses upon the nautical prodigal returned, "Elihu,"
appear on page 162.

Vitaï Lampada

SIR HENRY NEWBOLT

There's a breathless hush in the Close tonight—
Ten to make and the match to win—
A bumping pitch and a blinding light,
An hour to play and the last man in.
And it's not for the sake of a ribboned coat,
Or the selfish hope of a season's fame,
But his Captain's hand on his shoulder smote—
"Play up! play up! and play the game!"

The sand of the desert is sodden red—
Red with the wreck of a square that broke;
The Gatling's jammed and the Colonel dead,
And the Regiment blind with dust and smoke.
The river of death has brimmed his banks,
And England's far and Honour a name,
But the voice of a schoolboy rallies the ranks:
"Play up! play up! and play the game!"

This is the word that year by year,
While in her place the School is set,
Every one of her sons must hear,
And none that hears it dare forget.
This they all with a joyful mind
Bear through life like a torch in flame,
And falling fling to the host behind—
"Play up! play up! and play the game!"

In the earlier part of the nineteenth century little children were indoctrinated with such gentle virtues as honesty, charity, and industry. With the spread of British red over the map of the world, sterner, more pugnacious qualities were needed to serve the cause of Empire, and the lads of the Island Race were exhorted in *Boy's Own Paper* and other journals to fight a clean fight, keep a straight bat, maintain a stiff upper lip, and to be magnanimous towards a beaten foe. "Vitaï Lampada" (which may be translated as "Torches of Life") and Kipling's "If—" were typical of the imperial strain, and it even appeared in America in such works as "Alumnus Football" by Grantland Rice, which has the immortal lines:

> For when the One Great Scorer comes
> To write against your name,
> He marks—not that you won or lost—
> But how you played the game.

SIR HENRY JOHN NEWBOLT (1862–1938) was called to the bar, and his first steps towards a literary life were contributions to the *Law Digest*. In the nineties he began to write stories, a tragedy in blank verse, and such superb poems as "Drake's Drum," "Admirals All," and "The Fighting Téméraire." He also composed sensitive and romantic verse, joined the Admiralty and the Foreign Office in what used to be called the Great War, became an official naval historian, and was particularly assiduous in honorary work. It is, though, as the "nautical Kipling," as Walter de la Mare called him, that his name lives.

3
Love, Sweet Love

'Tis but the dalliance, the dalliance of youth and maid;
'Tis but the passion, the passion of vows that fade.

—"Love, Sweet Love"

Love, Sweet Love

FELIX MC GLENNON

Love, sweet love is the poet's theme;
Love, sweet love is the poet's dream.
What is the love of which they sing?
Only a phantom unreal thing.
'Tis but the dalliance, the dalliance of youth and maid;
'Tis but the passion, the passion of vows that fade.
'Tis not the Heav'n, the Heav'n-implanted glow
That true hearts call love, ah no, ah no!

See a mother gazing on her baby boy
With ecstatic eyes and heart that fills with joy;
He to her is purest gold without alloy;
For him she prays to Heav'n above!
How she guides his footsteps thro' this vale of strife;
Watches o'er his bedside when infection's rife,
Risking for her baby boy her health, her life.
    That is love, that is love!

Love, sweet love—how the word's misplaced!
Love, sweet love—how the word's disgraced!
What is a fond lover's glance?
What is a shy maiden's advance?
What is the pressure, the pressure of am'rous lips?
What is the pressure, the pressure of finger tips?
Only the pleasure, the joys of a passing day.
'Tis not the love that will live for aye.

See a father standing at his cottage door,
Watching baby in the gutter rolling o'er;
Laughing at his merry pranks—but hark, a roar!
    Help, oh help him, gracious Heav'n above!
Dashing down the road there comes a madden'd horse:
Out the father rushes with resistless force;
Saves the child—but there he lies, a mangled corse.
    That is love, that is love!

Oh, the love of a faithful friend!
True, true love that will never end!
Where can such friendship be found on earth?
In true hearts alone it findeth birth.
Friends meet friends, and they vow, they vow to cling.
Often, alas, doth their love, their love take wing.
Seldom, alas, can such faithful friendship be
As that of two comrades who went to sea.

When a squall had struck the ship and she was lost,
Clinging to a plank the chums were tempest-toss'd;
But the plank was water-logged and sank almost—
    One of them must meet his God above.
One of them said, "Jack, the plank will not hold two;
You've a wife and children, so I'll die for you.
Goodbye, Jack." He leaves the plank and sinks from view.
    That is love, that is love!

This song of 1889 contains two notable episodes that recur in various guises throughout Victorian popular literature: father saving his curly-pated child from a runaway horse (or carriage, or locomotive), and the shipwreck scene in which Jack surrenders his plank (or lifebelt, or raft) to a married messmate. Felix McGlennon was also the composer of a number of English music-hall songs, including the famous "Comrades."

"Curfew Must Not Ring Tonight"

ROSE HARTWICK THORPE

Slowly England's sun was setting o'er the hill-tops far away,
Filling the land with beauty at the close of one sad day,
And the last rays kissed the foreheads of a man and a maiden fair,
He with footsteps slow and weary—she with sunny, floating hair;
He with bowed head, sad and thoughtful, she with lips all cold and white,
Struggling to keep back the murmur,—"Curfew must not ring tonight."

"Sexton," Bessie's white lips faltered, pointing to the prison old,
With its turrets tall and gloomy, with its walls dark, damp and cold,
"I've a lover in that prison, doomed this very night to die
At the ringing of the curfew, and no earthly help is nigh!
Cromwell will not come till sunset," and her lips grew strangely white
As she breathed the husky whisper,—"Curfew must not ring tonight."

"Bessie," calmly spoke the sexton,—every word pierced her young heart
Like the piercing of an arrow, like a deadly poison dart—
"Long, long years I've rung the curfew from that gloomy, shadowed
        tower;
Every evening, just at sunset, it has told the twilight hour;
I have done my duty ever, tried to do it just and right,
Now I'm old I still must do it; curfew, it must ring tonight."

Wild her eyes and pale her features, stern and white her thoughtful brow,
And within her secret bosom Bessie made a solemn vow.
She had listened while the judges read without a tear or sigh,
"At the ringing of the curfew Basil Underwood *must die*."
And her breath came fast and faster, and her eyes grew large and bright;
In an undertone she murmured, "Curfew *must not* ring tonight."

She with quick steps bounded forward, sprang within the old church door,
Left the old man threading slowly paths so oft he'd trod before.
Not a moment paused the maiden, but with eye and cheek aglow
Mounted up the gloomy tower, where the bell swung to and fro,
As she climbed the dusty ladder on which fell no ray of light—
Up and up, her white lips saying, "Curfew must not ring tonight."

She has reached the topmost ladder; o'er her hangs the great dark bell;
Awful is the gloom beneath her, like the pathway down to hell!
Lo! the ponderous tongue is swinging, 'tis the hour of curfew now,
And the sight has chilled her bosom, stopped her breath, and paled her
    brow,
Shall she let it ring? No, never! flash her eyes with sudden light,
And she springs and grasps it firmly—"Curfew must not ring tonight."

Out she swung, far out—the city seemed a speck of light below,
'Twixt Heaven and earth her form suspended, as the bell swung to and
    fro!
And the sexton at the bell-rope, old and deaf, heard not the bell,
But he thought it still was ringing fair young Basil's funeral knell.
Still the maiden clung more firmly, and with trembling lips and white,
Said, to hush her heart's wild beating, *"Curfew shall not ring tonight."*

It was o'er; the bell ceased swaying; and the maiden stepped once more
Firmly on the dark old ladder, where for hundred years before
Human foot had not been planted. The brave deed that she had done
Should be told long ages after, as the rays of setting sun
Should illume the sky with beauty; agèd sires, with heads of white,
Long should tell the little children curfew did not ring that night.

O'er the distant hills came Cromwell; Bessie sees him, and her brow,
Full of hope and full of gladness, has no anxious traces now.
At his feet she tells her story, shows her hands all bruised and torn;
And her face, so sweet and pleading, yet with sorrow pale and worn,
Touched his heart with sudden pity, lit his eye with misty light:
"Go! your lover lives," said Cromwell; "Curfew shall not ring tonight."

This remarkable work exists in a number of versions: the present editor knows
of at least three, one of which has an additional concluding stanza:

    Wide they flung the massive portals, led the prisoner forth to die,
    All his bright young life before him. 'Neath the darkening English sky
    Bessie came with flying footsteps, eyes aglow with love-light sweet;
    Kneeling on the turf beside him, laid a pardon at his feet.
    In his brave, strong arms he clasped her, kissed the face upturned and white,
    Whispered, "Darling, you have saved me; curfew will not ring tonight."

ROSE HARTWICK THORPE (1850–1939), poetess and novelist, was born in Indiana. The one poem on which her reputation now rests was published in a Detroit newspaper when its author was only seventeen, and was based on an anonymous story called "Love and Loyalty." There are a number of unsympathetic parodies, but the most notable modern comment upon "Curfew Must Not Ring Tonight" came in the form of illustrations by the late James Thurber.

Lochinvar
from "Marmion," Canto V
SIR WALTER SCOTT

Oh! young Lochinvar is come out of the West,
Through all the wide Border his steed was the best;
And, save his good broadsword, he weapon had none,
He rode all unarmed, and he rode all alone.
So faithful in love, and so dauntless in war,
There never was knight like the young Lochinvar.

He stayed not for brake, and he stopped not for stone,
He swam the Eske river when ford there was none;
But, ere he alighted at Netherby gate,
The bride had consented, the gallant came late;
For a laggard in love, and a dastard in war,
Was to wed the fair Ellen of brave Lochinvar.

So boldly he entered the Netherby Hall,
Among bride's-men, and kinsmen, and brothers, and all.
Then spoke the bride's father, his hand on his sword
(For the poor craven bridegroom said never a word),
"Oh! come ye in peace here, or come ye in war,
Or to dance at our bridal, young Lord Lochinvar?"

"I long wooed your daughter, my suit you denied:—
Love swells like the Solway, but ebbs like its tide—
And now I am come, with this lost love of mine,
To lead but one measure, drink one cup of wine.
There are maidens in Scotland more lovely by far,
That would gladly be bride to the young Lochinvar."

The bride kissed the goblet; the knight took it up,
He quaffed at the wine, and he threw down the cup.
She looked down to blush, and she looked up to sigh,
With a smile on her lips, and a tear in her eye.

He took her soft hand, ere her mother could bar,—
"Now tread we a measure," said young Lochinvar.

So stately his form, and so lovely her face,
That never a hall such a galliard did grace;
While her mother did fret, and her father did fume,
And the bridegroom stood dangling his bonnet and plume;
And the bridesmaidens whispered, " 'Twere better by far
To have matched our fair cousin with young Lochinvar."

One touch of her hand, and one word in her ear,
When they reached the hall-door, and the charger stood near;
So light to the croupe the fair lady he swung,
So light to the saddle before her he sprung;
"She is won! we are gone! over bank, bush, and scaur;
They'll have fleet steeds that follow," quoth young Lochinvar.

There was mounting 'mong Graemes of the Netherby clan;
Forsters, Fenwicks, and Musgraves, they rode and they ran:
There was racing and chasing on Cannobie Lee,
But the lost bride of Netherby ne'er did they see.
So daring in love, and so dauntless in war,
Have ye e'er heard of gallant like young Lochinvar?

Ancient Gaelic poetry and medieval balladry so excited the literati of the eighteenth century that Chatterton and Macpherson ("translator" of Ossian) even
went so far as to forge it. Others imitated the forms, but only achieved a self-
consciously Gothick effect. It took a poet of Scott's calibre to turn the laconic,
succinct, basically unromantic ballad into highly successful full-blown romantic
verse.

SIR WALTER SCOTT (1771–1832) seems to have impressed Victorian anthologists (who had the pleasant habit of appending short biographies to their selections) less for his poetic and literary accomplishments than for his financial and social successes. In particular, they stressed that at his romantic mansion of Abbotsford he entertained visitors of all ranks, from the prince downward, and remarked on his honourable conduct after making the literally fatal mistake of forming intimate relations with James Ballantyne, a printer, and the firm of Constable, a publisher. After their failure, his personal liabilities amounted to £117,000, of which, in four years by the fruits of his pen, he repaid £70,000. The effort only ended in his bodily and mental collapse, and although the Admiralty provided a ship to take him to Italy in the hope of recovery, it was too late. He returned to Abbotsford to die, being consoled at the last by having read to him his favourite passages from the Bible.

The Deserter

BAYARD TAYLOR

" 'Deserter!' Well, Captain, the word's about right,
And it's uncommon queer I should run from a fight
Or the chance of a fight: I, raised in the land
Where boys, you might say, are born rifle in hand,
And who've fought all my life for the right of my ranch,
With the wily Apache and the cruel Comanche.

"But it's true, and I'll own it—I did run away.
'Drunk?' No, sir! I'd not tasted a drop all day;
But—smile if you will—I'd a dream in the night,
And I woke in a fever of sorrow and fright,
And I went for my horse; then up and away:
And I rode like the wind till the break of the day.

" 'What was it I dreamt?' I dreamed of my wife—
The true little woman that's better than life—
I dreamt of my boys—I have three—one is ten,—
The youngest is four—all brave little men;
Of my one baby girl, my pretty white dove!
The star of my home, the rose of my love!

"I saw the log-house on the clear San Antone,
For I knew that around it the grass had been mown;
For I felt, in my dream, the sweet breath of the hay—
I was there, for I lifted a jessamine spray;
And the dog that I loved heard my whispered command,
And whimpered, and put his big head in my hand.

"The place was so still! all the boys were at rest;
And the mother lay dreaming, the babe at her breast;
I saw the fair scene for a moment; then . . . stood
In a circle of flame, amid shrieking and blood!
The Comanche had the place!—Captain, spare me the rest!
You know what that means, for you come from the West.

[*87*]

"I woke with a start, and I had but one aim—
To save or revenge them! My head was aflame,
And my heart had stood still; I was mad I dare say,
For my horse fell dead at the dawn of the day.
Then I knew what I'd done; and with heart-broken breath,
When the boys found me out, I was praying for death.

" 'A pardon?' No, Captain—I did run away,
And the wrong to the flag it is right I should pay
With my life. It is not hard to be brave
When one's children and wife have gone over the grave.
Boys, take a good aim! When I turn to the West
Put a ball through my heart!—it is kindest and best."

He lifted his hat to the flag—bent his head,
And the prayer of his childhood solemnly said;
Shouted: "Comrades, adieu!"—spread his arms to the West—
And a rifle-ball instantly granted him rest.
But o'er his sad grave, by the Mexican sea,
Wives and mothers have planted a blossoming tree;
And maidens bring roses, and tenderly say,—
"It was love—sweetest love—led that soldier away."

JAMES BAYARD TAYLOR (1825–1878), who hailed from
Pennsylvania, was apprenticed to a printer, but like many Americans heard
Europe's call, left his job, went on a walking tour and wrote articles and an
immensely successful book about it, *Views Afoot; or, Europe Seen with Knap-
sack and Staff*. As a journalist he reported the Gold Rush, as a diplomat he
represented the United States in St. Petersburg and Berlin, as a scholar he was
non-resident Professor of German Literature at Cornell and translated *Faust,*
and he also flowered as a novelist and dramatist. Popular, facile, ambitious, and
nomadic, Taylor nonetheless considered his calling in life was that of a serious
poet, a belief that posterity, alas, has failed to confirm.

When I Was a King in Babylon

W. E. HENLEY

Or ever the knightly years were gone
With the old world to the grave,
I was a King in Babylon
And you were a Christian Slave.

I saw, I took, I cast you by,
I bent and broke your pride.
You loved me well, or I heard them lie,
But your longing was denied.
Surely I knew that by and by
You cursed your gods and died.

And a myriad suns have set and shone
Since then upon the grave
Decreed by the King in Babylon
To her that had been his Slave.

The pride I trampled is now my scathe,
For it tramples me again.
The old resentment lasts like death,
For you love, yet you refrain.
I break my heart on your hard unfaith,
And I break my heart in vain.

Yet not for an hour do I wish undone
The deed beyond the grave,
When I was a King in Babylon
And you were a Virgin Slave.

No more telling verses can have been written on the proprietorial Victorian attitude of man towards woman. In *The Age of Optimism*, James Laver quotes the example of the doughty Hon. Mrs. Norton, who fought her husband, who had deserted her, for her children and the money she earned by writing and yet could still say: "The natural position of women is inferiority to a man, that is a thing of God's appointing, not of man's devising."

WILLIAM ERNEST HENLEY (1849–1903), English poet, journalist, critic, and playwright, was a cripple from the age of twelve, and despite his extremely robust appearance was always in precarious health. His long treatment under Lister resulted in the powerful and moving *Hospital Verses*, which are undeservedly neglected today. His life was very full, devoted mainly to editing and criticism, but his poetry was extremely popular, especially in America, and Francis Thompson found "a rich and lovely verbal magic is mated with metre that comes and goes like the heaving of the Muse's bosom." He compiled *Lyra Heroica*, an anthology of stirring verse for boys. His enfeebled frame probably accounted for the strain of pugnacious patriotism to be found in his "England, My England":

> What have I done for you,
>   England, my England?
> What is there I would not do,
>   England, my own?
> With your glorious eyes austere,
> As the Lord were walking near,
> Whispering terrible things and dear
>   As the Song on your bugles blown,
>   England—
> Round the world on your bugles blown.

Oh, No! We Never Mention Her

THOMAS HAYNES BAYLY

Oh, no! we never mention her, her name is never heard;
My lips are now forbid to speak that once familiar word:
From sport to sport they hurry me, to banish my regret;
And when they win a smile from me, they think that I forget.

They bid me seek in change of scene the charms that others see;
But were I in a foreign land, they'd find no change in me.
'Tis true that I behold no more the valley where we met,
I do not see the hawthorn-tree; but how can I forget?

For oh! there are so many things recall the past to me,—
The breeze upon the sunny hills, the billows of the sea;
The rosy tint that decks the sky before the sun is set;—
Ay, every leaf I look upon forbids me to forget.

They tell me she is happy now, the gayest of the gay;
They hint that she forgets me too,—I heed not what they say:
Perhaps like me she struggles with each feeling of regret;
But if she loves as I have loved, she never can forget.

In the version of this touching work printed in *A Thousand and One Gems of
English Poetry*, "Oh, no! we never mention her" becomes, for some unexplained
reason, "Oh, no! we never mention *him*." A twentieth-century commentator,
more knowing than his predecessors, might suspect in poet or anthologist a certain regrettable amatory tendency not unknown among literary men.

THOMAS HAYNES BAYLY (1797–1839), born at Bath, was
extremely well-connected, wrote plays from the age of seven, and produced a
weekly paper at school at Winchester. Having flirted with law and the church,
he found his true avocations to lie with amateur theatricals and lyric poetry. The
considerable proceeds from his literary labours and his wife's dowry enabled him
to lead a pleasant social life, diversified by the composition of ballads, works

of fiction, and plays which were popular on the professional stage and also in august private circles. The cast of one production of *Perfection* included the Marchioness of Londonderry, Lord Castlereagh, and Sir Roger Griesly. The failure of certain coal-mines and a dishonest agent on his Irish properties temporarily resulted in a darker strain in Bayly's poetry, but a sojourn in France helped to restore his characteristic charm and playful fancy. He succumbed to brain-fever, dropsy, and jaundice, a sad conclusion to the career of a poet who repeated on sundry occasions his ambition to be a butterfly:

> What, though you tell me each gay little rover
> Shrinks from the breath of the first autumn day!
> Surely 'tis better, when summer is over,
> To die when all fair things are fading away.
> Some in life's winter may toil to discover
> Means of procuring a weary delay—
> I'd be a butterfly; living, a rover,
> Dying when fair things are fading away!
> —"Butterfly Life"

From "Maud"

LORD TENNYSON

Come into the garden, Maud,
   For the black bat, night, has flown,
Come into the garden, Maud,
   I am here at the gate alone;
And the woodbine spices are wafted abroad,
   And the musk of the rose is blown.

For a breeze of morning moves,
   And the planet of Love is on high,
Beginning to faint in the light that she loves
   On a bed of a daffodil sky,
To faint in the light of the sun that she loves,
   To faint in his light, and to die.

All night have the roses heard
   The flute, violin, bassoon;
All night has the casement jessamine stirr'd
   To the dancers dancing in tune;
Till a silence fell with the waking bird,
   And a hush with the setting moon.

I said to the lily, "There is but one
   With whom she has heart to be gay.
When will the dancers leave her alone?
   She is weary of dance and play."
Now half to the setting moon are gone,
   And half to the rising day;
Low on the sand and loud on the stone
   The last wheel echoes away.

I said to the rose, "The brief night goes
   In babble and revel and wine.
O young lord-lover, what sighs are those,
   For one that will never be thine?

But mine, but mine," so I sware to the rose,
"For ever and ever, mine."

And the soul of the rose went into my blood,
  As the music clashed in the hall;
And long by the garden lake I stood,
  For I heard your rivulet fall
From the lake to the meadow and on to the wood,
  Our wood, that is dearer than all;

From the meadow your walks have left so sweet
  That wherever a March-wind sighs
He sets the jewel-print of your feet
  In violets as blue as your eyes,
To the woody hollows in which we meet
  And the valleys of Paradise.

The slender acacia would not shake
  One long milk-bloom on the tree;
The white lake-blossom fell into the lake
  As the pimpernel dozed on the lea;
But the rose was awake all night for your sake,
  Knowing your promise to me;
The lilies and roses were all awake,
  They sigh'd for the dawn and thee.

Queen rose of the rosebud garden of girls,
  Come hither, the dances are done,
In gloss of satin and glimmer of pearls,
  Queen lily and rose in one;
Shine out, little head, sunning over with curls,
  To the flowers, and be their sun.

There has fallen a splendid tear
  From the passion-flower at the gate.
She is coming, my dove, my dear;
  She is coming, my life, my fate;
The red rose cries, "She is near, she is near";

And the white rose weeps, "She is late";
The larkspur listens, "I hear, I hear";
And the lily whispers, "I wait."

She is coming, my own, my sweet;
Were it ever so airy a tread,
My heart would hear her and beat,
Were it earth in an earthy bed;
My dust would hear her and beat,
Had I lain for a century dead;
Would start and tremble under her feet,
And blossom in purple and red.

"Maud" is a monodrama of tragic passion that shocked the polite world by its disgust for contemporary society and its justification of war. One critic remarked, "If an author pipe of adultery, fornication, murder and suicide, set him down as the practiser of those crimes." Tennyson replied mildly, "Adulterer I may be, fornicator I may be, suicide I am not yet." The neurotic hero tells of his feud against the old lord of the Hall, who has ruined his family, of his growing love for Maud, the lord's daughter, who is hymned in some of Tennyson's most lyrical passages. A fatal duel with Maud's brother, exile, and finally the discovery of a new and worthwhile life fighting in Britain's noble cause complete the drama.

The anthropomorphized flowers in the stanzas quoted above provide, incidentally, a fragrant glimpse of a crowded mid-Victorian garden.

There is a note on Alfred, Lord Tennyson on page 57.

My Mother

ANN TAYLOR

Who fed me from her gentle breast,
And hush'd me in her arms to rest,
And on my cheeks sweet kisses prest?
                              My Mother.

When sleep forsook my open eye,
Who was it sung sweet hushabye,
And rock'd me that I should not cry?
                              My Mother.

Who sat and watch'd my infant head,
When sleeping on my cradle bed?
And tears of sweet affection shed?
                              My Mother.

When pain and sickness made me cry,
Who gazed upon my heavy eye,
And wept for fear that I should die?
                              My Mother.

Who dress'd my doll in clothes so gay?
And taught me pretty how to play,
And minded all I had to say?
                              My Mother.

Who ran to help me when I fell,
And would some pretty story tell,
Or kiss the place to make it well?
                              My Mother.

Who taught my infant lips to pray,
And love GOD'S holy book and day,
And walk in wisdom's pleasant way?
My Mother.

And can I ever cease to be
Affectionate and kind to thee,
Who wast so very kind to me,
My Mother?

Ah, no! the thought I cannot bear,
And if GOD please my life to spare,
I hope I shall reward thy care,
My Mother.

When thou art feeble, old and gray,
My healthy arm shall be thy stay,
And I will soothe thy pains away,
My Mother.

And when I see thee hang thy head,
'Twill be my turn to watch *thy* bed,
And tears of sweet affection shed,
My Mother.

For could our Father in the skies,
Look down with pleased or loving eyes,
If ever I could dare despise
My Mother?

M R S . A N N G I L B E R T, *née* T A Y L O R (1782–1866), and her
sister Jane (1783–1866) were the daughters of Isaac Taylor, independent
minister and engraver. He instructed his children in the latter craft, but the
lively and talented family were happily occupied early in the new century in producing volumes of poetry for children: *Original Poems for Infant Minds,*
Rhymes for the Nursery, and *Hymns for Infant Minds.* Ann and Jane each
wrote about half of these; Ann's most famous piece was "My Mother" and

Jane's, "Twinkle, Twinkle, Little Star." The family settled in Essex, and this little flock of singing birds became known as "The Taylors of Ongar." In 1812 Ann's hand was sought in marriage by letter from the Reverend Joseph Gilbert, who had never seen her, but had heard her praises sung by her friends. Her later life was occupied by numerous children and literary pursuits, and she died a sweet-tempered old lady. "My Mother" is printed here with the last stanza as revised a few months before her death. One of Jane Taylor's poems may be found on page 198, and one of the pair's instructional verses for children in the note on page 4.

Bedouin Song

BAYARD TAYLOR

From the Desert I come to thee
  On a stallion shod with fire;
And the winds are left behind
  In the speed of my desire.
Under the window I stand,
  And the midnight hears my cry:
I love thee, I love but thee,
  With a love that shall not die
      Till the sun grows cold,
      And the stars are old,
      And the leaves of the Judgment
        Book unfold!

Look from thy window and see
  My passion and my pain;
I lie on the sands below,
  And I faint in thy disdain.
Let the night-winds touch thy brow
  With the heat of my burning sigh,
And melt thee to hear the vow
  Of a love that shall not die
      Till the sun grows cold,
      And the stars are old,
      And the leaves of the Judgment
        Book unfold!

My steps are nightly driven,
  By the fever in my breast,
To hear from thy lattice breathed
  The word that shall give me rest.
Open the door of thy heart,
  And open thy chamber door,

And my kisses shall teach thy lips
The love that shall fade no more
Till the sun grows cold,
And the stars are old,
And the leaves of the Judgment
Book unfold!

On page 68 there is a short comment upon the romantic idea of Arabia that blazed so splendidly from the mid-nineteenth century onwards. The translation by Edward William Lane in 1840 of the *Arabian Nights' Entertainments* kindled the flame; Bayard Taylor's "Bedouin Song" of 1855 (one of a number of his verses in similar vein), which was to be rendered in countless parlours by gentleman vocalists, fanned it; and the public imagination was well alight by the time Edward Fitzgerald had published his poetic version of *The Rubáiyát* of Omar Khayyám in 1859. It mattered little that this most exotic of all myths— a Middle-Eastern Never-Never Land of passion and pleasure, fatalistic and hedonistic—mingled Arab and Persian elements indiscriminately. It was the contrast with the worthy dullness of so much of Victorian life that mattered.

A note on Bayard Taylor appears on page 88.

The Cane-Bottom'd Chair
WILLIAM MAKEPEACE THACKERAY

In tattered old slippers that toast at the bars,
And a ragged old jacket perfumed with cigars,
Away from the world and its toils and its cares,
I've a snug little kingdom up four pair of stairs.

To mount to this realm is a toil, to be sure,
But the fire there is bright and the air rather pure;
And the view I behold on a sunshiny day
Is grand through the chimney-pots over the way.

This snug little chamber is cramm'd in all nooks
With worthless old knicknacks and silly old books,
And foolish old odds and foolish old ends,
Crack'd bargains from brokers, cheap keepsakes from friends.

Old armour, prints, pictures, pipes, china (all crack'd);
Old rickety tables, and chairs broken-backed;
A twopenny treasury, wondrous to see;
What matter? 'tis pleasant to you, friend, and me.

No better divan need the Sultan require,
Than the creaking old sofa that basks by the fire;
And 'tis wonderful, surely, what music you get
From the rickety, ramshackle, wheezy spinet.

That praying rug came from a Turcoman's camp;
By Tiber once twinkled that brazen old lamp;
A Mameluke fierce yonder dagger has drawn:
'Tis a murderous knife to toast muffins upon.

Long long through the hours, and the night, and the chimes
Here we talk of old books, and old friends, and old times;
As we sit in a fog made of rich Latakie
This chamber is pleasant to you, friend, and me.

But of all the cheap treasures that garnish my nest,
There's one that I love and I cherish the best;
For the finest of couches that's padded with hair
I never would change thee, my cane-bottom'd chair.

'Tis a bandy-legg'd, high-shoulder'd, worm-eaten seat,
With a creaking old back, and twisted old feet;
But since the fair morning when Fanny sat there
I bless thee and love thee, old cane-bottom'd chair.

If chairs have but feeling, in holding such charms,
A thrill must have pass'd through your wither'd old arms!
I look'd, and I long'd, and I wish'd in despair;
I wish'd myself turn'd to a cane-bottom'd chair.

It was but a moment she sat in this place,
She'd a scarf on her neck, and a smile on her face!
A smile on her face and a rose in her hair,
And she sat there and bloom'd in my cane-bottom'd chair.

And so I have valued my chair ever since
Like the shrine of a saint, or the throne of a prince;
Saint Fanny my patroness sweet I declare,
The queen of my heart and my cane-bottom'd chair.

When the candles burn low, and the company's gone,
In the silence of night as I sit here alone—
I sit here alone, but we yet are a pair—
My Fanny I see in my cane-bottom'd chair.

She comes from the past and revisits my room;
She looks as she then did, all beauty and bloom;
So smiling and tender, so fresh and so fair,
And yonder she sits in my cane-bottom'd chair.

WILLIAM MAKEPEACE THACKERAY (1811–1863) was a man of immense energy and huge talents (the *D.N.B.* reports that his large cranium housed a brain weighing 58½ ounces), whose novels are but the summit of a great literary mountain of journalism, satire, and hack-work. His verse, a minor activity but occupying 236 pages in the Collected Edition, varies from a pathetic little piece about an orphan in a snow-storm to comic doggerel in Cockney. There are several charming love poems, of which "The Cane-Bottom'd Chair," with its reminiscences of student life, is the best. One Victorian anthology, *Favourite English Poems and Poets,* found the tenth stanza too indelicate for inclusion. Fearlessly, we print it here.

The Engineer's Story

EUGENE J. HALL

Han'som, stranger? Yes, she's purty, an' ez peart ez she kin be.
Clever? W'y, she ain't no chicken, but she's good enough fur me.
What's her name? 'Tis kind o' common, yit I ain't ashamed to tell.
She's ole "Fiddler" Filkin's daughter, and her dad he calls her "Nell."

I wuz drivin' on the Central jist about a year ago,
On the run from Winnemucca up to Reno in Washoe.
There's no end o' skeery places. 'Tain't a road fur one who dreams,
With its curves an' awful tres'les over rocks an' mountain streams.

'Twuz an afternoon in August; we hed got behind an hour,
An' wuz tearin' up the mountain like a summer thunder-shower,
Round the bends an' by the ledges 'bout ez fast ez we could go,
With the mountain-peaks above us an' the river down below.

Ez we come nigh to a tres'le cros't a holler, deep an' wild,
Suddenly I saw a baby,—'twuz the station-keeper's child,—
Toddlin' right along the timbers with a bold an' fearless tread,
Right afore the locomotive, not a hundred rods ahead.

I jist jumped, an' grabbed the throttle, an' I fa'rly held my breath,
Fur I felt I couldn't stop her till the child was crushed to death,
When a woman sprang afore me like a sudden streak o' light,
Caught the boy, an' twixt the timbers in a second sank from sight.

I jist whis'l'd all the brakes on. An' we worked with might an' main,
Till the fire flew from the drivers, but we couldn't stop the train,
An' it rumbled on above her. How she screamed ez we rolled by!
An' the river roared below us,—I shell hear her till I die.

Then we stopped; the sun wuz shinin'; I ran back along the ridge,
An' I found her—dead? No, livin'! She wuz hangin' to the bridge,
Where she dropped down through the cross-ties with one arm about a sill.
An' the other round the baby, who wuz yellin' fur to kill.

So we saved 'em. She wuz gritty. She's ez peart ez she kin be;
Now we're married; she's no chicken, but she's good enough for me.
An' ef eny ask who owns her, w'y! I ain't ashamed to tell—
She's my wife. Ther' ain't none better than ole Filkin's daughter Nell.

One of a number of railroad recitations in this volume, "The Engineer's Story"
has a theme that occurs in several popular verses: hero and heroine wed as the
result of a plucky rescue. Here are three stanzas from "The Fireman's Wed-
ding" by W. A. Eaton:

> And there was the face at the window,
>   With its blank look of haggard despair—
> Her hands were clasped tight on her bosom,
>   And her white lips were moving in prayer. . . .
>
> When up sprang a sturdy young fireman,
>   As a sailor would climb up a mast;
> We saw him go in at the window,
>   And we cheered as though danger were past. . . .
>
> And now, sir, they're going to get married,
>   I bet you, she'll make a good wife;
> And who has the most right to have her?
>   Why, the fellow that saved her young life!

4
Strange Tales

His eyes—how they twinkled! his dimples how merry!
His cheeks were like roses, his nose like a cherry!

—"A Visit from St. Nicholas"

The Raven

EDGAR ALLAN POE

Once upon a midnight dreary, while I ponder'd weak and weary,
Over many a quaint and curious volume of forgotten lore—
While I nodded, nearly napping, suddenly there came a tapping,
As of some one gently rapping, rapping at my chamber door.
" 'Tis some visitor," I muttered, "tapping at my chamber door—
                Only this and nothing more."

Ah, distinctly I remember it was in the bleak December,
And each separate dying ember wrought its ghost upon the floor.
Eagerly I wish'd the morrow;—vainly I had sought to borrow
From my books surcease of sorrow—sorrow for the lost Lenore—
For the rare and radiant maiden whom the angels name Lenore—
                Nameless here for evermore.

And the silken sad uncertain rustling of each purple curtain
Thrill'd me—fill'd me with fantastic terrors never felt before;
So that now, to still the beating of my heart, I stood repeating,
" 'Tis some visitor entreating entrance at my chamber door—
Some late visitor entreating entrance at my chamber door;
                This it is, and nothing more."

Presently my soul grew stronger, hesitating then no longer,
"Sir," said I, "or madam, truly your forgiveness I implore;
But the fact is I was napping, and so gently you came rapping,
And so faintly you came tapping, tapping at my chamber door,
That I scarce was sure I heard you"—here I open'd wide the door;—
                Darkness there, and nothing more.

Deep into the darkness peering, long I stood there, wondering, fearing,
Doubting, dreaming dreams no mortal ever dared to dream before;
But the silence was unbroken, and the stillness gave no token,
And the only word there spoken was the whispered word, "Lenore!"
This I whispered, and an echo murmured back the word, "Lenore!"—
                Merely this, and nothing more.

Back into my chamber turning, all my soul within me burning,
Soon again I heard a tapping, something louder than before.
"Surely," said I, "surely that is something at my window lattice;
Let me see, then, what thereat is, and this mystery explore—
Let my heart be still a moment, and this mystery explore:—
          'Tis the wind, and nothing more."

Open here I flung the shutter, when, with many a flirt and flutter,
In there stepp'd a stately Raven of the saintly days of yore.
Not the least obeisance made he; not a minute stopp'd or stay'd he;
But, with mien of lord or lady, perch'd above my chamber door—
Perch'd upon a bust of Pallas, just above my chamber door—
          Perch'd, and sat, and nothing more.

Then this ebony bird beguiling my sad fancy into smiling,
By the grave and stern decorum of the countenance it wore:
"Though thy crest be shorn and shaven, thou," I said, "art sure no craven;
Ghastly, grim, and ancient Raven, wandering from the nightly shore,
Tell me what thy lordly name is on the night's Plutonian shore?"
          Quoth the Raven, "Nevermore."

Much I marvelled this ungainly fowl to hear discourse so plainly,
Though its answer little meaning, little relevancy bore:
For we cannot help agreeing that no living human being
Ever yet was blessed with seeing bird above his chamber door—
Bird or beast upon the sculptured bust above his chamber door
          With such name as "Nevermore."

But the Raven, sitting lonely on that placid bust, spoke only
That one word, as if his soul in that one word he did outpour;
Nothing further then he uttered, not a feather then he fluttered,
Till I scarcely more than muttered—"Other friends have flown before,
On the morrow *he* will leave me, as my hopes have flown before."
          Then the bird said, "Nevermore "

Startled by the stillness broken by reply so aptly spoken,
"Doubtless," said I, "what it utters is its only stock and store,
Caught from some unhappy master, whom unmerciful disaster

Followed fast and followed faster, till his songs one burden bore—
Till the dirges of his hope this melancholy burden bore—
                              Of 'Never, nevermore.' "

But the Raven still beguiling all my sad soul into smiling,
Straight I wheeled a cushioned seat in front of bird, and bust, and door;
Then upon the velvet sinking, I betook myself to linking
Fancy into fancy, thinking what this ominous bird of yore—
What this grim, ungainly, ghastly, gaunt and ominous bird of yore
                              Meant in croaking, "Nevermore."

Thus I sat engaged in guessing, but no syllable expressing
To the fowl whose fiery eyes now burned into my bosom's core;
This and more I sat divining, with my head at ease reclining,
On the cushion's velvet lining, that the lamp-light gloated o'er,
But whose violet velvet lining, with the lamp-light gloating o'er
                              She shall press, ah, nevermore.

Then methought the air grew denser, perfumed from an unseen censer
Swung by seraphim, whose footfalls tinkled on the tufted floor.
"Wretch," I cried, "thy God hath lent thee—by these angels he hath sent
       thee
Respite—respite and nepenthe from my memories of Lenore!
Quaff, oh quaff this kind nepenthe, and forget this lost Lenore!"
                              Quoth the Raven, "Nevermore."

"Prophet," said I, "thing of evil!—prophet still, if bird or devil!
Whether tempter sent, or whether tempest tossed thee here ashore
Desolate, yet all undaunted, on this desert land enchanted,
On this home by horror haunted—tell me truly, I implore,
Is there—*is* there balm in Gilead?—tell me—tell me, I implore!"
                              Quoth the Raven, "Nevermore."

"Prophet," said I, "thing of evil!—prophet still, if bird or devil!—
By that Heaven that bends above us—by that God we both adore—
Tell this soul with sorrow laden if within the distant Aidenn,
It shall clasp a sainted maiden whom the angels name Lenore—
Clasp a rare and radiant maiden whom the angels name Lenore?"
                              Quoth the Raven, "Nevermore."

"Be that word our sign of parting, bird or fiend!" I shriek'd, upstarting,
"Get thee back into the tempest and the night's Plutonian shore!
Leave no black plume as a token of that lie thy soul hath spoken!
Leave my loneliness unbroken!—quit the bust above my door!"
Take thy beak from out my heart, and take thy form from off my door!"
　　　　　　　　Quoth the Raven, "Nevermore."

And the Raven, never flitting, still is sitting, still is sitting,
On the pallid bust of Pallas, just above my chamber door;
And his eyes have all the seeming of a demon's that is dreaming,
And the lamp-light o'er him streaming throws his shadow on the floor,
And my soul from out that shadow that lies floating on the floor,
　　　　　　　　Shall be lifted—nevermore.

EDGAR ALLAN POE (1809–1849) rivalled Lord Byron as the
provocation for head-wagging over a misspent life. A child of singular beauty
and precocious talents, he was orphaned at the age of two, when his actor
parents both died within a week. His foster-parents, John Allan, a tobacco
exporter, and his wife, were ill-rewarded by their charge, for he acquired a
fondness for excitants at the University of Virginia, ran away from a commercial
career, joined the army, and was expelled from West Point. He married his
cousin, a girl of thirteen, who with her mother devoted much tolerant care to
him, but by the time he was publishing poems and stories in the early thirties the
pattern of his life was fixed: periods of energy and hope alternating with attacks
of despair and inebriation. Nevertheless, Poe's fame and influence were world-
wide; Baudelaire was one of his many admirers. His tragedy was that of the
alcoholic who could not hold his liquor; a very small quantity could have dis-
astrous effects. At the last he joined the Sons of Temperance, but a relapse
followed shortly after and he died in a coma.

An Indian Mother About to Destroy Her Child

JAMES MONTGOMERY

Awhile she lay all passive to the touch
Of those small fingers, and the soft, soft lips
Soliciting the sweet nutrition thence,
While yearning sympathy crept around her heart,
She felt her spirit yielding to the charm,
That wakes the parent in the fellest bosom,
And binds her to her little one for ever,
If once completed—but she broke—she broke it.

For she was brooding o'er her sex's wrongs,
And seem'd to lie among a nest of scorpions,
That stung remorse to frenzy:—forth she sprung,
And with collected might a moment stood,
Mercy and misery struggling in her thoughts,
Yet both impelling her to one dire purpose.
There was a little grave already made,
But two spans long, in the turf floor beside her,
By him who was the father of that child;
Thence had he sallied when the work was done,
To hunt, to fish, to ramble on the hills,
Till all was peace again within that dwelling,
His haunt,—his den,—his anything but home!
Peace? no—till the new-comer was despatch'd,
Whence it should ne'er return, to break the stupor
Of unawaken'd conscience in himself.

She pluck'd the baby from her flowing breast,
And o'er its mouth, yet moist with nature's beverage,
Bound a white lotus-leaf to still its cries;
Then laid it down in that untimely grave,
As tenderly as though 'twere rock'd to sleep
With songs of love, and afraid to wake it:
Soon as she felt it touch the ground she started,
Hurried the damp earth over it; then fell

[*113*]

Flat on the heaving heap, and crush'd it down
With the whole burden of her grief, exclaiming,
"Oh, that my mother had done so to me!"
Then in a swoon forgot, a little while,
Her child, her sex, her tyrant, and herself.

JAMES MONTGOMERY (1771–1854), son of an Ulster-Scottish missionary of the Moravian persuasion, neglected his scholastic studies to compose epic poems, including one in the manner of Milton, in which the Archangel Michael takes Satan unawares and lops off a wing. He joined the *Sheffield Register* as a clerk and ended up as its proprietor, landing twice in prison for libel. In later years he was justly renowned in Sheffield as a very worthy and philanthropic citizen, serving the Muse as well as the community by writing long, heroic poems, notably "Greenland" about the Moravian missions to that country, and over a hundred hymns. His libertarian sentiments were particularly acceptable in America, where children learned from *McGuffey's Fifth Eclectic Reader* his lengthy but defiant ballad on the Swiss patriot, Arnold von Winkelried:

> "Make way for Liberty!" he cried;
> Made way for Liberty, and died.

The *D.N.B.* remarks that "He is largely indebted for his fame to the approbation of religious circles, better judges of his sentiments than of his poetry."

Asleep at the Switch

AUTHOR UNKNOWN

The first thing that I remember was Carlo tugging away,
With the sleeves of my coat fast in his teeth, pulling as much as to say:
"Come, master, awake, and tend to the switch, lives now depend upon you,
Think of the souls in the coming train and the graves you're sending them
    to;
Thing of the mother and babe at her breast, think of the father and son,
Think of the lover, and loved one, too, think of them doomed every one
To fall, as it were, by your very hand, into yon fathomless ditch,
Murdered by one who should guard them from harm, who now lies asleep
    at the switch."

I sprang up amazed, scarce knew where I stood, sleep had o'er-mastered me
    so;
I could hear the wind hollowly howling and the deep river dashing below,
I could hear the forest leaves rustling as the trees by the tempest were
    fanned,
But what was that noise at a distance? That—I could not understand!
I heard it at first indistinctly, like the rolling of some muffled drum,
Then nearer and nearer it came to me, and made my very ears hum;
What is this light that surrounds me and seems to set fire to my brain?
What whistle's that yelling so shrilly! Oh, God! I know now—it's the
    train.

We often stand facing some danger, and seem to take root to the place;
So I stood with this demon before me, its heated breath scorching my face,
Its headlight made day of the darkness, and glared like the eyes of some
    witch;
The train was almost upon me, before I remembered the switch.
I sprang to it, seized it wildly, the train dashing fast down the track,
The switch resisted my efforts, some devil seemed holding it back;
On, on, came the fiery-eyed monster and shot by my face like a flash;
I swooned to the earth the next moment, and knew nothing after the crash.

How long I laid there unconscious 'twere impossible for me to tell,
My stupor was almost a heaven, my waking almost a hell—
For I then heard the piteous moaning and shrieking of husbands and wives,
And I thought of the day we all shrink from, when I must account for their
  lives;
Mothers rushed like maniacs, their eyes staring madly and wild;
Fathers, losing their courage, gave way to their grief like a child;
Children searching for parents, I noticed as by me they sped,
And lips that could form naught but "Mamma," were calling for one
  perhaps dead.
My mind was made up in a second, the river should hide me away;
When, under the still burning rafters, I suddenly noticed there lay
A little white hand, she who owned it was doubtless an object of love
To one whom her loss would drive frantic, tho' she guarded him now from
  above;
I tenderly lifted the rafters and quietly laid them one side;
How little she thought of her journey, when she left for this last fatal ride;
I lifted the last log from off her, and while searching for some spark of life,
Turned her little face up in the starlight, and recognized—Maggie, my
  wife!

Oh, Lord! Thy scourge is a hard one, at a blow Thou has shattered my
  pride:
My life will be one endless night-time, with Maggie away from my side;
How often we've sat down and pictured the scenes in our long happy life;
How I'd strive through all of my life-time to build up a home for my wife.
How people would envy us always in our cosy and neat little nest,
When I would do all the labour, and Maggie should all the day rest;
How one of God's blessings might cheer us, when some day I p'r'aps
  should be rich.
But all of my dreams have been shattered, while I lay there asleep at the
  switch.

I fancied I stood on my trial, the jury and judge I could see,
And every eye in the court room was steadfastly fixed upon me,
And fingers were pointing in scorn, till I felt my face blushing red,
And the next thing I heard were the words, "Hung by the neck until
  dead."

Then I felt myself pulled once again, and my hand caught tight hold of a
  dress,
And I heard, "What's the matter, dear Jim? You've had a bad nightmare,
  I guess."
And there stood Maggie, my wife, with never a scar from the ditch,
I'd been taking a nap in my bed and had not been asleep at the switch.

From the moment when William Huskisson, M.P., was run down by the locomotive "Dart" at the opening of the Manchester and Liverpool railway in 1830,
the iron road has provided poets with ample inspiration for tales of disaster and
narrow escape. The inattentive employee dozing at the switch in the days of
single-line working, in particular, seems to have been a popular subject. Here is
the prelude to a collision in a tunnel, recorded by G. Manville Fenn:

> I hardly had roared out them words to poor Jack,
>   When we dashed by the box with a leap;
> And there, in a moment, I saw, leaning back,
>   The signalman—*helpless!—asleep!*
> The next flash ahead showed an engine's two lamps—
>   My God! I can't tell you my fears,
> "Turn steam off!—turn on!" Why, look here, my face damps
>   As I tell you the tale after years.
>   —"The Pitch-In: An Engine Driver's Story"

Good Words printed a metrical report of an actual incident (which inspired
more than one bard) in which a signalman had to choose between the down-
train and his baby playing between the rails. He shifts the points, saves the
express, and:

> There's a rush in his ears, though the train has passed;
>   He gropes for he cannot see,
> To the place where the laughing baby crawled,
>   Where the mangled limbs must be.
> But he hears a cry that is only of fear—
>   His joy seems too great to bear.
> For, his duty done, God saw to his son—
>   The train had not touched a hair!
>   —"A Fact"

"Asleep at the Switch" was recited by the American Harry Bruno in his
famous Railroad Specialty. Other, more tragic stories by Bret Harte and J. G.
Whittier appear on pages 240 and 242.

The Deacon's Masterpiece, or,
The Wonderful "One-Hoss Shay"
A Logical Story

OLIVER WENDELL HOLMES

Have you heard of the wonderful one-hoss shay,
That was built in such a logical way
It ran a hundred years to a day,
And then, of a sudden, it—ah, but stay,
I'll tell you what happened without delay,
Scaring the parson into fits,
Frightening people out of their wits,—
Have you ever heard of that, I say?

Seventeen hundred and fifty-five.
Georgius Secundus was then alive,—
Snuffy old drone from the German hive.
That was the year when Lisbon-town
Saw the earth open and gulp her down,
And Braddock's army was done so brown,
Left without a scalp to its crown.
It was on the terrible Earthquake-day
That the Deacon finished the one-hoss shay.

Now in building of chaises, I tell you what,
There is always somewhere a weakest spot,—
In hub, tire, felloe, in spring or thill,
In panel, or crossbar, or floor, or sill,
In screw, bolt, thoroughbrace,—lurking still,
Find it somewhere you must and will,—
Above or below, or within or without,—
And that's the reason, beyond a doubt,
That a chaise *breaks down,* but doesn't *wear out.*

But the Deacon swore (as deacons do,
With an "I dew vum," or an "I tell *yeou*")

He would build one shay to beat the taown
'N' the keounty 'n' all the kentry raoun';
It should be so built that it couldn't break daown:
"Fur," said the Deacon, " 't's mighty plain
Thut the weakes' place mus' stan' the strain;
'N' the way t' fix it, uz I maintain,
    Is only jest
T' make that place uz strong uz the rest."

So the Deacon inquired of the village folk
Where he could find the strongest oak,
That couldn't be split nor bent nor broke,—
That was for spokes and floor and sills;
He sent for lancewood to make the thills;
The crossbars were ash, from the straightest trees,
The panels of white-wood, that cuts like cheese,
But lasts like iron for things like these;
The hubs of logs from the "Settler's ellum,"—
Last of its timber,—they couldn't sell 'em,
Never an axe had seen their chips,
And the wedges flew from between their lips,
Their blunt ends frizzled like celery tips;
Step and prop-iron, bolt and screw,
Spring, tire, axle, and linchpin too,
Steel of the finest, bright and blue;
Thoroughbrace bison-skin, thick and wide;
Boot, top, dasher, from tough old hide
Found in the pit when the tanner died.
That was the way he "put her through."
"There!" said the Deacon, "naow she'll dew!"

Do! I tell you, I rather guess
She was a wonder, and nothing less!
Deacon and deaconess dropped away,
Colts grew horses, beards turned gray,
Children and grandchildren—where were they?

But there stood the stout old one-hoss shay
As fresh as on Lisbon-earthquake-day!

EIGHTEEN HUNDRED;—it came and found
The Deacon's masterpiece strong and sound.
Eighteen hundred increased by ten;—
"Hahnsum kerridge" they called it then.
Eighteen hundred and twenty came;—
Running as usual; much the same.
Thirty and forty at last arrive,
And then came fifty, and FIFTY-FIVE.

Little of all we value here
Wakes on the morn of its hundredth year
Without both feeling and looking queer.
In fact, there's nothing that keeps its youth,
So far as I know, but a tree and truth.
(This is a moral that runs at large;
Take it.—You're welcome.—No extra charge.)

FIRST OF NOVEMBER,—the Earthquake-day,—
There are traces of age in the one-hoss shay,
A general flavor of mild decay,
But nothing local, as one may say.
There couldn't be,—for the Deacon's art
Had made it so like in every part
That there wasn't a chance for one to start.
For the wheels were just as strong as the thills,
And the floor was just as strong as the sills,
And the panels just as strong as the floor,
And the whipple-tree neither less nor more,
And the back-crossbar as strong as the fore,
And spring and axle and hub *encore*.
And yet, *as a whole*, it is past a doubt
In another hour it will be *worn out!*

First of November, fifty-five!
This morning the parson takes a drive.
Now, small boys, get out of the way!
Here comes the wonderful one-hoss shay,
Drawn by a rat-tailed, ewe-necked bay.
"Huddup!" said the parson.—Off went they.
The parson was working his Sunday's text,—
Had got to *fifthly*, and stopped perplexed
At what the—Moses—was coming next.
All at once the horse stood still,
Close by the meet'n'-house on the hill.
First a shiver, and then a thrill,
Then something decidedly like a spill,—
And the parson was sitting upon a rock,
At half past nine by the meet'n'-house clock,—
Just the hour of the Earthquake shock!
What do you think the parson found,
When he got up and stared around?
The poor old chaise in a heap or mound,
As if it had been to the mill and ground!
You see, of course, if you're not a dunce,
How it went to pieces all at once,—
All at once, and nothing first,—
Just as bubbles do when they burst.

End of the wonderful one-hoss shay.
Logic is logic. That's all I say.

Many commentators state that the Wonderful One-Hoss Shay represents the
Calvinist system, the uncompromising creed built upon iron logic. Certainly,
the author, who was of strict Calvinist Puritan descent, never lost an opportunity
to air his hatred of the creed.

OLIVER WENDELL HOLMES, Sr. (1809–1894), born in Cambridge, Massachusetts, was the Harvard Brahmin *in excelsis*. For him Boston was "the hub of the universe." First destined for the law, Holmes turned to medicine and expressed advanced ideas, gained from his studies in Paris, some of them anticipating the discoveries of Pasteur and Lord Lister. It is his reputation as an incomparable wit and magnificent talker, however, that has brought him his greatest fame. As a writer, he could turn his hand to essays and verse, grave or gay—or more usually an amalgam of both, as the occasion demanded. His "Autocrat" papers are a unique blend of anecdote, poetry, and speculation on an astonishing variety of subjects; his interests ranged from boxing to philosophy. Like many vivacious men who lacked inches, Holmes loved to dominate an audience, particularly when it consisted of the gentler sex. Vain, garrulous, and of a formidable intelligence, he nevertheless appears to have inspired affection in almost everyone he met—with the possible exception of his son, who was too like him.

The Fairy Folk

WILLIAM ALLINGHAM

Up the airy mountain,
  Down the rushy glen,
We daren't go a-hunting,
  For fear of little men;
Wee folk, good folk,
  Trooping all together;
Green jacket, red cap,
  And white owl's feather.

Down along the rocky shore
  Some make their home,
They live on crispy pancakes
  Of yellow tide-foam;
Some in the reeds
  Of the black mountain-lake,
With frogs for their watch-dogs,
  All night awake.

High on the hill-top
  The old king sits;
He is now so old and gray
  He's nigh lost his wits.
With a bridge of white mist
  Columbkill he crosses,
On his stately journeys
  From Slieveleague to Rosses;

Or going up with music,
  On cold starry nights,
To sup with the Queen
  Of the gay Northern Lights.

They stole little Bridget
  For seven years long;
When she came down again
  Her friends were all gone.

They took her lightly back,
  Between the night and morrow;
They thought that she was fast asleep,
  But she was dead with sorrow.
They have kept her ever since
  Deep within the lakes,
On a bed of flag leaves,
  Watching till she wakes.

By the craggy hillside,
  Through the mosses bare,
They have planted thorn-trees
  For pleasure here and there.
Is any man so daring
  As dig one up in spite?
He shall find the thornies set
  In his bed at night.

Up the airy mountain,
  Down the rushy glen,
We daren't go a-hunting,
  For fear of little men;
Wee folk, good folk,
  Trooping all together;
Green jacket, red cap,
  And white owl's feather.

WILLIAM ALLINGHAM (1824–1889), son of an Irish bank manager, spent a great deal of his life as a customs officer in Ulster. He visited London frequently, however, becoming rather a protégé of Leigh Hunt, and he met Carlyle, Tennyson, and Coventry Patmore. He also struck up an intimate friendship with Rossetti. His sweet, graceful verse, mostly with an Irish background, was quietly successful. On retirement from the customs, he settled in London as editor of *Fraser's Magazine*.

A Visit from St. Nicholas

CLEMENT CLARKE MOORE

'Twas the night before Christmas, when all through the house
Not a creature was stirring, not even a mouse;
The stockings were hung by the chimney with care,
In hopes that St. Nicholas soon would be there;
The children were nestled all snug in their beds,
While visions of sugar-plums danced in their heads;
And mamma in her 'kerchief, and I in my cap,
Had just settled our brains for a long winter's nap,
When out on the lawn there arose such a clatter,
I sprang from the bed to see what was the matter.
Away to the window I flew like a flash,
Tore open the shutters and threw up the sash.
The moon on the breast of the new-fallen snow
Gave the lustre of mid-day to objects below,
When, what to my wondering eyes should appear,
But a miniature sleigh, and eight tiny reindeer,
With a little old driver, so lively and quick,
I knew in a moment it must be St. Nick.
More rapid than eagles his coursers they came,
And he whistled, and shouted, and called them by name;
"Now, *Dasher*! now, *Dancer*! now *Prancer* and *Vixen*!
On, *Comet*! on, *Cupid*! on, *Donder* and *Blitzen*!
To the top of the porch! to the top of the wall!
Now dash away! dash away! dash away all!"
As dry leaves that before the wild hurricane fly,
When they meet with an obstacle, mount to the sky;
So up to the house-top the coursers they flew,
With the sleigh full of Toys, and St. Nicholas too.
And then, in a twinkling, I heard on the roof
The prancing and pawing of each little hoof.
As I drew in my head, and was turning around,
Down the chimney St. Nicholas came with a bound.
He was dressed all in fur, from his head to his foot,
And his clothes were all tarnished with ashes and soot;

A bundle of Toys he had flung on his back,
And he looked like a pedlar just opening his pack.
His eyes—how they twinkled! his dimples how merry!
His cheeks were like roses, his nose like a cherry!
His droll little mouth was drawn up like a bow,
And the beard of his chin was as white as the snow;
The stump of a pipe he held tight in his teeth,
And the smoke it encircled his head like a wreath;
He had a broad face and a little round belly,
That shook when he laughed, like a bowlful of jelly.
He was chubby and plump, a right jolly old elf,
And I laughed when I saw him, in spite of myself;
A wink of his eye and a twist of his head,
Soon gave me to know I had nothing to dread.
He spoke not a word, but went straight to his work,
And filled all the stockings; then turned with a jerk,
And laying his finger aside of his nose,
And giving a nod, up the chimney he rose;
He sprang to his sleigh, to his team gave a whistle,
And away they all flew like the down of a thistle.
But I heard him exclaim, ere he drove out of sight,
"Happy Christmas to all, and to all a good-night."

This is one of the earliest literary manifestations of that jolly Dutch-German
figure who, later in the nineteenth century, was to acquire a scarlet coat, brush
off the soot, and hide his pipe, ready to change into that now rather shop-soiled
symbol of Commercial Yule.

C L E M E N T C L A R K E M O O R E (1779–1863) was born in New
York, son of an Episcopal clergyman who was loyal to Great Britain during the
Revolution but nevertheless became a bishop and president of Columbia. Clement
C. Moore was a scholar, Professor of Oriental Languages at the General Theological Seminary in New York, compiler of a Hebrew Lexicon. This one poem
of his that survives from a body of sentimental verse was written for his children
at Christmas, 1822, and was sent without his knowledge to the Troy *Sentinel,*
where it appeared anonymously a year later.

The Enchanted Shirt

COLONEL JOHN HAY

FYTTE YE FIRSTE: *wherein it shall be shown how ye Truthe is too mightie a Drugge for such as be of Feeble Temper.*

The king was sick. His cheek was red,
  And his eye was clear and bright;
He ate and drank with a kingly zest,
  And peacefully snored at night.

But he said he was sick, and a king should know,
  And doctors came by the score.
They did not cure him. He cut off their heads,
  And sent to the schools for more.

At last two famous doctors came,
  And one was as poor as a rat,
He had passed his life in studious toil,
  And never found time to grow fat.

The other had never looked into a book;
  His patients gave him no trouble:
If they recovered, they paid him well;
  If they died, their heirs paid double.

Together they looked at the royal tongue,
  As the king on his couch reclined;
In succession they thumped his august chest,
  But no trace of disease could find.

The old sage said, "You're as sound as a nut."
  "Hang him up!" roared the king in a gale—
In a ten-knot gale of royal rage;
  The other leech grew a shade pale;

But he pensively rubbed his sagacious nose,
  And thus his prescription ran:
The king will be well, if he sleeps one night
  In the Shirt of a Happy Man.

FYTTE YE SECONDE: *telleth of ye searche for ye Shirte,
and how it was nighe founde, but was notte for reasons
qu: are sayd or sung.*

Wide o'er the realm the couriers rode,
  And fast their horses ran,
And many they saw, and to many they spoke,
  But they found no Happy Man.

They found poor men who would fain be rich,
  And rich who thought they were poor;
And men who twisted their waists in stays,
  And women that shorthose wore.

They saw two men by the roadside sit,
  And both bemoaned their lot;
For one had buried his wife, he said,
  And the other one had not.

At last they came to a village gate,
  A beggar lay whistling there!
He whistled, and sang, and laughed, and rolled
  On the grass in the soft June air.

The weary courtiers paused and looked
  At the scamp so blithe and gay;
And one of them said, "Heaven save you, friend!
  You seem to be happy to-day."

"Oh yes, fair sirs," the rascal laughed,
  And his voice rang free and glad;
"An idle man has so much to do
  That he never has time to be sad."

"This is our man," the courtier said;
  "Our luck has led us aright.
I will give you a hundred ducats, friend,
  For the loan of your shirt to-night."

The merry blackguard lay back on the grass,
  And laughed till his face was black;
"I would do it, Got wot," and he roared with the fun,
  "But I haven't a shirt to my back."

FYTTE YE THIRDE: *shewing how Hys Majestie the King*
came at last to sleepe in a Happie Man his Shirte.

Each day to the king the reports came in
  Of his unsuccessful spies,
And the sad panorama of human woes
  Passed daily under his eyes.

And he grew ashamed of his useless life,
  And his maladies hatched in gloom;
He opened his windows and let in the air
  Of the free heaven into his room.

And out he went in the world, and toiled
  In his own appointed way;
And the people blessed him, the land was glad,
  And the king was well and gay.

See page 13 for a note on Colonel John Hay.

The Jackdaw of Rheims
from *The Ingoldsby Legends*

REVEREND R. H. BARHAM

The Jackdaw sat on the Cardinal's chair!
  Bishop, and abbot, and prior were there;
  Many a monk, and many a friar,
  Many a knight, and many a squire,
With a great many more of lesser degree,—
In sooth a goodly company;
And they served the Lord Primate on bended knee.
    Never, I ween,
    Was a prouder seen,
Read of in books, or dreamt of in dreams,
Than the Cardinal Lord Archbishop of Rheims!

    In and out
    Through the motley rout
That little Jackdaw kept hopping about;
    Here and there,
    Like a dog in a fair,
    Over comfits and cates,
    And dishes and plates,
Cowl and cope, and rochet and pall
Mitre and crosier! he hopp'd upon all!
    With a saucy air,
    He perch'd on the chair
Where, in state, the great Lord Cardinal sate
In the great Lord Cardinal's great red hat;
    And he peer'd in the face
    Of his Lordship's Grace,
With a satisfied look, as if he would say,
"We two are the greatest folks here today!"
    And the priests, with awe,
    As such freaks they saw,
Said, "The Devil must be in that little Jackdaw!"

The feast was over, the board was clear'd
The flawns and the custards had all disappear'd,
And six little Singing-boys,—dear little souls!
In nice clean faces, and nice white stoles,
 Came, in order due,
  Two by two,
Marching that grand refectory through!
A nice little boy held a golden ewer,
Emboss'd and fill'd with water, as pure
As any that flows between Rheims and Namur,
Which a nice little boy stood ready to catch
In a fine golden hand-basin made to match.
Two nice little boys, rather more grown,
Carried lavender-water, and eau de Cologne;
And a nice little boy had a nice cake of soap,
Worthy of washing the hands of the Pope.
 One little boy more
  A napkin bore,
Of the best white diaper, fringed with pink,
And a Cardinal's Hat mark'd in "permanent ink."

The great Lord Cardinal turns at the sight
Of these nice little boys dress'd all in white:
 From his finger he draws
  His costly turquoise;
And, not thinking at all about little Jackdaws,
 Deposits it straight
  By the side of his plate,
While the nice little boys on his Eminence wait;
Till, when nobody's dreaming of any such thing,
That little Jackdaw hops off with the ring!

  . . . .

 There's a cry and a shout,
  And a deuce of a rout,
And nobody seems to know what they're about,
But the monks have their pockets all turn'd inside out,
 The friars are kneeling,

And hunting, and feeling
The carpet, the floor, and the walls and the ceiling.
The Cardinal drew off each plum-colour'd shoe,
And left his red stockings exposed to the view;
 He peeps, and he feels
 In the toes and the heels;
They turn up the dishes,—they turn up the plates,—
They take up the poker and poke out the grates,
 They turn up the rugs,
 They examine the mugs:—
 But no! no such thing;—
 They can't find THE RING!
And the Abbot declared that, "when nobody twigg'd it,
Some rascal or other had popp'd in, and prigg'd it!"

The Cardinal rose with a dignified look,
He call'd for his candle, his bell, and his book!
 In holy anger, and pious grief,
 He solemnly cursed that rascally thief!
He cursed him at board, he cursed him in bed!
From the sole of his foot to the crown of his head!
He cursed him in sleeping, that every night
He should dream of the devil, and wake in a fright;
He cursed him in eating, he cursed him in drinking,
He cursed him in coughing, in sneezing, and winking;
He cursed him in sitting, in standing, in lying;
He cursed him in walking, in riding, in flying;
He cursed him in living, he cursed him in dying!—
Never was heard such a terrible curse!!
 But what gave rise
 To no little surprise,
Nobody seem'd one penny the worse!

 The day was gone,
 The night came on,
The Monks and the Friars they search'd till dawn;
 When the Sacristan saw,
 On crumpled claw,

Come limping a poor little lame Jackdaw!
　　No longer gay,
　　As on yesterday;
His feathers all seem'd to be turn'd the wrong way;—
His pinions droop'd—he could hardly stand,—
His head was as bald as the palm of your hand;
　　His eye so dim,
　　So wasted each limb,
That, heedless of grammar, they all cried, "THAT'S HIM!—
That's the scamp that has done this scandalous thing!
That's the thief that has got my Lord Cardinal's ring!"
　　The poor little Jackdaw,
　　When the monks he saw,
Feebly gave vent to the ghost of a caw;
And turn'd his bald head, as much as to say,
"Pray be so good as to walk this way!"
　　Slower and slower
　　He limp'd on before,
Till they came to the back of the belfry door,
　　Where the first thing they saw,
　　Midst the sticks and the straw,
Was the RING, in the nest of that little Jackdaw!

Then the great Lord Cardinal call'd for his book,
And off that terrible curse he took;
　　The mute expression
　　Served in lieu of confession,
And, being thus coupled with full restitution,
The Jackdaw got plenary absolution!

　　—When those words were heard,
　　That poor little bird
Was so changed in a moment, 'twas really absurd.
　　He grew sleek, and fat;
　　In addition to that,
A fresh crop of feathers came thick as a mat!
　　His tail waggled more
　　Even than before;

But no longer it wagg'd with an impudent air,
No longer he perch'd on the Cardinal's chair.
   He hopp'd now about
   With a gait devout;
At Matins, at Vespers, he never was out;
And, so far from any more pilfering deeds,
He always seem'd telling the Confessor's beads.
If any one lied,—or if any one swore,—
Or slumber'd in prayer-time and happened to snore,
   That good Jackdaw
   Would give a great "Caw!"
As much as to say, "Don't do so any more!"
While many remark'd, as his manners they saw,
That they "never had known such a pious Jackdaw!"
   He long lived the pride
   Of that country side,
And at last in the odour of sanctity died;
   When, as words were too faint
   His merits to paint,
The Conclave determined to make him a Saint;
And on newly-made Saints and Popes, as you know,
It's the custom, at Rome, new names to bestow,
So they canonized him by the name of Jim Crow!

REVEREND RICHARD HARRIS BARHAM (1788–
1845) hailed from Tappington Everard in Kent, was originally intended for
the bar, but took orders and for some years was a minor canon at St. Paul's. A
stillborn novel was followed by humorous verses and the publication of *The
Ingoldsby Legends* in *Bentley's Miscellany*. Acclaim was immediate and lasting.
Barham adapted the French metrical *conte* for his exuberant grotesqueries on
medieval themes, a side of the Gothic revival now less familiar than the high-
minded architecture of Pugin or the romanticism of Keats's *Eve of St. Agnes*.
Needless to say, many worthy contemporaries found Barham farcical and irreverent, his humour inferior to poets such as Hood because, as the *D.N.B.* puts
it, his gaiety was "not equally purified and ennobled by being dashed with tears."

Bishop Hatto and the Rats

ROBERT SOUTHEY

The summer and autumn had been so wet,
That in winter the corn was growing yet,
'Twas a piteous sight to see all around
The corn lie rotting on the ground.

Every day the starving poor
They crowded around Bishop Hatto's door,
For he had a plentiful last year's store,
And all the neighbourhood could tell
His granaries were furnished well.

At last Bishop Hatto appointed a day
To quiet the poor without delay,
He bade them to his great barn repair,
And they should have food for the winter there.

Rejoiced the tidings good to hear,
The poor folks flocked from far and near,
The great barn was full as it could hold
Of women and children, and young and old.

Then when he saw it could hold no more,
Bishop Hatto he made fast the door,
And whilst for mercy on Christ they call,
He set fire to the barn and burnt them all.

I' faith, 'tis an excellent bonfire! quoth he,
And the country is greatly obliged to me,
For ridding it these times forlorn
Of rats that only consume the corn.

So then to his palace returnèd he,
And he sate down to supper merrily,
And he slept that night like an innocent man;
But Bishop Hatto never slept again.

In the morning as he entered the hall,
Where his picture hung against the wall,
A sweat like death all over him came,
For the rats had eaten it out of the frame.

As he look'd there came a man from his farm,
He had a countenance white with alarm.
My lord, I opened your granaries this morn,
And the rats had eaten all your corn.

Another came running presently,
And he was pale as pale could be,
Fly! my lord bishop, fly! quoth he,
Ten thousand rats are coming this way—
The Lord forgive you for yesterday!

I'll go to my tower on the Rhine, replied he,
'Tis the safest place in Germany;
The walls are high, and the shores are steep,
And the tide is strong, and the water deep.

Bishop Hatto fearfully hastened away,
And he cross'd the Rhine without delay,
And reach'd his tower in the island, and barr'd
All the gates secure and hard.

He laid him down and closed his eyes—
But soon a scream made him arise.
He started, and saw two eyes of flame
On his pillow, from whence the screaming came.

He listen'd and look'd;—it was only the cat;
But the bishop he grew more fearful for that,
For she sate screaming, mad with fear,
At the army of rats that were drawing near.

For they have swum the river so deep,
And they have climb'd the shores so steep,

And now by thousands up they crawl
To the holes and windows in the wall.

Down on his knees the bishop fell,
And faster and faster his beads did he tell,
As louder and louder drawing near
The saw of their teeth without he could hear.

And in at the windows, and in at the door,
And through the walls, by thousands they pour,
And down from the ceiling, and up through the floor,
From the right and the left, from behind and before,
From within and without, from above and below,
And all at once to the bishop they go.

They have whetted their teeth against the stones,
And now they pick the bishop's bones,
They gnawed the flesh from every limb,
For they were sent to do judgment on him!

Hatto II, archbishop of Mainz from 968 to 970, was as wicked as Hatto I, who suffered the equally unpleasant legendary end of being cast into the crater of Mount Etna. The medieval tale on which Southey based his poem records that Hatto caught people stealing corn during a famine and burnt them alive in a barn. Their dying screams he compared to the squeaking of mice. In an attempt to escape his fate, he was reputed to have built the Mäuseturm, the Mouse Tower, on a rock mid-stream in the Rhine at Bingen. In fact, the Tower was built to collect river tolls.

The legend—or Southey's version of it—is referred to in Longfellow's "The Children's Hour." He describes how he is besieged by the "blue-eyed banditti," and, incidentally, moves Hatto's see from Mainz to Bingen in the process:

> They almost devour me with kisses,
> Their arms about me entwine,
> Till I think of the Bishop of Bingen
> In his Mouse-Tower on the Rhine!

The parallel, one might think, is a little grisly.

A short biography of Southey appears on page 44.

Ballad

HANS BREITMANN (CHARLES G. LELAND)

Der noble Ritter Hugo
Von Schwillensaufenstein,
Rode out mit shpeer und helmet,
Und he coom to de panks of de Rhine.

Und oop dere rose a meermaid,
Vot hadn't got nodings on,
Und she say, "Oh, Ritter Hugo,
Vhere you goes mit yourself alone?"

And he says, "I rides in de creenwood,
Mit helmet und mit shpeer,
Til I cooms into em Gasthaus,
Und dere I trinks some beer."

Und den outshpoke de maiden
Vot hadn't got nodings on:
"I ton't dink mooch of beoplesh
Dat goes mit demselfs alone.

"You'd petter coom down in de wasser,
Vhere dere's heaps of dings to see,
Und hafe a shplendid tinner
Und drafel along mit me.

"Dere you sees de fisch a schwimmin',
Und you catches dem efery von:"—
So sang dis wasser maiden
Vot hadn't got nodings on.

"Dere is drunks all full mit money
In ships dat vent down of old;
Und you helpsh yourself, by dunder!
To shimmerin' crowns of gold.

"Shoost look at dese shpoons und vatches!
Shoost see dese diamant rings!
Coom down and fill your bockets,
Und I'll giss you like efery dings.

"Vot you vantsh mit your schnapps und lager?
Coom down into der Rhine!
Der ish pottles der Kaiser Charlemagne
Vonce filled mit gold-red wine!"

Dat fetched him—he shtood all shpellpound;
She pooled his coat-tails down,
She drawed him oonder der wasser,
De maiden mit nodings on.

The reader will note that although the Ritter is equipped with medieval spear and helmet, he wears a Victorian frock-coat, for the maiden is able to yank him into the Rhine by his coat-tails.

The German-American ballad was a remarkable manifestation of the dialect poem, so vigorously developed by Colonel John Hay, Will Carleton, and Bret Harte. Inspiration came from the "scrapple English" of the "Pennsylvania Dutch" (it was easy to confuse the Deutsch with the Dutch) and the Hans Breitmann ballads became world-famous and widely imitated. A notable follower of Charles G. Leland was Charles Follen Adams, whose Leedle Yawcob Strauss verses (see the specimen on page 30) were quite as popular as Breitmann verses, especially as they introduced a new sentimental note.

The Breitmann Ballads are probably, despite surface appearances, the most erudite and thoughtful comic poems ever written. The prototype of Hans Breitmann, the central character and "author," was the thrifty, solid German immigrant who also possessed a soldier's propensity for looting, fighting, swearing, and drinking lager beer: "a man of desperate courage whenever a cent could be made," as Nicholas Trübner remarked. The subject matter, nevertheless, was wide and learned, embracing Teutonic myth and philosophy, medieval Latinity, and American politics. Leland admired his rumbustious, crafty, old-student hero; his laughter was affectionate, he said, because "the Germans, as a race, and I might say as individuals, are superior to any others on the American continent."

CHARLES GODFREY LELAND (1824–1903), born and bred in Philadelphia, where he was admitted to the Bar, exchanged law for literature, journalism, German studies, and research into gipsy history and language. He edited *Graham's Magazine*, in which "Hans Breitmann's Barty," the first of the canon, appeared, and launched the *Continental Magazine*. The ballads themselves were not, to begin with, intended for public consumption; they merely helped to fill up letters to a friend.

5
The Rolling Deep

The skipper he stood beside the helm,
His pipe was in his mouth.

—"The Wreck of the Hesperus"

The Wreck of the Hesperus

HENRY WADSWORTH LONGFELLOW

It was the schooner Hesperus,
   That sailed the wintry sea;
And the skipper had taken his little daughtèr,
   To bear him company.

Blue were her eyes as the fairy flax,
   Her cheeks like the dawn of day,
And her bosom white as the hawthorn-buds,
   That ope in the month of May.

The skipper he stood beside the helm,
   His pipe was in his mouth,
And he watched how the veering flaw did blow,
   The smoke now west, now south.

Then up and spake an old sailòr,
   Had sailed the Spanish Main,
"I pray thee, put into yonder port,
   For I fear a hurricane.

"Last night, the moon had a golden ring,
   And tonight no moon we see!"
The skipper, he blew a whiff from his pipe,
   And a scornful laugh laughed he.

Colder and louder blew the wind,
   A gale from the north-east;
The snow fell hissing in the brine,
   And the billows frothed like yeast.

Down came the storm, and smote amain
   The vessel in its strength;

She shuddered and paused, like a frighted steed,
   Then leaped her cable's length.

"Come hither! come hither! my little daughtèr,
   And do not tremble so;
For I can weather the roughest gale,
   That ever wind did blow."

He wrapped her warm in his seaman's coat,
   Against the stinging blast;
He cut a rope from a broken spar,
   And bound her to the mast.

"O father! I hear the church-bells ring,
   O say, what may it be?"
" 'Tis a fog-bell on a rock-bound coast!"
   And he steered for the open sea.

"O father! I hear the sound of guns,
   O say what may it be?"
"Some ship in distress, that cannot live
   In such an angry sea!"

"O father! I see a gleaming light,
   O say what may it be?"
But the father answered never a word,
   A frozen corpse was he.

Lashed to the helm, all stiff and stark,
   With his face turned to the skies,
The lantern gleamed through the gleaming snow
   On his fixed and glassy eyes.

Then the maiden clasped her hands and prayed
   That savèd she might be;
And she thought of Christ who stilled the wave
   On the lake of Galilee.

And fast through the midnight dark and drear,
    Through the whistling sleet and snow,
Like a sheeted ghost, the vessel swept
    Towards the reef of Norman's Woe.

And ever the fitful gusts between
    A sound came from the land;
It was the sound of the trampling surf,
    On the rocks and the hard sea-sand.

The breakers were right beneath her bows,
    She drifted a dreary wreck,
And a whooping billow swept the crew
    Like icicles from her deck.

She struck where the white and fleecy waves
    Looked soft as carded wool,
But the cruel rocks they gored her side
    Like the horns of an angry bull.

Her rattling shrouds, all sheathed in ice,
    With the masts went by the board;
Like a vessel of glass, she stove and sank,
    Ho! ho! the breakers roared!

At day-break, on the bleak sea-beach,
    A fisherman stood aghast,
To see the form of a maiden fair,
    Lashed close to a drifting mast.

The salt sea was frozen on her breast,
    The salt tears in her eyes;
And he saw her hair, like the brown sea-weed,
    On the billows fall and rise.

Such was the wreck of the Hesperus,
   In the midnight and the snow!
Christ save us all from a death like this,
   On the reef of Norman's Woe!

Written swiftly at midnight on December 30, 1839, this poem was Longfellow's horrified reaction to news of the schooner *Hesperus*'s running onto
Norman's Woe, off Gloucester. The sea delivered twenty corpses to the beach,
one of them lashed to a spar.

There is a note on Longfellow on page 39.

The Yankee Man-of-War

AUTHOR UNKNOWN

'Tis of a gallant Yankee ship that flew the stripes and stars,
And the whistling wind from the west-nor'-west blew through the pitch-
    pine spars;
With her starboard tacks aboard, my boys, she hung upon the gale;
On an autumn night we raised the light on the old Head of Kinsale.

It was a clear and cloudless night, and the wind blew steady and strong,
As gayly over the sparkling deep our good ship bowled along;
With the foaming seas beneath her bow the fiery waves she spread,
And bending low her bosom of snow, she buried her lee cat-head.

There was no talk of short'ning sail by him who walked the poop,
And under the press of her pond'ring jib, the boom bent like a hoop!
And the groaning water-ways told the strain that held her stout main-tack,
But he only laughed as he glanced aloft at a white and silvery track.

The mid-tide meets in the Channel waves that flow from shore to shore,
And the mist hung heavy upon the land from Featherstone to Dunmore,
And that sterling light in Tusker Rock where the old bell tolls each hour,
And the beacon light that shone so bright was quench'd on Waterford
    Tower.

The nightly robes our good ship wore were her whole topsails three,
Her spanker and her standing jib—the courses being free,
"Now, lay aloft! my heroes bold, not a moment must be passed!"
And royals and top-gallant sails were quickly on each mast.

What looms upon our starboard bow? What hangs upon the breeze?
'Tis time our good ship hauled her wind abreast the old Saltees,
For by her ponderous press of sail and by her consorts four
We saw our morning visitor was a British man-of-war.

Up spake our noble Captain then, as a shot ahead of us past—
"Haul snug your flowing courses! lay your topsail to the mast!"

Those Englishmen gave three loud hurrahs from the deck of their covered
   ark,
And we answered back by a solid broadside from the decks of our patriot
   bark.

"Out booms! out booms!" our skipper cried, "out booms and give her
   sheet,"
And the swiftest keel that was ever launched shot ahead of the British
   fleet,
And amidst a thundering shower of shot, with stun'-sails hoisting away,
Down the North Channel Paul Jones did steer just at the break of day.

John Paul Jones, America's first great naval hero, delivered a blow to the
legend of British mastery of the seas that the Island Race prefers to forget.
Furthermore, it still manages to ignore the startling American maritime successes in the War of 1812. As Ogden Nash has remarked, "every English
schoolboy knows that John Paul Jones was only an unfair American pirate."

   This splendid ballad has a number of variant stanzas; the text printed here
comes from Stedman's *An American Anthology* of 1900 and Walsh's *Patriotic
and Naval Songster* of 1898.

A Wet Sheet and a Flowing Sea

ALLAN CUNNINGHAM

A wet sheet and a flowing sea,
A wind that follows fast,
And fills the white and rustling sail,
And bends the gallant mast;
And bends the gallant mast, my boys,
Awhile, like the eagle free,
Away the good ship flies, and leaves
Old England on the lee.

O for a soft and gentle wind!
I hear a fair one cry;
But give to me the snoring breeze,
And white waves heaving high;
And white waves heaving high, my boys,
The good ship tight and free—
The world of waters is our home,
And merry men are we.

There's tempest in yon hornèd moon,
And lightning in yon cloud;
And hark the music, mariners!
The wind is piping loud;
The wind is piping loud, my boys,
The lightning flashing free—
While the hollow oak our palace is,
Our heritage the sea.

A "sheet" in nautical parlance is not a sail but the rope attached to the lower corner of a sail to control its position. When a boat is running before the wind, the mainsail is almost at a right angle to the vessel, the mainsheet dipping continually into the water. Incidentally, the author of this most famous sea song was a landsman.

ALLAN CUNNINGHAM (1784–1842) trained as a stonemason in Scotland, but he had a marked poetical bent, attending Burns' funeral, becoming a friend of Hogg, the Ettrick shepherd, walking to Edinburgh and back to catch a glimpse of Scott, and composing songs. These he showed to R. H. Cromek, who was on a literary collecting tour. Cromek showed little interest, so Cunningham, with true Scottish resource, dressed up his verses as old Scottish songs and resubmitted them. This time Cromek reacted with great enthusiasm and published them in *Remains of Nithsdale and Galloway Song* in 1810. Cunningham came to make his fortune in London, finding a post as secretary to Sir Francis Chantry, the sculptor. An industrious man with a large family, he also turned out quantities of verse and stories in Scottish dialect, romances and *Lives of the Eminent British Painters, Sculptors and Architects* in six volumes. A bluff and hearty man, his friends accorded him the sobriquet of "honest Allan Cunningham."

The Story of a Stowaway

CLEMENT SCOTT

Come, my lad, and sit beside me; we have often talked before
Of the hurricane and tempest, and the storms on sea and shore:
When we read of deed and daring, done for dear old England's sake,
We have cited Nelson's duty, and the enterprise of Drake;
'Midst the fever'd din of battle, roll of drum, and scream of fife,
Heroes pass in long procession, calmly yielding up their life.
Pomps and pageants have their glory, in cathedral aisles are seen
Marble effigies; but seldom of the mercantile marine.
If your playmates love adventure, bid them gather round at school,
Whilst you tell them of a hero, Captain Strachan of Liverpool.

Spite of storm and stress of weather, in a gale that lash'd the land,
On the *Cyprian* screw steamer, there the captain took his stand.
He was no fair-weather sailor, and he often made the boast
That the ocean safer sheltered than the wild Carnarvon coast.
He'd a good ship underneath him, and a crew of English form,
So he sailed from out the Mersey in the hurricane and storm.
All the luck was dead against him—with the tempest at its height,
Fires expired and rudders parted, in the middle of the night
Sails were torn and rent asunder. Then he spoke with bated breath:
"Save yourselves, my gallant fellows! we are drifting to our death!"

Then they looked at one another, and they felt the awful shock,
When, with a louder crash than tempest, they were dashed upon a rock.
All was over now and hopeless; but across those miles of foam
They could hear the shouts of people, and could see the lights of home.
"All is over!" screamed the Captain. "You have answered duty's call.
Save yourselves! I cannot help you! God have mercy on us all!"
So they rushed about like madmen, seizing belt, and oar, and rope—
For the sailor knows where life is, there's the faintest ray of hope—
Then, amidst the wild confusion, at the dreaded dawn of day,
From the hold of that doomed vessel crept a wretched Stowaway!

Who shall tell the saddened story of this miserable lad?
Was it wild adventure stirred him, was he going to the bad?
Was he thief, or bully's victim, or a runaway from school,
When he stole that fatal passage from the port of Liverpool?
No one looked at him, or kicked him, 'midst the paralysing roar
All alone he felt the danger, and he saw the distant shore.
Over went the gallant fellows, when the ship was breaking fast,
And the Captain with his lifebelt—he prepared to follow last;
But he saw a boy neglected, with a face of ashy grey,
"Who are you?" roared out the Captain. "I'm the boy what stow'd away!"

There was scarce another second left to think what he could do,
For the fatal ship was sinking—death was ready for the two.
So the Captain called the outcast—as he faced the tempest wild—
From his own waist took the lifebelt—and he bound it round the child!
"I can swim, my little fellow! Take the belt, and make for land.
Up, and save yourself!" The outcast humbly knelt to kiss his hand.
With the lifebelt round his body then the urchin cleared the ship;
Over went the gallant Captain, with a blessing on his lip.
But the hurricane howled louder than it ever howled before,
As the Captain and the stowaway were making for the shore!

When you tell this gallant story to your playfellows at school,
They will ask you of the hero, Captain Strachan, of Liverpool.
You must answer: They discovered, on the beach at break of day,
Safe—the battered, breathing body of the little Stowaway;
And they watched the waves of wreckage and they searched the cruel
    shore,
But the man who tried to save the little outcast—was no more.

                .   .   .   .

When they speak of English heroes, tell this story where you can,
To the everlasting credit of the bravery of man,
Tell it out in tones of triumph or with tears and quickened breath,
"Manhood's stronger far than storms, and Love is mightier than Death!"

CLEMENT WILLIAM SCOTT (1841–1904) is known today chiefly as the forthright drama critic of the *Daily Telegraph*, from which pulpit he called down fire and brimstone on the monstrous Ibsenite invasion of the British theatre. He found journalism to be his real calling while he was still a junior clerk in the War Office, and when he retired, without ever having been promoted, he devoted himself to writing theatre reviews, adapting the plays of Sardou into English, travelling, and writing sentimental verse, much of it specifically for recitation. Shipwreck is a recurring theme; other typical pieces are "The Wreck of the Indian Chief" and "The Women of Mumbles Head."

Casabianca

MRS. HEMANS

The boy stood on the burning deck
  Whence all but he had fled;
The flame that lit the battle's wreck
  Shone round him o'er the dead.

Yet beautiful and bright he stood,
  As born to rule the storm;
A creature of heroic blood,
  A proud, though childlike form.

The flames roll'd on—he would not go
  Without his father's word;
That father, faint in death below,
  His voice no longer heard.

He call'd aloud—"Say, father, say
  If yet my task is done!"
He knew not that the chieftain lay
  Unconscious of his son.

"Speak, father!" once again he cried,
  "If I may yet be gone!"
And but the booming shots replied,
  And fast the flames roll'd on.

Upon his brow he felt their breath,
  And in his waving hair,
And looked from that lone post of death,
  In still yet brave despair;

And shouted but once more aloud,
  "My father, must I stay?"
While o'er him fast, through sail and shroud
  The wreathing fires made way.

They wrapt the ship in splendour wild,
  They caught the flag on high,
And stream'd above the gallant child,
  Like banners in the sky.

There came a burst of thunder sound—
  The boy—oh! where was he?
Ask of the winds that far around
  With fragments strewed the sea!—

With mast, and helm, and pennon fair,
  That well had borne their part;
But the noblest thing which perished there
  Was that young faithful heart.

This most recited of all the Gems in this collection celebrates an actual incident.
Louis de Casabianca was the Corsican commander of the French ship *L'Orient*
during the Battle of the Nile. His son, about thirteen years old, remained at his
post after the vessel had taken fire and all the guns been abandoned, perishing
in the explosion when the flames reached the powder. It is said that Casabianca,
mortally wounded, blew up his ship to prevent its capture by the English. André
Chenier also commemorated this event in verse.

The parodies of "Casabianca" are numberless. Here is just one, in typical
schoolboy vein:

The boy stood in the waiting room
  Whence all but he had fled;
His waistcoat was unbuttoned,
  His mouth was gorged with bread.

"My fifteenth cup of tea," he cried,
  In accents loud and wild,
"Another crust before I bust!"
  He was a greedy child.

With a roar that rent the firmament,
  The boy, oh, where was he?
Ask of the maids that mopped it up,
  The breadcrumbs and the tea.

FELICIA DOROTHEA HEMANS, *née* BROWNE (1793–1835), came of Irish, German, Italian, and Lancashire blood and was born into what Lady Bracknell called "the purple of commerce." Her father, George Browne, was a Liverpool merchant, and her three brothers distinguished themselves in the army, in the Irish police, and as assistant deputy commissary-general in Upper Canada. Her first volume of poems, published when she was fifteen, attracted the attentions of Shelley, whose enthusiastic letters had to be stopped by Felicia's mamma. She married an Irish soldier, who bestowed upon her five children in six years and then decamped for ever. Equally prolific on paper, Mrs. Hemans published annually books of patriotic, pathetic, and devotional poetry. "Few poets, living or dead, have written so much," said *The Book of Gems*, "or written so well." Her admirers were drawn from all stations in life, including her fellow bards, Scott, Wordsworth (who commemorated her in his "Epitaphs"), and Byron, as well as Bishop Heber and the Countess of Blessington. A prey to constant bad health, she faded away and died in Ireland, leaving behind her a noble corpus of poems which have, says the *D.N.B.*, "singular grace and tenderness, and exhibit an ardent sympathy with chivalry in every form." She is, indeed, the undisputed Poetess Laureate of the parlour.

A Leap for Life

WALTER COLTON

Old Ironsides at anchor lay,
 In the harbour of Mahon;
A dead calm rested on the bay—
 The waves to sleep had gone;
When little Hal, the captain's son,
 A lad both brave and good,
In sport, up shroud and rigging ran,
 And on the main truck stood!

A shudder shot through every vein;
 All eyes were turned on high!
There stood the boy, with dizzy brain,
 Between the sea and sky.
No hold had he above, below;
 Alone he stood in air;
To that far height none dared to go—
 No aid could reach him there.

We gazed, but not a man could speak!
 With horror all aghast—
In groups, with pallid brow and cheek,
 We watched the quivering mast.
The atmosphere grew thick and hot,
 And of a lurid hue;
As riveted unto the spot,
 Stood officers and crew.

The father came on deck. He gasped,
 "O God! Thy will be done!"
Then suddenly a rifle grasped,
 And aimed it at his son.
"Jump, far out, boy, into the wave!
 Jump, or I fire," he said.
"That only chance your life can save;
 Jump, jump, boy!" He obeyed.

He sunk—he rose—he lived—he moved,
  And for the ship struck out.
On board we hailed the boy beloved
  With many a manly shout.
The father drew, in silent joy,
  Those wet arms round his neck,
And folded to his heart his boy—
  Then fainted on the deck.

"Old Ironsides" was the popular name for the frigate *Constitution,* famous for her role in the War of 1812. There is a celebrated poem about her by Oliver Wendell Holmes, written to protest—effectively, as it turned out—against the proposal to break her up. It runs:

Ay, tear her tattered ensign down!
  Long has it waved on high,
And many an eye has danced to see
  That banner in the sky;
Beneath it rung the battle-shout,
  And burst the cannon's roar:
The meteor of the ocean air
  Shall sweep the clouds no more!

Her deck, once red with heroes' blood,
  Where knelt the vanquished foe,
When winds were hurrying o'er the flood
  And waves were white below,
No more shall feel the victor's tread,
  Or know the conquered knee:
The harpies of the shore shall pluck
  The eagle of the sea!

O better that her shattered hulk
  Should sink beneath the wave!
Her thunders shook the mighty deep,
  And there should be her grave:
Nail to the mast her holy flag,
  Set every threadbare sail,
And give her to the god of storms,
  The lightning and the gale!

[*158*]

The frigate was saved, not only from destruction, but also from the god of storms. She was rebuilt, saw further service, and is now preserved at Charlestown, Massachusetts.

W A L T E R C O L T O N (1797–1851) came from Vermont, and grew up to be a Congregationalist minister, chaplain in the U.S. Navy, nautical writer and founder of California's first newspaper. Gardner Quincy Colton, his brother, experimented with laughing gas, inspiring its use as a dental anaesthetic.

The Old Navy

FREDERICK MARRYAT

The captain stood on the carronade: "First lieutenant," says he,
"Send all my merry men aft here, for they must list to me;
I haven't the gift of the gab, my sons—because I'm bred to the sea;
That ship there is a Frenchman, who means to fight with we.
  And odds bobs, hammer and tongs, long as I've been to sea,
  I've fought 'gainst every odds—but I've gained the victory!

"That ship there is a Frenchman, and if we don't take *she*,
'Tis a thousand bullets to one, that she will capture *we*;
I haven't the gift of the gab, my boys; so each man to his gun;
If she's not mine in half an hour, I'll flog each mother's son.
  For odds bobs, hammer and tongs, long as I've been to sea,
  I've fought 'gainst every odds—and I've gained the victory!"

We fought for twenty minutes, when the Frenchman had enough;
"I little thought," said he, "that your men were of such stuff";
Our captain took the Frenchman's sword, a low bow made to *he*;
"I haven't the gift of the gab, Mounsieur, but polite I wish to be.
  And odds bobs, hammer and tongs, long as I've been to sea,
  I've fought 'gainst every odds—and I've gained the victory!"

Our captain sent for all of us: "My merry men," said he,
"I haven't the gift of the gab, my lads, but yet I thankful be:
You've done your duty handsomely, each man stood to his gun;
If you hadn't, you villains, as sure as day, I'd have flogged each mother's
    son.
  For odds bobs, hammer and tongs, as long as I'm at sea,
  I'll fight 'gainst every odds—and I'll gain the victory!"

Carronades were naval cannon of very large bore but short range, used in close
engagements and normally mounted on the poop or the fo'c'sle, where they may
be seen on H.M.S. *Victory*. The name comes from the foundry on the banks of
the Carron near Falkirk where they were first made.
  This *tour de force* of a poem was extravagant enough in Victorian eyes to

cause W. E. Henley, in the Introduction to his anthology of verse for boys, *Lyra Heroica*, to admit that its inclusion there would cause distress to the sensitive.

CAPTAIN FREDERICK MARRYAT (1792–1848) had a life that reads like one of his own rollicking yarns. Son of the M.P. for Sandwich, he ran away from school several times, not actually reaching the sea until his father signed him on as a midshipman aboard the frigate *Impérieuse*. His naval career was crammed with excitement and sea-fights; he won the Royal Humane Society's gold medal for gallantry in saving life at sea, and held certificates for jumping overboard to save upwards of a dozen persons. He retired from the Royal Navy to write the novels and boys' stories—among them *Peter Simple*, *Mr. Midshipman Easy*, and *Masterman Ready*—that stirred generations of stout-hearted lads. He was incautious enough, after two years in the United States and Canada, to publish his outspoken diaries: his books were burned and his effigy hanged as a reprisal by the infuriated victims. Edgar Allan Poe found his work "mediocre," too.

Elihu

ALICE CARY

"*O sailor, tell me, tell me true,*
Is my little lad—my Elihu—
    A sailing in your ship?"
The sailor's eyes were dimmed with dew.
"Your little lad? your Elihu?"
    He said with trembling lip;
    "What little lad—what ship?"

What little lad?—as if there could be
Another such a one as he!
    "What little lad, do you say?"
"Why, Elihu, that took to the sea
The moment I put him off my knee.
    It was just the other day
    The *Gray Swan* sailed away."

The other day? The sailor's eyes
Stood wide open with surprise.
    "The other day?—the *Swan?*"
His heart began in his throat to rise.
"Ay, ay, sir; here in the cupboard lies
    The jacket he had on."
    "And so your lad is gone!"—

"Gone with the *Swan.*" "And did she stand
With her anchor clutching hold of the sand,
    For a month, and never stir?"
"Why, to be sure! I've seen from the land,
Like a lover kissing his lady's hand,
    The wild sea kissing her—
    A sight to remember, sir."

"But, my good mother, do you know,
All this was twenty years ago?

I stood on the *Gray Swan*'s deck,
And to that lad I saw you throw—
Taking it off, as it might be so—
    The kerchief from your neck."
    "Ay, and he'll bring it back."

"And did the little lawless lad,
That has made you sick, and made you sad,
    Sail with the *Gray Swan*'s crew?"
"Lawless! the man is going mad;
The best boy mother ever had;
    Be sure, he sailed with the crew—
    What would you have him do?"

"And he has never written line,
Nor sent you word, nor made you sign,
    To say he was alive?"
"Hold—if 'twas wrong, the wrong is mine;
Besides, he may be in the brine;
    And could he write from the grave?
    Tut, man! what would you have?"

"Gone twenty years! a long, long cruise;
'Twas wicked thus your love to abuse;
    But if the lad still live,
And come back home, think you you can
Forgive him?" "Miserable man!
    You're mad as the sea; you rave—
    What have I to forgive?"

The sailor twitched his shirt so blue,
And from within his bosom drew
    The kerchief. She was wild:
"My God!—my Father!—is it true?
My little lad—my Elihu?
And is it?—is it? is it you?
    My blessed boy—my child—
    My dead—my living child!"

Connoisseurs of the lachrymose will note with approval the insertion of an extra line in the final stanza in order to wring yet more tears from the impressionable auditor. The present editor rejects as corrupt the emendation of "gorge" for "heart" in the fourth line of the third verse.

There is a short comment on the poetical sisters Alice and Phoebe Cary on page 74.

Drake's Drum

SIR HENRY NEWBOLT

Drake he's in his hammock an' a thousand mile away,
   (Capten, art tha sleepin' there below?),
Slung atween the round shot in Nombre Dios Bay,
   An' dreamin' arl the time o' Plymouth Hoe.
Yarnder lumes the Island, yarnder lie the ships,
   Wi' sailor lads a-dancin' heel-an'-toe,
An' the shore-lights flashin', an' the night-tide dashin',
   He sees et arl so plainly as he saw et long ago.

Drake he was a Devon man, an' rüled the Devon seas,
   (Capten, art tha sleepin' there below?),
Rovin' tho' his death fell, he went wi' heart at ease,
   An' dreamin' arl the time o' Plymouth Hoe.
"Take my drum to England, hang et by the shore,
   Strike et when your powder's runnin' low;
If the Dons sight Devon, I'll quit the port o' Heaven,
   An' drum them up the Channel as we drumm'd them long ago."

Drake he's in his hammock till the great Armadas come,
   (Capten, art tha sleepin' there below?),
Slung atween the round shot, listenin' for the drum,
   An' dreamin' arl the time o' Plymouth Hoe.
Call him on the deep sea, call him up the Sound,
   Call him when ye sail to meet the foe;
Where the old trade's plyin' an' the old flag's flyin'
   They shall find him ware an' wakin', as they found him long ago!

After years of harrying the Spaniards, acting the filibuster for Elizabeth and bringing home shiploads of treasure, finally playing a leading part in the defeat of the "glorious Armada," Sir Francis Drake retired to Plymouth. The queen ordered him to sea again in 1594, to command an expedition to the West Indies. Things went wrong even before the fleet of twenty-seven sail put out from Plymouth the next year. The Spaniards were ready to receive the English and no booty was taken. Sick of dysentery and vexation, Drake died off Porto Bello, and his body was committed to the deep.

A note on Sir Henry Newbolt may be found on page 76.

Jim Bludso of the Prairie Belle

COLONEL JOHN HAY

Wall, no! I can't tell whar he lives,
    Becase he don't live, you see;
Leastways, he's got out of the habit
    Of livin' like you and me.
Whar have you been for the last three year
    That you haven't heard folks tell
How Jimmy Bludso passed in his checks
    The night of the Prairie Belle?

He weren't no saint,—them engineers
    Is all pretty much alike,—
One wife in Natchez-under-the-Hill
    And another one here, in Pike;
A keerless man in his talk was Jim,
    And an awkward hand in a row,
But he never flunked, and he never lied,—
    I reckon he never knowed how.

And this was all the religion he had,—
    To treat his engine well;
Never be passed on the river;
    To mind the pilot's bell;
And if ever the Prairie Belle took fire,—
    A thousand times he swore
He'd hold her nozzle agin the bank
    Till the last soul got ashore.

All boats has their day on the Mississip,
    And her day come at last,—
The Movastar was a better boat,
    But the Belle she *wouldn't* be passed.
And so she come tearin' along that night—
    The oldest craft on the line—
With a nigger squat on her safety-valve,
    And her furnace crammed, rosin and pine.

The fire burst out as she clared the bar,
  And burnt a hole in the night,
And quick as a flash she turned, and made
  For that willer-bank on the right.
There was runnin' and cursin', but Jim yelled out,
  Over all the infernal roar,
"I'll hold her nozzle agin the bank
  Till the last galoot's ashore."

Through the hot, black breath of the burnin' boat
  Jim Bludso's voice was heard,
And they all had trust in his cussedness,
  And knowed he would keep his word.
And, sure's you're born, they all got off
  Afore the smokestacks fell,—
And Bludso's ghost went up alone
  In the smoke of the Prairie Belle.

He weren't no saint,—but at jedgment
  I'd run my chance with Jim,
'Longside of some pious gentleman
  That wouldn't shake hands with him.
He seen his duty, a dead-sure thing,—
  And went for it thar and then;
And Christ ain't a going to be too hard
  On a man that died for men.

This Pike County Ballad (see page 12) is in true epic style, with classic use of
repetition: " 'I'll hold her nozzle agin the bank/Till the last galoot's ashore.' "
Colonel John Hay and Bret Harte were early in the field with this kind of
character narrative, so well suited to dramatic recitation and exploited by Will
Carleton, Clement Scott, George R. Sims, and other poets.

The Lifeboat

GEORGE R. SIMS

Been out in the lifeboat often? Ay, ay, sir, oft enough.
When it's rougher than this? Lor' bless you! this ain't what *we* calls rough!
It's when there's a gale a-blowin', and the waves run in and break
On the shore with a roar like thunder and the white cliffs seem to shake;
When the sea is a hell of waters, and the bravest holds his breath
As he hears the cry for the lifeboat—his summons maybe to death—
That's when we call it rough, sir; but, if we can get her afloat,
There's always enough brave fellows ready to man the boat.

You've heard of the Royal Helen, the ship as was wrecked last year?
Yon be the rock she struck on—the boat as went out be here;
The night as she struck was reckoned the worst as ever we had,
And this is a coast in winter where the weather be awful bad.
The beach here was strewed with wreckage, and to tell you the truth, sir,
        then
Was the only time as ever we'd a bother to get the men.
The single chaps was willin', and six on 'em volunteered,
But most on us here is married, and the wives that night was skeered.

Our women ain't chicken-hearted when it comes to savin' lives,
But death that night looked certain—and our wives be only wives:
Their lot ain't bright at the best, sir; but here, when the man lies dead,
'Taint only a husband missin', it's the children's daily bread;
So our women began to whimper and beg o' the chaps to stay—
I only heard on it after, for that night I was kept away.
I was up at my cottage, yonder, where the wife lay nigh her end,
She'd been ailin' all the winter, and nothing 'ud make her mend.

The doctor had given her up, sir, and I knelt by her side and prayed,
With my eyes as red as a babby's, that Death's hand might yet be stayed.
I heerd the wild wind howlin', and I looked on the wasted form,
And thought of the awful shipwreck as had come in the ragin' storm;
The wreck of my little homestead—the wreck of my dear old wife,
Who'd sailed with me forty years, sir, o'er the troublous waves of life,

And I looked at the eyes so sunken, as had been my harbour lights,
To tell of the sweet home haven in the wildest, darkest nights.

She knew she was sinkin' quickly—she knew as her end was nigh,
But she never spoke o' the troubles as I knew on her heart must lie,
For we'd had one great big sorrow with Jack, our only son—
He'd got into trouble in London as lots o' lads ha' done;
Then he'd bolted his masters told us—he was allus what folks call wild.
From the day as I told his mother, her dear face never smiled.
We heerd no more about him, we never knew where he went,
And his mother pined and sickened for the message he never sent.
I had my work to think of; but she had her grief to nurse,
So it eat away at her heartstrings, and her health grew worse and worse.
And the night as the Royal Helen went down on yonder sands,
I sat and watched her dyin', holdin' her wasted hands.
She moved in her doze a little, then her eyes were opened wide,
And she seemed to be seekin' somthin', as she looked from side to side;
Then half to herself she whispered, "Where's Jack, to say good-bye?
It's hard not to see my darlin', and kiss him afore I die!"

I was stoopin' to kiss and soothe her, while the tears ran down my cheek,
And my lips were shaped to whisper the words I couldn't speak,
When the door of the room burst open, and my mates were there outside
With the news that the boat was launchin'. "You're wanted!" their leader
    cried.
"You've never refused to go, John; you'll put these cowards right.
There's a dozen of lives maybe, John, as lie in our hands tonight!"
'Twas old Ben Brown, the captain; he'd laughed at the women's doubt.
We'd always been first on the beach, sir, when the boat was goin' out.

I didn't move, but I pointed to the white face on the bed—
"I can't go, mate," I murmured; "in an hour she may be dead.
I cannot go and leave her to die in the night alone."
As I spoke Ben raised his lantern, and the light on my wife was thrown;
And I saw her eyes fixed strangely with a pleading look on me,
While a tremblin' finger pointed through the door to the ragin' sea.
Then she beckoned me near, and whispered, "Go, and God's will be done!
For every lad on that ship, John, is some poor mother's son."

Her head was full of the boy, sir—she was thinking, maybe, some day
For lack of a hand to help him his life might be cast away.
"Go, John, and the Lord watch o'er you! and spare me to see the light,
And bring you safe," she whispered, "out of the storm tonight."
Then I turned and kissed her softly, and tried to hide my tears,
And my mates outside, when they saw me, set up three hearty cheers;
But I rubbed my eyes wi' my knuckles, and turned to old Ben and said,
"I'll see her again, maybe, lad, when the sea gives up its dead."

We launched the boat in the tempest, though death was the goal in view,
And never a one but doubted if the craft could live it through;
But our boat she stood it bravely, and, weary and wet and weak,
We drew in hail of the vessel we had dared so much to seek.
But just as we come upon her she gave a fearful roll,
And went down in the seethin' whirlpool with every livin' soul!
We rowed for the spot, and shouted, for all around was dark—
But only the wild wind answered the cries from our plungin' bark.

I was strainin' my eyes and watchin', when I thought I heard a cry,
And I saw past our bows a somethin' on the crest of a wave dashed by;
I stretched out my hand to seize it. I dragged it aboard, and then
I stumbled, and struck my forrud, and fell like a log on Ben.
I remember a hum of voices, and then I knowed no more
Till I came to my senses here, sir—here, in my home ashore.
My forrud was tightly bandaged, and I lay on my little bed—
I'd slipped, so they told me arter, and a rulluck had struck my head.

Then my mates came in and whispered; they'd heard I was comin' round.
At first I could scarcely hear 'em, it seemed like a buzzin' sound;
But as my head got clearer, and accustomed to hear 'em speak,
I knew as I'd lain like that, sir, for many a long, long week.
I guessed what the lads was hidin', for their poor old shipmate's sake.
I could see by their puzzled faces they'd got some news to break;
So I lifts my head from the pillow, and I says to old Ben, "Look here!
I'm able to bear it now, lad—tell me, and never fear."

Not one on 'em ever answered, but presently Ben goes out,
And the others slinks away like, and I says, "What's this about?

Why can't they tell me plainly as the poor old wife is dead?"
Then I fell again on the pillows, and I hid my achin' head;
I lay like that for a minute, till I heard a voice cry "John!"
And I thought it must be a vision as my weak eyes gazed upon;
For there by the bedside, standin' up and well was my wife.
And who do ye think was with her? Why, Jack, as large as life.

It was him as I'd saved from drownin' the night as the lifeboat went
To the wreck of the Royal Helen; 'twas that as the vision meant.
They'd brought us ashore together, he'd knelt by his mother's bed,
And the sudden joy had raised her like a miracle from the dead;
And mother and son together had nursed me back to life,
And my old eyes woke from darkness to look on my son and wife.
Jack? He's our right hand now, sir; 'twas Providence pulled him
   through—
He's allus the first aboard her when the lifeboat wants a crew.

The "Elihu" story told again, with rather more picturesque detail. A note on
George R. Sims may be found on page 29.

6

Poor but Honest

*An exile from home, splendour dazzles in vain;
O, give me my lowly thatched cottage again!*

—"Home, Sweet Home"

Home, Sweet Home

JOHN HOWARD PAYNE

'Mid pleasures and palaces though we may roam,
Be it ever so humble, there's no place like home;
A charm from the sky seems to hallow us there,
Which, seek through the world, is ne'er met with elsewhere.
    Home, Home, sweet, sweet Home!
There's no place like Home! there's no place like Home!

An exile from home, splendour dazzles in vain;
O, give me my lowly thatched cottage again!
The birds singing gayly, that came at my call,—
Give me them,—and the peace of mind, dearer than all!
    Home, Home, sweet, sweet Home!
There's no place like Home! there's no place like Home!

How sweet 't is to sit 'neath a fond father's smile,
And the cares of a mother to soothe and beguile!
Let others delight 'mid new pleasures to roam,
But give me, oh, give me, the pleasures of home!
    Home, Home, sweet, sweet Home!
There's no place like Home! there's no place like Home!

To thee I'll return, overburdened with care;
The heart's dearest solace will smile on me there;
No more from that cottage again will I roam;
Be it ever so humble, there's no place like home.
    Home, Home, sweet, sweet Home!
There's no place like Home! there's no place like Home!

A number of variants of this evergreen gem exist, but the present editor must leave to some future scholar the compilation of a Variorum Edition of "Home, Sweet Home." The version printed here has the authority of E. C. Stedman's *An American Anthology,* 1900, but it is worth quoting a stanza that occurs in some collections.

I gaze on the moon as I trace the drear wild,
And feel that my parent now thinks of her child;
She looks on that moon from her own cottage door,
Through woodbines whose fragrance shall cheer me no more.
Home, Home, etc.

JOHN HOWARD PAYNE (1791–1852), perpetually impecu-
nious, seems to have made the unfortunate error of selling his libretto of the
opera, *Clari; or , the Maid of Milan,* for an outright fee, receiving no royalties.
It contained the song "Home, Sweet Home," set to music that Sir Henry Bishop
had previously composed for a poem by Thomas Haynes Bayly. "Home, Sweet
Home" is said to have sold 100,000 copies in the year of its first performance,
1823. But perhaps rough justice was done, after all, for in 1818 J. K. Paulding
had published in America "The Backwoodsman," which contained the lines:

> Whate'er may happen, whereso'er we roam,
> However homely, still there's naught like home.

Payne, an American actor, was dogged by ill luck and financial embarrassment.
He lived for some years in England and wooed Mary Shelley, widow of the poet,
in vain. He finished his life as American consul in Tunis.

The Village Blacksmith

HENRY WADSWORTH LONGFELLOW

Under a spreading chestnut tree
The village smithy stands;
The smith, a mighty man is he,
With large and sinewy hands;
And the muscles of his brawny arms
Are strong as iron bands.

His hair is crisp, and black, and long,
His face is like the tan;
His brow is wet with honest sweat,
He earns whate'er he can;
And looks the whole world in the face,
For he owes not any man.

Week out, week in, from morn till night,
You can hear his bellows blow;
You can hear him swing his heavy sledge
With measured beat and slow,
Like sexton ringing the village bell,
When the evening sun is low.

And children coming home from school
Look in at the open door:
They love to see the flaming forge,
And hear the bellows roar,
And catch the burning sparks that fly
Like chaff from a threshing floor.

He goes on Sunday to the church,
And sits among his boys,
He hears the parson pray and preach,
He hears his daughter's voice
Singing in the village choir,
And it makes his heart rejoice.

It sounds to him like her mother's voice,
Singing in Paradise!
He needs must think of her once more,
How in her grave she lies;
And with his hard, rough hand he wipes
A tear from out his eyes.

Toiling, rejoicing, sorrowing,
Onward through life he goes;
Each morning sees some task begin,
Each evening sees it close;
Something attempted, something done,
Has earned a night's repose.

Thanks—thanks to thee, my worthy friend,
For the lesson thou hast taught!
Thus at the flaming forge of life
Our fortunes must be wrought,—
Thus on its sounding anvil shaped
Each burning deed and thought!

The original mighty man is said to have been one of the poet's New England ancestors, | a | blacksmith | in | Newbury. Other commentators consider | that | the smithy that inspired Longfellow was situated on Brattle Street, Cambridge, Massachusetts.

Of the many parodies, the most original may be that anonymous work quoted by Arnold Silcock in his Private Collection, *Verse and Worse:*

Under a spreading gooseberry bush the village burglar lies,
The burglar is a hairy man with whiskers round his eyes
And the muscles of his brawny arms keep off the little flies.

He goes on Sunday to the church to hear the Parson shout.
He puts a penny in the plate and takes a pound note out
And drops a conscience-stricken tear in case he is found out.

A note on Longfellow appears on page 39.

[*178*]

Song of the Shirt

THOMAS HOOD

With fingers weary and worn,
  With eyelids heavy and red,
A woman sat, in unwomanly rags,
  Plying her needle and thread,—
    Stitch! stitch! stitch!
In poverty, hunger, and dirt,
  And still, with a voice of dolorous pitch,
She sang the "Song of the Shirt."

"Work! work! work!
While the cock is crowing aloof!
  And work—work—work,
Till the stars shine through the roof!
  It's oh! to be a slave
  Along with the barbarous Turk,
Where woman has never a soul to save,
  If this is Christian work!

"Work—work—work,
Till the brain begins to swim,
  Work—work—work,
Till the eyes are heavy and dim!
  Seam, and gusset, and band,
  Band, and gusset, and seam,
Till over the buttons I fall asleep,
  And sew them on in a dream.

"Oh! men with sisters dear!
  Oh, men with mothers and wives!
It is not linen you're wearing out,
  But human creatures' lives!
    Stitch—stitch—stitch,
  In poverty, hunger, and dirt,
Sewing at once, with a double thread,
  A shroud as well as a shirt.

"But why do I talk of death,
   That phantom of grisly bone?
I hardly fear his terrible shape,
   It seems so like my own,—
   It seems so like my own,
   Because of the fasts I keep.
O God! that bread should be so dear,
   And flesh and blood so cheap!

   "Work—work—work,
   My labour never flags;
And what are its wages? A bed of straw,
   A crust of bread,—and rags,—
That shattered roof,—and this naked floor,—
   A table,—a broken chair,—
And a wall so blank, my shadow I thank
   For sometimes falling there!

   "Work—work—work!
From weary chime to chime!
   Work—work—work,
As prisoners work for crime!
   Band, and gusset, and seam,
   Seam, and gusset, and band,
Till the heart is sick, and the brain benumbed,
   As well as the weary hand.

   "Work—work—work,
In the dull December light,
   And work—work—work,
When the weather is warm and bright—
While underneath the eaves
   The brooding swallows cling,
As if to show me their sunny backs,
   And twit me with the Spring.

"Oh, but to breathe the breath
   Of the cowslip and primrose sweet—

With the sky above my head,
   And the grass beneath my feet;
For only one sweet hour!
   To feel as I used to feel,
Before I knew the woes of want,
   And the walk that costs a meal;

"Oh, but for one short hour!
   A respite, however brief!
No blessed leisure for love or hope,
   But only time for grief!
A little weeping would ease my heart,
   But in their briny bed
My tears must stop, for every drop
   Hinders needle and thread!"

With fingers weary and worn,
   With eyelids heavy and red,
A woman sat, in unwomanly rags,
   Plying her needle and thread,—
      Stitch! stitch! stitch!
   In poverty, hunger, and dirt,
And still, with a voice of dolorous pitch—
   Would that its tone could reach the Rich!—
She sang this "Song of the Shirt."

"Some of his poems he enclosed in crystal tear drops," wrote Mr. Thornbury of Hood in *Two Centuries of Song*. So fond was the poet himself of this truly powerful evocation of the miseries of the Poor, that he wished to have one single line inscribed on his tombstone:

"He sang the 'Song of the Shirt' "

This was, in fact, one of the most quoted and anthologized poems of the last century and actually did much to relieve the evil conditions under which poor women were forced to sew "slop-work." Other bards found it of use in further-ing pious aims: a J. Nott wrote the words and a G. F. King the music

of a version for Simeon Smith to render during his Popular Temperance
Musical Evenings. Here are the first two stanzas:

Temperance Song of the Shirt

With fingers lightsome and slim,
And eyes of joyous gleam,
A woman sat in her temperance home,
Plying her sewing machine.
Stitch, stitch, stitch,
No poverty near her nor dirt,
But still with a voice of sonorous pitch
She sang this song of the shirt:

"Work, work, work,
Aye cheerfully with a will;
And work, work, work,
With God above us still,
It's oh! to be a slave,
To brandy, wine, or beer,
As if man had not a soul to save,
And nothing on earth was dear."

THOMAS HOOD (1799–1845), son of a London bookseller, was of a
delicate constitution that prevented him continuing his training first in a counting
house, then as an engraver. Publisher friends of his father gave him the post of
assistant sub-editor of the *London Magazine*, providing him with the opportunity to meet De Quincey, Hazlitt, and Lamb. He began to write whimsical,
pathetic, and humorous verse and prose, including "Eugene Aram's Dream"
and "Miss Kilmansegg," defying the consumption and monetary troubles that
plagued him. Jesting in the face of death, a nightingale with a thorn at his breast,
it is not surprising that he should catch the lively sympathy of a very wide public.

The Old Arm-Chair

ELIZA COOK

I love it! I love it! And who shall dare
To chide me for loving that old arm-chair?
I've treasured it long as a sainted prize;
I've bedewed it with tears, and embalmed it with sighs.
'Tis bound by a thousand bands to my heart;
Not a tie will break, not a link will start.
Would ye learn the spell?—a mother sat there;
And a sacred thing is that old arm-chair.

In childhood's hour I lingered near
The hallowed seat with list'ning ear;
And gentle words that mother would give,
To fit me to die, and teach me to live.
She told me shame would never betide
With truth for my creed, and God for my guide;
She taught me to lisp my earliest prayer,
As I knelt beside that old arm-chair.

I sat and watched her many a day,
When her eyes grew dim, and her locks were grey;
And I almost worshipped her when she smiled,
And turned from her Bible to bless her child.
Years rolled on; but the last one sped—
My idol was shattered; my earth-star fled.
I learnt how much the heart can bear,
When I saw her die in that old arm-chair.

'Tis past! 'tis past! But I gaze on it now
With quivering breath and sobbing brow:
'Twas there she nursed me; 'twas there she died:
And memory flows with lava tide.
Say it is folly, and deem me weak,
While the scalding drops start down my cheek;
But I love it! I love it! and cannot tear
My soul from a mother's old arm-chair.

E L I Z A   C O O K (1818–1889), born in London, the youngest of a brasier's eleven children, was precocious enough to rise above her humble situation and publish her first volume, *Lays of a Wild Harp*, at the age of seventeen. She contributed verses to various papers anonymously, until the editor of the *Weekly Dispatch*, who printed "The Old Arm-Chair," inserted a notice in his columns appealing to her to reveal her identity. Success encouraged her to bring out *Eliza Cook's Journal*, a mild and moral periodical brought to a premature end by her lack of journalistic ability and her bad health. Declining to the state of a confirmed invalid, her later years were brightened by a Civil List pension of £100, royalties from her publishers, and her rather wilting reputation as a poetess of sincere domestic sentiment and fervent patriotism.

My Mother's Bible

G. P. MORRIS

This book is all that's left me now,—
Tears will unbidden start,—
With faltering lip and throbbing brow
I press it to my heart.
For many generations past
Here is our family tree;
My mother's hands this Bible clasped,
She, dying, gave it me.

Ah! well do I remember those
Whose names these records bear;
Who round the hearthstone used to close,
After the evening prayer,
And speak of what these pages said
In tones my heart would thrill!
Though they are with the silent dead,
Here are they living still!

My father read this holy book
To brothers, sisters, dear;
How calm was my poor mother's look,
Who loved God's word to hear!
Her angel face,—I see it yet!
What thronging memories come!
Again that little group is met
Within the walls of home!

Thou truest friend man ever knew,
Thy constancy I've tried;
When all were false, I found thee true,
My counselor and guide.
The mines of earth no treasures give
That could this volume buy;
In teaching me the way to live,
It taught me how to die.

From the seventeenth century onwards the family Bible was handed down from father to son for a reason other than its role as a staunch provider of religious and moral sustenance. Upon the flyleaf parental pens recorded the births, marriages, and deaths of successive generations: it was the family history in concrete form.

"My Mother's Bible" belongs to the relic or souvenir school of poetry, in which a possession of a deceased loved one is the subject of tearful nostalgia. Chairs are particularly favored—see the preceding poem and Thackeray's effusion on page 99—but other objects can provoke the starting tear. Clocks, in particular, can start an additional sob with their relevance to the inexorable passage of time. In H. C. Work's song, "Grandfather's Clock," you will remember,

> . . . it stopped short, never to go again,
> When the old man died.

GEORGE POPE MORRIS (1802–1864) went from Philadelphia, Pennsylvania, to New York to make a career in journalism. When he was twenty-one he founded the *New York Mirror and Ladies' Literary Gazette* in association with Samuel Woodworth, author of "The Old Oaken Bucket" (see page 258), publishing such notabilities as William Cullen Bryant and Walt Whitman. When the paper had become the *Evening Mirror* after a period as the *New Mirror*, he printed Edgar Allan Poe's "The Raven," which appears on page 109 of this collection. Morris was a member of the talented Knickerbocker School, writers who made New York a literary center in the first half of the nineteenth century; he also tried his hand at stories and drama successfully, at operetta rather less so.

Over the Hill to the Poor-House

WILL CARLETON

Over the hill to the poor-house I'm trudgin' my weary way—
I, a woman of seventy, and only a trifle grey—
I, who am smart an' chipper, for all the years I've told,
As many another woman that's only half as old.

Over the hill to the poor-house—I can't quite make it clear!
Over the hill to the poor-house—it seems so horrid queer!
Many a step I've taken, a-toilin' to and fro,
But this is a sort of journey I never thought to go.

What is the use of heapin' on me a pauper's shame?
Am I lazy or crazy? am I blind or lame?
True, I am not so supple, nor yet so awful stout;
But charity ain't no favour, if one can live without.

I am willin' an' anxious and ready any day
To work for a decent livin', and pay my honest way;
For I can earn my victuals, an' more too, I'll be bound,
If anybody only is willin' to have me round.

Once I was young an' han'some—I was, upon my soul—
Once my cheeks were roses, my eyes as black as coal;
And I can't remember, in them days, of hearin' people say,
For any kind of a reason, that I was in their way.

'Tain't no use of boastin', or talkin' over free,
But many a house an' home was open then to me;
Many a han'some offer I had from likely men,
And nobody ever hinted that I was a burden then.

And when to John I was married, sure he was good and smart,
But he and all the neighbours would own I done my part;
For life was all before me, an' I was young and strong,
And I worked the best that I could in tryin' to get along.

And so we worked together; and life was hard but gay,
With now and then a baby for to cheer us on our way;
Till we had half a dozen, an' all growed clean an' neat,
An' went to school like others, an' had enough to eat.

So we worked for the childr'n, and raised 'em every one;
Worked for 'em summer and winter, just as we ought to've done;
Only perhaps we humored 'em, which some good folks condemn,
But every couple's childr'n's a heap the best of them.

Strange how much we think of our blessed little ones!—
I'd have died for my daughters, I'd have died for my sons;
And God He made that rule of love; but when we're old and grey
I've noticed it sometimes somehow fails to work the other way.

Strange, another thing; when our boys an' girls were grown,
And when, exceptin' Charley, they'd left us there alone;
When John, he nearer an' nearer come, an' nearer seemed to be,
The Lord of Hosts, He come one day, an' took him away from me.

Still I was bound to struggle, an' never to cringe or fall—
Still I worked for Charley, for Charley was now my all;
And Charley was pretty good to me, with scarce a word or frown,
Till at last he went a-courtin', and brought a wife from town.

She was somewhat dressy, an' hadn't a pleasant smile—
She was quite conceity, and carried a heap o' style;
But if ever I tried to be friends, I did with her, I know,
But she was hard and proud, an' I couldn't make it go.

She had an edication, an' that was good for her;
But when she twitted me on mine, 'twas carryin' things too fur;
An' I told her once 'fore company (an' it almost made her sick),
That I never swallowed a grammar, or e't a 'rithmetic.

So 'twas only a few days before the thing was done—
They was a family of themselves, and I another one;
And a very little cottage one family will do,
But I never have seen a house that was big enough for two.

An' I never could speak to suit her, never could please her eye,
An' it made me independent, an' then I didn't try;
But I was terribly staggered, an' felt it like a blow,
When Charley turned ag'in me, an' told me I could go.

I went to live with Susan, but Susan's house was small,
And she was always a-hintin' how snug it was for us all;
And what with her husband's sisters, and what with childr'n three,
'Twas easy to discover that there wasn't room for me.

An' then I went to Thomas, the oldest son I've got,
For Thomas's buildings'd cover the half of an acre lot;
But all the childr'n was on me—I couldn't stand their sauce—
And Thomas said I needn't think I was comin' there to boss.

An' then I wrote to Rebecca, my girl who lives out west,
And to Isaac, not far from her—some twenty miles at best;
And one of 'em said 'twas too warm there for any one so old,
And t'other had an opinion the climate was too cold.

So they have shirked and slighted me, and shifted me about—
So they have well-nigh soured me, an' wore my old heart out;
But still I've borne up pretty well, an' wasn't much put down,
Till Charley went to the poor-master, an' put me on the town.

Over the hill to the poor-house—my childr'n dear, good-by!
Many a night I've watched you when only God was nigh;
And God'll judge between us; but I will always pray
That you shall never suffer the half I do today.

Readers affected by this tale of filial ingratitude will be cheered to learn that the
poet provided a sequel, "Over the Hill from the Poor-House," in which a black-
sheep son, long given up for dead, appears from the West to rescue his mother.
The prodigal can be sure that on Judgment Day, however blotted his record in
the big book,

> My good old Christian mother, you'll see,
> Will be sure to stand right up for me.

WILLIAM McKENDREE CARLETON (1845–1912) was born on a Michigan farm, his rural upbringing providing him with a rich vein of poetical ore for his dialect ballads that gained a world-wide popularity. Will Carleton worked as a newspaperman and wrote stories, but his great reputation was made reciting his own verse on lecture tours. His subject-matter embraced city life, too, and even a noted Scottish disaster, with a piece (rivalling in vigour the account by the poet McGonagall) entitled "The Death-Bridge of the Tay":

Down, down, through the dark the train plunges, with speed unaccustomed and
    dire;
It glows with its last dying beauty—it gleams like a hailstorm of fire!

The Clown's Baby

It was out on the Western frontier—
　　The miners, rugged and brown,
Were gathered around the posters;
　　The circus had come to town!
The great tent shone in the darkness
　　Like a wonderful palace of light!
And rough men crowded the entrance—
　　Shows didn't come every night!

Not a woman's face among them;
　　Many a face that was bad,
And some that were only vacant,
　　And some that were very sad.
And behind a canvas curtain
　　In a corner of the place,
The clown with chalk and vermilion,
　　Was "making up" his face.

A weary-looking woman,
　　With a smile that still was sweet,
Sewed on a little garment,
　　With a cradle at her feet.
Pantaloon stood ready and waiting;
　　It was time for the going on,
But the clown in vain searched wildly;
　　The "property baby" was gone!

He murmured, impatiently hunting,
　　"It's strange that I cannot find—
There! I've looked in every corner;
　　It must have been left behind!"
The miners were stamping and shouting,
　　They were not patient men.
The clown bent over the cradle—
　　"I must take *you*, little Ben."

The mother started and shivered,
  But trouble and want were near;
She lifted her baby gently;
  "You'll be *very* careful, dear?"
"Careful? You foolish darling,"—
  How tenderly it was said!
What a smile shone through the chalk and paint,—
  "I love each hair of his head!"

The noise rose into an uproar,
  Misrule for the time was king;
The clown, with a foolish chuckle,
  Bolted into the ring.
But as, with a squeak and a flourish,
  The fiddles closed their tune,
"You'll hold him as if he was made of glass?"
  Said the clown to the pantaloon.

The jovial fellow nodded;
  "I've a couple myself," he said,
"I know how to handle 'em, bless you!
  Old fellow, go ahead!"
The fun grew fast and furious,
  And not one of all the crowd
Had guessed that the baby was alive,
  When he suddenly laughed aloud.

Oh, that baby-laugh! It was echoed
  From the benches with a ring.
And the roughest customer there sprang up
  With, "Boys, it's the real thing!"
The ring was jammed in a minute,
  Not a man that did not strive
For a "shot at holding the baby"—
  The baby that was "alive!"

He was thronged by kneeling suitors
  In the midst of the dusty ring,

And he held his court right royally,—
    The fair little baby-king,—
Till one of the shouting courtiers,
    A man with a bold, hard face,
The talk, for miles, of the country,
    And the terror of the place;

Raised the little king to his shoulder,
    And chuckled, "Look at that!"
As the chubby fingers clutched his hair
    Then, "Boys, hand round the hat."
There never was such a hatful
    Of silver, and gold, and notes;
People are not always penniless
    Because they don't wear coats!

And then, "Three cheers for the baby!"
    I tell you, those cheers were meant,
And the way in which they were given
    Was enough to raise the tent.
And then there was sudden silence,
    And a gruff old miner said,
"Come, boys, enough of this rumpus;
    It's time it was put to bed."

So, looking a little sheepish,
    But with faces strangely bright,
The audience, somewhat lingeringly,
    Flocked out into the night.
And the bold-faced leader chuckled,
    "He wasn't a bit afraid!
He's as game as he is good-looking—
    Boys, that was the show that *paid*."

Here is graphic confirmation of the commercial advantages of innocence and purity, a cornerstone of the Victorian Protestant ethic. The poem also illustrates the theatrical truism that seasoned performers are no match for animals or babies.

"Margaret Vandegrift" was the pen-name of M A R G A R E T T H O M S O N J A N V I E R (1844–1913), born in New Orleans, sister of the writer, Thomas Allibone Janvier. She won acclaim as the authoress of such children's books as *The Absent-Minded Fairy, and Other Verses* and *The Dead Doll, and Other Verses.*

The Sluggard

DR. ISAAC WATTS

'Tis the voice of the sluggard; I heard him complain,
"You have wak'd me too soon, I must slumber again,"
As the door on its hinges, so he on his bed,
Turns his sides and his shoulders and his heavy head.

"A little more sleep, and a little more slumber";
Thus he wastes half his days, and his hours without number,
And when he gets up, he sits folding his hands,
Or walks about sauntering, or trifling he stands.

I pass'd by his garden, and saw the wild briar,
The thorn and the thistle grow broader and higher;
The clothes that hang on him are turning to rags;
And his money still wastes till he starves or he begs.

I made him a visit, still hoping to find
That he took better care for improving his mind:
He told me his dreams, talked of eating and drinking;
But he scarce reads his Bible, and never loves thinking.

Said I then to my heart, "Here's a lesson for me,"
This man's but a picture of what I might be:
But thanks to my friends for their care in my breeding,
Who taught me betimes to love working and reading.

Lewis Carroll's little friend Alice Liddell must have recited this didactic poem on sundry Sunday afternoons, for he made it the starting point of a verse that has entirely eclipsed the original:

'Tis the voice of the Lobster: I heard him declare
"You have baked me too brown, I must sugar my hair."
As a duck with its eyelids, so he with his nose
Trims his belt and his buttons, and turns out his toes.
When the sands are all dry, he is gay as a lark,
And will talk in contemptuous tones of the Shark:
But, when the tide rises and sharks are around,
His voice has a timid and tremulous sound.

"That's different from what *I* used to say when I was a child," said the Gryphon.

There is a short note on Dr. Watts on page 23.

The Mistake

AUTHOR UNKNOWN

Mamma, there's Rachel making hay,
For all 'tis such a sultry day!
For my part I can scarcely stir,
And how much worse it is for her,
All day beneath the burning sun;
It really ought not to be done.

'Tis proper, Sophy, to be sure,
To pity and relieve the poor;
But do not waste your pity here,
Work is not hard to her, my dear;
It makes her healthy, strong, and gay
And is as pleasant as your play.
We've each our task; and they may
        boast
The happiest life, who do the most.
None needs our pity half so much
As idlers,—always pity such.

This improving Gem comes from a tiny volume entitled *The Mother's Fables in Verse, Designed, Through the Medium of Amusement, to Correct Some of the Faults and Follies of Children,* published in London in 1812. The question-and-answer poem was a popular means of juvenile indoctrination in the early nineteenth century. On page 198 is another example from the gentle pen of Jane Taylor (see page 97). One of her *Hymns for Infant Minds,* it must have cheered many tots depressed by early intimations of mortality.

CHILD

Tell me, mamma, if I must die
One day, as little baby died;
And look so very pale, and lie
Down in the pit-hole by his side?

Shall I leave dear papa and you,
And never see you any more?
Tell me, mamma, if this is true;
I did not know it was before.

MAMMA

'Tis true, my love, that you must die;
The God who made you says you must;
And every one of us shall lie,
Like the dear baby, in the dust.

These hands, and feet, and busy head,
Shall waste and crumble right away;
But though your body shall be dead,
There is a part which can't decay.

The Lips That Touch Liquor Shall Never Touch Mine

HARRIET A. GLAZEBROOK

Alice Lee stood awaiting her lover one night,
Her cheeks flushed and glowing, her eyes full of light.
She had placed a sweet rose 'mid her wild flowing hair;
No flower of the forest e'er looked half so fair
As she did that night, as she stood by the door
Of the cot where she dwelt by the side of the moor.

She heard a quick step coming over the moor,
And a merry voice which she had oft heard before;
And ere she could speak a strong arm held her fast,
And a manly voice whispered, "I've come, love, at last.
I'm sorry that I've kept you waiting like this,
But I know you'll forgive me, then give me a kiss."

But she shook the bright curls on her beautiful head,
And she drew herself up while quite proudly she said,
"Now, William, I'll prove if you really are true,
For you say that you love me—I don't think you do;
If really you love me you must give up the wine,
For the lips that touch liquor shall never touch mine."

He looked quite amazed. "Why, Alice, 'tis clear
You really are getting quite jealous, my dear."
"In that you are right," she replied; "for, you see,
You'll soon love the liquor far better than me.
I'm jealous, I own, of the poisonous wine,
For the lips that touch liquor shall never touch mine."

He turned, then, quite angry. "Confound it!" he said,
"What nonsense you've got in your dear little head;
But I'll see if I cannot remove it from hence."
She said, " 'Tis not nonsense, 'tis plain common-sense:
And I mean what I say, and this you will find,
I don't often change when I've made up my mind."

He stood all irresolute, angry, perplexed:
She never before saw him look half so vexed;
But she said, "If he talks all his life I won't flinch";
And he talked, but he never could move her an inch.
He then bitterly cried, with a look and a groan,
"O Alice, your heart is as hard as a stone."

But though her heart beat in his favour quite loud,
She still firmly kept to the vow she had vowed;
And at last, without even a tear or a sigh,
She said, "I am going, so, William, goodbye."
"Nay, stay," he then said, "I'll choose one of the two—
I'll give up the liquor in favour of you."

Now, William had often great cause to rejoice
For the hour he had made sweet Alice his choice;
And he blessed through the whole of a long, useful life,
The fate that had given him his dear little wife.
And she, by her firmness, won to us that night
One who in our cause is an ornament bright.

Oh! that each fair girl in our abstinence band
Would say: "I'll ne'er give my heart or my hand
Unto one who I ever had reason to think
Would taste one small drop of the vile, cursed drink";
But say, when you are wooed, "I'm a foe to the wine,
And the lips that touch liquor shall never touch mine."

Directness and the common touch ranked high among the literary standards of
the Band of Hope and other disciples of the White Ribbon. They were also cath-
olic enough to embrace "Think Before You Drink," which is to be found in the
temperance section of *The Home and Platform Elocutionist*. Set by the editor,
George Stedman Wordsworth, M.A., among a collection of stern if picturesque
pieces, it carries no indication that it is other than completely serious in intention:

> He who thinks before he drinks
> Will nothing drink but water,
> He who drinks before he thinks
> Will drink what no one ought to.

The piece that follows shows the temperance movement in another characteristic mood: sustained moral outrage.

Price of a Drink

JOSEPHINE POLLARD

"Five cents a glass!" Does anyone think
That this is really the price of a drink?
"Five cents a glass," I hear you say,
"Why, that isn't very much to pay."
Ah, no, indeed; 'tis a very small sum
You are passing over with finger and thumb;
And if that were all that you gave away
It wouldn't be very much to pay.

The price of a drink! Let him decide
Who has lost his courage and lost his pride,
And lies a groveling heap of clay
Not far removed from a beast today.

The price of a drink! Let that one tell
Who sleeps tonight in a murderer's cell,
And feels within him the fires of hell.
Honor and virtue, love and truth,
All the glory and pride of youth,
Hopes of manhood, the wreath of fame,
High endeavor and noble aim,
These are treasures thrown away,
As the price of a drink, from day to day.

"Five cents a glass!" How Satan laughed
As over the bar the young man quaffed
The beaded liquor, for the demon knew
The terrible work that drink would do;
And before morning the victim lay
With his life-blood ebbing swiftly away.
And that was the price he paid, alas!
For the pleasure of taking a social glass.

The price of a drink! If you want to know
What some are willing to pay for it, go
Through that wretched tenement, over there
With dingy window and broken stair;
Where foul disease like a vampire crawls
With outstretched wings o'er the moldy walls.
There poverty dwells with her hungry brood,
Wild-eyed as demons, for lack of food;
There violence deals its cruel blow;
And innocent ones are thus accursed
To pay the price of another's thirst.

"Five cents a glass!" Oh, if that were all
The sacrifice would, indeed, be small!
But the money's worth is the least amount
We pay, and whoever will keep account,
Will learn the terrible waste and blight
That follows the ruinous appetite.
"Five cents a glass!" Does anyone think
That is really the price of a drink.

If this piece seems somewhat overemphatic, the reader is referred to a vitupera-
tive effusion by an anonymous New York lady, "Go, Feel What I Have Felt,"
the last stanza of which runs:

Tell me I hate the bowl,—
    Hate is a feeble word;
I loathe, abhor, my very soul
    By strong disgust is stirred
Whene'er I see, or hear, or tell
Of the DARK BEVERAGE OF HELL!

In the Workhouse: Christmas Day

GEORGE R. SIMS

It is Christmas Day in the Workhouse,
   And the cold bare walls are bright
With garlands of green and holly,
   And the place is a pleasant sight:
For with clean-washed hands and faces,
   In a long and hungry line
The paupers sit at the tables
   For this is the hour they dine.
And the guardians and their ladies,
   Although the wind is east,
Have come in their furs and wrappers,
   To watch their charges feast;
To smile and be condescending,
   Put pudding on pauper plates,
To be hosts at the workhouse banquet
   They've paid for—with the rates.

Oh, the paupers are meek and lowly
   With their "Thank'ee kindly, mum's"
So long as they fill their stomachs,
   What matter it whence it comes?
But one of the old men mutters,
   And pushes his plate aside:
"Great God!" he cries; "but it chokes me!
   For this is the day *she* died."

The guardians gazed in horror,
   The master's face went white;
"Did a pauper refuse the pudding?"
   "Could their ears believe aright?"
Then the ladies clutched their husbands,
   Thinking the man would die,
Struck by a bolt, or something,
   By the outraged One on high.

But the pauper sat for a moment,
　　Then rose 'mid a silence grim,
For the others had ceased to chatter
　　And trembled in every limb.
He looked at the guardians' ladies,
　　Then, eyeing their lords, he said,
"I eat not the food of villains
　　Whose hands are foul and red:

"Whose victims cry for vengeance
　　From their dank, unhallowed graves."
"He's drunk!" said the workhouse master,
　　"Or else he's mad and raves."
"Not drunk or mad," cried the pauper,
　　"But only a hunted beast,
Who, torn by the hounds and mangled,
　　Declines the vulture's feast.

"I care not a curse for the guardians,
　　And I won't be dragged away.
Just let me have the fit out,
　　It's only Christmas Day
That the black past comes to goad me,
　　And prey on my burning brain;
I'll tell you the rest in a whisper,—
　　I swear I won't shout again.

"Keep your hands off me, curse you!
　　Hear me right out to the end.
You come here to see how paupers
　　The season of Christmas spend.
You come here to watch us feeding,
　　As they watch the captured beast.
Hear why a penniless pauper
　　Spits on your paltry feast.

"Do you think I will take your bounty,
　　And let you smile and think

You're doing a noble action
    With the parish's meat and drink?
Where is my wife, you traitors—
    The poor old wife you slew?
Yes, by the God above us,
    My Nance was killed by you!

"Last winter my wife lay dying,
    Starved in a filthy den;
I had never been to the parish,—
    I came to the parish then.
I swallowed my pride in coming,
    For, ere the ruin came,
I held up my head as a trader,
    And I bore a spotless name.

"I came to the parish, craving
    Bread for a starving wife,
Bread for the woman who'd loved me
    Through fifty years of life;
And what do you think they told me,
    Mocking my awful grief?
That 'the House' was open to us,
    But they wouldn't give 'out relief.'

"I slunk to the filthy alley—
    'Twas a cold, raw Christmas eve—
And the bakers' shops were open,
    Tempting a man to thieve;
But I clenched my fists together,
    Holding my head awry,
So I came to her empty-handed
    And mournfully told her why.

"Then I told her 'the House' was open;
    She had heard of the ways of *that*,
For her bloodless cheeks went crimson,
    And up in her rags she sat,

Crying, 'Bide the Christmas here, John,
    We've never had one apart;
I think I can bear the hunger,—
    The other would break my heart.'

"All through that eve I watched her,
    Holding her hand in mine,
Praying the Lord, and weeping,
    Till my lips were salt as brine.
I asked her once if she hungered,
    And as she answered 'No,'
The moon shone in at the window
    Set in a wreath of snow.

"Then the room was bathed in glory,
    And I saw in my darling's eyes
The far-away look of wonder
    That comes when the spirit flies;
And her lips were parched and parted,
    And her reason came and went,
For she raved of our home in Devon,
    Where our happiest years were spent.

"And the accents long forgotten,
    Came back to the tongue once more,
For she talked like the country lassie
    I woo'd by the Devon shore.
Then she rose to her feet and trembled,
    And fell on the rags and moaned,
And, 'Give me a crust—I'm famished—
    For the love of God!' she groaned.

"I rushed from the room like a madman,
    And flew to the workhouse gate,
Crying, 'Food for a dying woman!'
    And the answer came, 'Too late.'
They drove me away with curses;
    Then I fought with a dog in the street,

And tore from the mongrel's clutches
   A crust he was trying to eat.

"Back, through the filthy by-lanes!
   Back, through the trampled slush!
Up to the crazy garret,
   Wrapped in an awful hush.
My heart sank down at the threshold,
   And I paused with a sudden thrill,
For there in the silv'ry moonlight
   My Nance lay, cold and still.

"Up to the blackened ceiling
   The sunken eyes were cast—
I knew on those lips all bloodless
   My name had been the last;
She'd called for her absent husband—
   O God! had I but known!—
Had called in vain, and in anguish
   Had died in that den—*alone.*

"Yes, there, in a land of plenty,
   Lay a loving woman dead,
Cruelly starved and murdered
   For a loaf of the parish bread.
At yonder gate, last Christmas,
   I craved for a human life.
You, who would feast us paupers,
   What of my murdered wife!

.   .   .   .   .   .

"There, get ye gone to your dinners;
   Don't mind me in the least;
Think of the happy paupers
   Eating your Christmas feast;
And when you recount their blessings
   In your smug parochial way,
Say what you did for *me*, too,
   Only last Christmas Day."

Innumerable "straight men" on the music-hall stage have begun a recitation of this work, to be interrupted inevitably by "I say, I say, I say! A very funny thing happened to me on the way to the theatre . . ." Diligent research has not yet discovered exactly why this poem, which has a certain grim power, has become part of a theatrical tradition, a tradition shared with "The Green Eye of the Yellow God." Parodists, too, have shown scant respect for the reformist zeal that gripped George R. Sims when he composed this ballad. There are many parodies, mostly rather gross—even when accorded the decent fig-leaves of asterisks. Here, however, is a specimen. Readers with delicate susceptibilities are advised to cease reading this note at once.

> It was Christmas Day in the workhouse,
> That season of good cheer.
> The paupers' hearts were merry,
> Their bellies full of beer.
> The pompous workhouse master,
> As he strode about the halls,
> Wished them a Merry Christmas,
> But the paupers answered "*****!"
> This angered the workhouse master,
> Who swore by all the gods
> That he'd stop their Christmas pudden,
> The dirty rotten ****.
> Then up spake a bald-headed pauper,
> His face as bold as brass,
> "You can keep your Christmas pudden
> And stick it up your ***!"

Here we have, in fact, the only example in this volume of exactly what the lower classes (the parodist can only have come from an inferior station) thought of well-meaning middle-class verse about their problems.

A brief note about George R. Sims appears on page 29.

The Pauper's Drive

THOMAS NOEL

There's a grim one-horse hearse in a jolly round trot,
To the churchyard a pauper is going, I wot;
The road it is rough and the hearse has no springs;
And hark to the dirge which the sad driver sings:
  Rattle his bones over the stones!
  He's only a pauper, whom nobody owns!

O, where are the mourners? Alas! there are none—
He has left not a gap in the world now he's gone—
Not a tear in the eye of child, woman, or man;
To the grave with his carcass as fast as you can:
  Rattle his bones over the stones!
  He's only a pauper, whom nobody owns!

What a jolting, and creaking, and splashing and din!
The whip how it cracks, and the wheels how they spin!
How the dirt, right and left, o'er the hedges is hurled!
The pauper at length makes a noise in the world!
  Rattle his bones over the stones!
  He's only a pauper, whom nobody owns!

Poor pauper defunct! he has made some approach
To gentility, now that he's stretched in a coach!
He's taking a drive in his carriage at last;
But it will not be long, if he goes on so fast!
  Rattle his bones over the stones!
  He's only a pauper, whom nobody owns!

You bumpkins! who stare at your brother conveyed—
Behold what respect to a cloddy is paid!
And be joyful to think, when by death you're laid low,
You've a chance to the grave like a gemman to go!
  Rattle his bones over the stones!
  He's only a pauper, whom nobody owns!

But a truce to this strain; for my soul it is sad,
To think that a heart in humanity clad
Should make, like the brutes, such a desolate end,
And depart from the light without leaving a friend!
Bear soft his bones over the stones!
Though a pauper, he's one whom his Maker yet owns.

THOMAS NOEL (1799–1861) was a clergyman's son, educated at Merton College, Oxford, who burst upon the world as a poet with a series of stanzas on proverbs and scriptural texts, entitled *The Cottage Muse* (printed at Maidenhead). He had something of a love affair with the Thames, about which he wrote pretty verses, living in great seclusion near Maidenhead. His wife came, down river, from Twickenham. He maintained a friendship, in correspondence only, with Miss Mitford. In 1858 he was ill-advised enough to leave the Thames and settle at Brighton, where he died less than three years later.

The African Chief

WILLIAM CULLEN BRYANT

Chained in the market-place he stood—
    A man of giant frame,
Amid the gathering multitude,
    That shrunk to hear his name;
All stern of look, and strong of limb,
    His dark eye on the ground:—
And silently they gaze on him,
    As on a lion bound.

Vainly, but well, that chief had fought—
    He was a captive now;
Yet pride, that fortune humbles not,
    Was written on his brow.
The scars his dark broad bosom wore,
    Showed warrior true and brave;
A prince among his tribe before—
    He could not be a slave!

Then to his conqueror he spake—
    "My brother is a king;
Undo this necklace from my neck,
    And take this bracelet ring,
And send me where my brother reigns,
    And I will fill thy hands
With store of ivory from the plains,
    And gold-dust from the sands."

"Not for thy ivory nor thy gold,
    Will I unbind thy chain;
That fettered hand shall never hold
    The battle-spear again.
A price thy nation never gave
    Shall yet be paid for thee;
For thou shalt be the Christian's slave,
    In lands beyond the sea."

Then wept the warrior-chief, and bade
   To shred his locks away,
And, one by one, each heavy braid
   Before the victor lay.
Thick were the plaited locks, and long;
   And deftly hidden there,
Shone many a wedge of gold, among
   The dark and crispèd hair.
"Look, feast thy greedy eyes with gold,
   Long kept for sorest need;
Take it—thou askest sums untold,—
   And say that I am freed.
Take it!—my wife, the long, long day
   Weeps by the cocoa-tree,
And my young children leave their play,
   And ask in vain for me."

"I take thy gold—but I have made
   Thy fetters fast and strong,
And ween that by the cocoa-shade
   Thy wife will wait thee long."
Strong was the agony that shook
   The captive's frame to hear,
And the proud meaning of his look
   Was changed to mortal fear.

His heart was broken—crazed his brain;
   At once his eye grew wild;
He struggled fiercely with his chain;
   Whispered, and wept, and smiled:
Yet wore not long those fatal bands;
   For soon at close of day,
They drew him forth upon the sands,
   The foul hyena's prey.

The thrifty, articulate and tragic hero is a direct descendant of Rousseau's noble savage, uncorrupted by the evils of civilization. The "peculiar institution" of slavery activated the pens of many American poets and novelists during the first half of the nineteenth century; Longfellow's "The Slave's Dream":

> Beside the ungathered rice he lay,
> His sickle in his hand;
> His breast was bare, his matted hair
> Was buried in the sand.
> Again, in the mist and shadow of sleep,
> He saw his Native Land,

and the divinely composed *Uncle Tom's Cabin; or, Life Among the Lowly* ("God wrote the book," said Harriet Beecher Stowe, "I took His dictation") are but two further passionate examples. Their effect on the public conscience did much to hasten the onset of the Civil War.

W I L L I A M   C U L L E N   B R Y A N T (1794–1878), born at Cummington, Massachusetts, was a serious child who prayed that he might become a poet, despite discouragement from a sternly Puritanical father. Nevertheless, he published a poem entitled "The Progress of Knowledge" when he was rising thirteen. He had to leave college for financial reasons and studied law, which he abominated. In 1817 his "Thanatopsis" appeared and he found himself famous. He married, abandoned the legal profession, went to New York, edited a magazine and later joined the *Evening Post*, working his way up to the editor's chair. His death from sunstroke and a fall was regarded as a national calamity.

7
Tragic Ends

*Think, too, how to beauty
They oft owe their fall,
And what may through vice
Be the fate of you all.*

—"Village-Born Beauty"

Eliza

DR. ERASMUS DARWIN

Now stood Eliza on the wood-crown'd height
O'er Minden's plains spectatress of the fight;
Sought with bold eye amid the bloody strife
Her dearer self, the partner of her life;
From hill to hill the rushing host pursued,
And view'd his banner, or believed she view'd.
Pleased with the distant roar, with quicker tread,
Fast by his hand one lisping boy she led;
And one fair girl, amid the loud alarm,
Slept on her kerchief, cradled on her arm:
While round her brows bright beams of honour dart,
And love's warm eddies circle round her heart.
—Near and more near th'intrepid beauty press'd,
Saw through the driving smoke his dancing crest,
Heard the exulting shout—"They run!—they run!"
"He's safe!" she cried, "he's safe! the battle's won!"
—A ball now hisses through the airy tides
(Some Fury wings it, and some Demon guides),
Parts the fine locks her graceful head that deck,
Wounds her fair ear, and sinks into her neck;
The red stream issuing from her azure veins
Dyes her white veil, her ivory bosom stains.
—"Ah me!" she cried, and sinking on the ground,
Kiss'd her dear babes, regardless of the wound:
"Oh, cease not yet to beat, thou vital urn,
Wait, gushing life, oh! wait my love's return!"—
Hoarse barks the wolf, the vulture screams from far,
The angel, Pity, shuns the walks of war;—
"Oh spare, ye war-hounds, spare their tender age!
On me, on me," she cried, "exhaust your rage!"
Then with weak arms, her weeping babes caress'd,
And sighing, hid them in her blood-stain'd vest.

From tent to tent th'impatient warrior flies,
Fear in his heart, and frenzy in his eyes:
Eliza's name along the camp he calls,
Eliza echoes through the canvas walls;
Quick through the murmuring gloom his footsteps tread,
O'er groaning heaps, the dying and the dead,
Vault o'er the plain,—and in the tangled wood,—
Lo! dead Eliza—weltering in her blood!
Soon hears his listening son the welcome sounds,
With open arms and sparkling eyes he bounds:
"Speak low," he cries, and gives his little hand,
"Mamma's asleep upon the dew-cold sand;
Alas! we both with cold and hunger quake—
Why do you weep? Mamma will soon awake."
—"She'll wake no more!" the hopeless mourner cried,
Upturn'd his eyes, and clasp'd his hands, and sigh'd;
Stretch'd on the ground, awhile entranced he lay,
And press'd warm kisses on the lifeless clay:
And then upsprung with wild convulsive start,
And all the father kindled in his heart:
"Oh Heaven!" he cried, "my first rash vow forgive!
These bind to earth, for these I pray to live."
Round his chill babes he wrapp'd his crimson vest,
And clasp'd them sobbing, to his aching breast.

DR. ERASMUS DARWIN (1731–1802) was a physician of
remarkable energy, irascibility, and eccentricity, in his evolutionist theories a
forerunner of his famous grandson, Charles. He graduated M.B. at Cambridge,
and failing to attract patients at Nottingham moved to Lichfield. There he bota-
nized, married twice, ruled his family with a rod of iron, invented an ingenious
equipage (which broke his knee-cap), and converted most of the local gentry into
water-drinkers. He restricted himself to English wines, thus reducing temptation
to a minimum and enabling him to become almost a total abstainer. Nevertheless, he had his lapses, and it is recorded that he once swam a river in his clothes
while intoxicated, afterwards repairing to Nottingham market-place, where, in
a tub, he lectured the citizens upon prudence and sanitary regulations. His scien-
tific theories and philosophizing were expressed in sturdy heroic couplets, espe-

cially in *The Botanic Garden*. In Part II of this, *The Loves of the Plants,* occurs "Eliza," which seems to have been singularly popular for more than a century. Darwin was even something of a prophet, as witness the following lines from *The Botanic Garden* which represent both the civil and military uses of aviation:

> Soon shall thy arm, unconquer'd Steam! afar
> Drag the slow barge, or drive the rapid car;
> Or on wide-waving wings expanded bear
> The flying-chariot through the fields of air.
> Fair crews triumphant, leaning from above,
> Shall wave their fluttering kerchiefs as they move;
> Or warrior-bands alarm the gaping crowd,
> And armies shrink beneath the shadowy cloud.

The Mistletoe Bough

THOMAS HAYNES BAYLY

The mistletoe hung in the castle hall,
The holly branch shone on the old oak wall;
And the baron's retainers were blithe and gay,
And keeping their Christmas holiday.
The baron beheld with a father's pride
His beautiful child, young Lovell's bride;
While she with her bright eyes seem'd to be
The star of the goodly company.

"I'm weary of dancing now;" she cried;
"Here tarry a moment—I'll hide—I'll hide!
And, Lovell, be sure thou'rt first to trace
The clue to my secret lurking place."
Away she ran—and her friends began
Each tower to search, and each nook to scan;
And young Lovell cried, "Oh where dost thou hide?
I'm lonesome without thee, my own dear bride."

They sought her that night! and they sought her next day!
And they sought her in vain when a week pass'd away!
In the highest—the lowest—the loneliest spot,
Young Lovell sought wildly—but found her not.
And years flew by, and their grief at last
Was told as a sorrowful tale long past;
And when Lovell appeared, the children cried,
"See! the old man weeps for his fairy bride."

At length an oak chest, that had long lain hid,
Was found in the castle—they raised the lid—
And a skeleton form lay mouldering there,
In the bridal wreath of that lady fair!
Oh! sad was her fate!—in sportive jest
She hid from her lord in the old oak chest.
It closed with a spring!—and, dreadful doom,
The bride lay clasp'd in her living tomb!

Was the opening of the third stanza in Lewis Carroll's mind when he was writing "The Hunting of the Snark"? Fit the fifth opens with:

They sought it with thimbles, they sought it with care;
They pursued it with forks and hope.

A short biography of the immensely popular Thomas Haynes Bayly may be found on page 91.

The Forced Bridal

AUTHOR UNKNOWN

I saw her on the bridal night:
Rich jewels decked her hair;
But in her eye—once sparkling bright—
I marked a yearning care.
Before the altar, side by side,
Without a smile or word,
They stood—the bridegroom and the bride—
The victim and her lord!

Upon her cold and pallid brow
There hung a single gem;
It needed but her passive vow
To gain a diadem!
That vow was uttered—still the bride
Before the altar stands;
With heightened form and seeming pride,
She listens to the banns.

Her hair fell o'er her angel face,
In glowing wreaths of jet;
Upon her head, her lord would place
His jewelled coronet.
Why shrank she back? A stolid look
His guilty eye did meet;
He gazed—the tightened heart-strings broke—
A corpse was at his feet!

In haste around the prostrate bride
Her lord's attendants crowd,
And scores of friends are at her side
With notes of pity loud.
They loose her robe—the star has set!
Her shining locks they part—
Her temples chafe—but all too late—
The wound's A BROKEN HEART!

Perhaps this mid-Victorian maiden's young Lochinvar had overslept—or his train had been late—with tragic consequences.

The Inchcape Rock
ROBERT SOUTHEY

No stir in the air, no stir in the sea;
The ship was still as she could be;
Her sails from heaven received no motion;
Her keel was steady in the ocean.

Without either sign or sound of their shock,
The waves flowed over the Inchcape Rock;
So little they rose, so little they fell,
They did not move the Inchcape Bell.

The worthy Abbot of Aberbrothok
Had placed that bell on the Inchcape Rock;
On a buoy in the storm it floated and swung,
And over the waves its warning rung.

When the rock was hid by the surge's swell,
The mariners heard the warning bell;
And then they knew the perilous rock,
And blest the Abbot of Aberbrothok.

The sun in heaven was shining gay,
All things were joyful on that day;
The sea birds screamed as they wheeled around,
And there was joyance in their sound.

The buoy of the Inchcape Bell was seen,
A darker speck on the ocean green.
Sir Ralph the Rover walked his deck,
And he fixed his eye on the darker speck.

He felt the cheering power of Spring;
It made him whistle; it made him sing;
His heart was mirthful to excess;
But the Rover's mirth was wickedness.

His eye was on the Inchcape float;
Quoth he, "My men, put out the boat,
And row me to the Inchcape Rock,
And I'll plague the Abbot of Aberbrothok."

The boat is lowered; the boatmen row,
And to the Inchcape Rock they go.
Sir Ralph bent over from the boat,
And he cut the bell from the Inchcape float.

Down sank the bell with a gurgling sound;
The bubbles rose and burst around.
Quoth Sir Ralph, "The next who comes to the Rock
Won't bless the Abbot of Aberbrothok."

Sir Ralph the Rover sailed away;
He scoured the seas for many a day;
And now, grown rich with plundered store,
He steers his course for Scotland's shore.

So thick a haze o'erspreads the sky
They cannot see the sun on high;
The wind hath blown a gale all day;
At evening it hath died away.

On deck the Rover takes his stand;
So dark it is they see no land.
Quoth Sir Ralph, "It will be lighter soon;
For there is the dawn of the rising moon."

"Canst hear," said one, "the breaker's roar?
For methinks we should be near the shore."
"Now where we are I cannot tell;
But I wish I could hear the Inchcape Bell!"

They hear no sound; the swell is strong;
Though the wind hath fallen they drift along,
Till the vessel strikes with a shivering shock,—
"Oh heavens! it is the Inchcape Rock!"

Sir Ralph the Rover tore his hair;
He cursed himself in his despair.
The waves rush in on every side;
The ship is sinking beneath the tide.

But even now, in his dying fear
One dreadful sound could the Rover hear—
A sound as if, with the Inchcape Bell,
The fiends in triumph were ringing his knell.

A short biography of Robert Southey appears on page 44.

The Mother in the Snow-Storm

SEBA SMITH

The cold winds swept the mountain's height,
  And pathless was the dreary wild,
And 'mid the cheerless hours of night,
  A mother wandered with her child;
As through the drifting snows she pressed
The babe was sleeping on her breast.

And colder still the wind did blow,
  And darker hours of night came on,
And deeper grew the drifting snow;
  Her limbs were chilled, her strength was gone:
"O God!" she cried, in accents wild,
"If I must perish, save my child!"

She stripped her mantle from her breast
  And bared her bosom to the storm,
And round the child she wrapped the vest,
  And smiled to think her babe so warm.
With one cold kiss one tear she shed,
And sunk upon her snowy bed.

At dawn a traveller passed by,
  And saw her 'neath a snowy veil;
The frost of death was in her eye,
  Her cheek was cold, and hard, and pale;
He moved the robe from off the child—
The babe looked up and sweetly smiled!

Another version of Seba Smith's tragic tale occurs, anonymously, in Ira D. Sankey's *Sacred Songs and Solos.* Here a variant first stanza and an additional final stanza explain, with true temperance fervour, just what the mother was doing out in such adverse weather:

A drunkard reached his cheerless home,
The storm without was dark and wild,
He forced his weeping wife to roam,
A wand'rer friendless with her child;
As through the falling snow she pressed
The babe was sleeping on her breast. . . .

Shall this sad warning plead in vain?
Poor thoughtless one, it speaks to you;
Now break the tempter's cruel chain,
No more your dreadful way pursue:
Renounce the cup; to Jesus fly—
Immortal soul, why will you die?

In this version, it is "the cruel husband" and not "a traveller" who discovers the frozen corpse.

S E B A S M I T H (1792–1868) grew up in Maine, worked as a teacher, wrote some poetry, contributed to Portland newspapers, founded his own, the Portland *Courier*, and married Elizabeth Prince. Better known as Elizabeth Oakes Smith, she was a novelist, poet, and advocate of women's rights. Smith's main reputation is that of a humorist: under the name of Major Jack Dowling, he contributed satirical letters on Maine politicians and President Jackson to the *Courier*. Imitators shamelessly appropriated the name of Jack Dowling, but he was the precursor of such famous comic oracles as Artemus Ward and Hosea Biglow.

Village-Born Beauty

AUTHOR UNKNOWN

See the star-breasted villain,
  To yonder cot bound,
Where the sweet honeysuckle
  Entwines it round,
Yet sweeter, far sweeter,
  Than flower e'er seen,
Is the poor hedger's daughter,
  The pride of the green.
But more, never more,
  Will she there please all eyes;
Her peace of mind withers,
  Her happiness flies!
She pauses, sighs, trembles,
  And yet dares to roam,
The village-born beauty's
  Seduced from her home.

From a post-chaise and four
  She's in London set down,
Where robbed of her virtue,
  She's launched on the town;
Her carriage, her servants,
  And jewels so gay,
Tell how high she is kept,
  And o'er all bears the sway;
At the opera—the playhouse,
  The parks and elsewhere,
Her beauty outrivals
  Each beauty that's there;
And while, big with envy,
  Her downfall they tell,
The village-born beauty
  O'er all bears the belle.

But soon from indifference,
  Caprice, or what not—
She's turned on the world—
  By her keeper forgot;
Yet, fond to be flattered,
  And fettered in vice,
She's this man's or that,
  As he comes to her price;
At length, growing stale,
  All her finery sold,
In the bloom of her youth,
  Through disease looking old,
Forsook by her lovers,
  And sought for no more,
The village-born beauty,
  Becomes quite impure.

Up lanes and through alleys
  She now takes her way,
Exposed to all weathers
  By night and by day:
Cold, houseless and shivering,
  And wet to the skin,
With glass after glass
  Drowns her sorrows in gin;
Distress'd, sore and ragged,
  Sad, friendless and poor,
She's borne to some garret,
  Or workhouse obscure;
Breathes a prayer hope to heaven
  A sinner to save!
When the village-born beauty
  Is laid in the grave.

Then pity, ye fair ones,
   Nor be too severe,
And give a frail sister
   The boon of a tear!
When prone to condemn them,
   Reflect, think awhile—
That the heart often bleeds
   When the face wears a smile.

Think, too, how to beauty
   They oft owe their fall,
And what may through vice
   Be the fate of you all;
And O, while sweet innocence
   Bears the proud sway,
May hell seize the villain
   That smiles to betray.

Obviously, the anonymous composer of "Village-Born Beauty" knew the text
of the classic street ballad "She Was Poor but She Was Honest" and wished to
tame it for a middle-class audience. Note the moralizing at the end; the final
stanza of the ballad is far more realistic:

   It's the same the whole world over:
      It's the poor what gets the blame,
   It's the rich what gets the pleasure;
      Ain't it all a blooming shame?

The Face Upon the Floor

H. ANTOINE D'ARCY

'Twas a balmy summer evening, and a goodly crowd was there,
Which well-nigh filled Joe's barroom on the corner of the square,
And as songs and witty stories came through the open door
A vagabond crept slowly in and posed upon the floor.

"Where did it come from?" someone said: "The wind has blown it in."
"What does it want?" another cried, "Some whisky, rum or gin?"
"Here, Toby, seek him, if your stomach's equal to the work—
I wouldn't touch him with a fork, he's as filthy as a Turk."

This badinage the poor wretch took with stoical good grace;
In fact, he smiled as though he thought he'd struck the proper place.
"Come, boys, I know there's kindly hearts among so good a crowd—
To be in such good company would make a deacon proud.

"Give me a drink—that's what I want—I'm out of funds, you know;
When I had cash to treat the gang, this hand was never slow.
What? You laugh as though you thought this pocket never held a sou;
I once was fixed as well, my boys, as any one of you.

"There, thanks; that's braced me nicely; God bless you one and all;
Next time I pass this good saloon, I'll make another call.
Give you a song? No, I can't do that, my singing days are past;
My voice is cracked, my throat's worn out, my lungs are going fast.

"Say! Give me another whisky, and I'll tell you what I'll do—
I'll tell you a funny story, and a fact, I promise, too.
That I was ever a decent man not one of you would think;
But I was, some four or five years back. Say, give me another drink.

"Fill her up, Joe, I want to put some life into my frame—
Such little drinks, to a bum like me, are miserably tame;
Five fingers—there, that's the scheme—and corking whisky, too.
Well, here's luck, boys; and, landlord, my best regards to you.

"You've treated me pretty kindly, and I'd like to tell you how
I came to be the dirty sot you see before you now.
As I told you, once I was a man, with muscle, frame and health,
And, but for a blunder, ought to have made considerable wealth.

"I was a painter—not one that daubed on bricks and wood
But an artist, and, for my age, was rated pretty good.
I worked hard at my canvas and was bidding fair to rise,
For gradually I saw the star of fame before my eyes.

"I made a picture, perhaps you've seen, 'tis called the "Chase of Fame,"
It brought me fifteen hundred pounds and added to my name.
And then I met a woman—now comes the funny part—
With eyes that petrified my brain, and sunk into my heart.

"Why don't you laugh? 'Tis funny that the vagabond you see
Could ever love a woman and expect her love for me;
But 'twas so, and for a month or two her smiles were freely given,
And when her loving lips touched mine it carried me to heaven.

"Did you ever see a woman for whom your soul you'd give,
With a form like the Venus Milo, too beautiful to live;
With eyes that would beat the Koh-i-noor, and a wealth of chestnut hair?
If so, 'twas she, for there never was another half so fair.

"I was working on a portrait, one afternoon in May,
Of a fair-haired boy, a friend of mine, who lived across the way,
And Madeline admired it, and, much to my surprise,
Said that she'd like to know the man who had such dreamy eyes.

"It didn't take long to know him, and before the month had flown
My friend had stolen my darling, and I was left alone;
And, ere a year of misery had passed above my head,
The jewel I had treasured so had tarnished and was dead.

"That's why I took to drink, boys. Why, I never saw you smile,
I thought you'd be amused and laughing all the while.
Why, what's the matter, friend? There's a teardrop in your eye,
Come, laugh, like me; 'tis only babes and women that should cry.

"Say, boys, if you give me just another whisky, I'll be glad,
And I'll draw right here a picture of the face that drove me mad.
Give me that piece of chalk with which you mark the baseball score—
You shall see the lovely Madeline upon the barroom floor."

Another drink, and with chalk in hand the vagabond began
To sketch a face that well might buy the soul of any man.
Then, as he placed another lock upon the shapely head,
With a fearful shriek, he leaped and fell across the picture—dead.

This tragic and graphic recitation is also known as *The Face on the Barroom Floor*. Its authorship has been disputed for many years. *The Reader's Encyclopedia of American Literature* records that the first appearance in print was in 1872, in the Ashtabula, Ohio, *Sentinel* published by John Henry Titus (1853?–1947). This, however, appears to have been a poor version compared to that printed fifteen years later in the New York *Dispatch* and reproduced above. Appended to the *Dispatch* text was the name of the actor, Hugh Antoine d'Arcy. The barroom setting has been identified—by tradition—with "Joe's" on Union Square, New York, now vanished. As late as 1934 Titus was taking legal action to support his claim to the title.

The piece has an astonishing durability. As recently as November, 1968, Ron Moody recited it with great feeling at the Royal Command Variety Performance in London, before an appreciative audience which included Queen Elizabeth the Queen Mother and the Prince of Wales.

This affecting tale is not unique in popular verse. It belongs to the family of verses about artists or musicians who appear mysteriously to draw a picture or play upon some musical instrument with passion and brilliance. They then either walk away without a word, or expire on the spot from a broken heart. "The Shooting of Dan McGrew" by Robert Service has elements of this genre; another example is Henry Lamb's song, "The Volunteer Organist":

A man then staggered down the aisle,
Whose clothes were old and torn,
How strange a drunkard seem'd to me
In church on Sunday morn.
But when he touch'd the organ keys
Without a single word,
The melody that followed was
The sweetest ever heard.

The High Tide on the Coast of Lincolnshire
(1571)

JEAN INGELOW

The old mayor climbed the belfry tower,
   The ringers ran by two, by three;
"Pull, if ye never pulled before;
   Good ringers pull your best," quoth he.
"Play uppe, play uppe, O Boston bells!
Ply all your changes, all your swells,
   Play uppe 'The Brides of Enderby.' "

Men say it was a stolen tyde—
   The Lord that sent it, He knows all;
But in myne ears doth still abide
   The message that the bells let fall:
And there was nought of strange, beside
The flights of mews and peewits pied
   By millions crouched on the old sea wall.

I sat and spun within the doore,
   My thread brake off, I raised myne eyes;
The level sun, like ruddy ore,
   Lay sinking in the barren skies,
And dark against day's golden death
She moved where Lindis wandereth,
   My sonne's faire wife, Elizabeth.

"Cusha! Cusha! Cusha!" calling,
Ere the early dews were falling,
   Farre away I heard her song.
"Cusha! Cusha!" all along
Where the reedy Lindis floweth,
   Floweth, floweth;
From the meads where melick groweth
Faintly came her milking song—

"Cusha! Cusha! Cusha!" calling,
"For the dews will soone be falling;
Leave your meadow grasses mellow,
   Mellow, mellow;
Quit your cowslips, cowslips yellow;
Come uppe Whitefoot, come uppe Lightfoot,
Quit the stalks of parsley hollow,
   Hollow, hollow;
Come uppe Jetty, rise and follow,
From the clovers lift your head;
Come uppe Whitefoot, come uppe Lightfoot,
Come uppe Jetty, rise and follow,
Jetty, to the milking shed."

If it be long, ay, long ago,
   When I beginne to think howe long,
Againe I hear the Lindis flow,
   Swift as an arrowe, sharpe and strong;
And all the aire, it seemeth mee,
Bin full of floating bells (sayth shee),
That ring the tune of Enderby.

Alle fresh the level pasture lay,
   And not a shadowe mote be seene,
Save where full fyve good miles away
   The steeple towered from out the greene;
And lo! the great bell farre and wide
Was heard in all the country side
That Saturday at eventide.

The swanherds where their sedges are
   Moved on in sunset's golden breath,
The shepherde lads I heard afarre,
   And my sonne's wife, Elizabeth;
Till floating o'er the grassy sea
Came downe that kyndly message free,
The "Brides of Mavis Enderby."

Then some looked uppe into the sky,
   And all along where Lindis flows
To where the goodly vessels lie,
   And where the lordly steeple shows.
They sayde, "And why should this thing be?
What danger lowers by land or sea?
They ring the tune of Enderby!

"For evil news from Mablethorpe,
   Of pyrate galleys warping down;
For shippes ashore beyond the scorpe,
   They have not spared to wake the towne:
But while the west bin red to see,
And storms be none, and pyrates flee,
Why ring 'The Brides of Enderby'?"

I looked without, and lo! my sonne
   Came riding downe with might and main:
He raised a shout as he drew on,
   Till all the welkin rang again,
"Elizabeth! Elizabeth!"
(A sweeter woman ne'er drew breath
Than my sonne's wife, Elizabeth.)

"The olde sea wall (he cried) is downe,
   The rising tide comes on apace,
And boats adrift in yonder towne
   Go sailing uppe the market-place."
He shook as one that looks on death:
"God save you, mother!" straight he saith;
"Where is my wife, Elizabeth?"

"Good sonne, where the Lindis winds away,
   With her two bairns I marked her long;
And ere yon bells beganne to play
   Afar I heard her milking song."
He looked across the grassy lea,
To right, to left, "Ho Enderby!"
They rang "The Brides of Enderby!"

With that he cried and beat his breast;
   For lo! along the river's bed
A mighty eygre reared his crest,
   And uppe the Lindis raging sped.
It swept with thunderous noises loud;
Shaped like a curling snow-white cloud,
Or like a demon in a shroud.

And rearing Lindis backward pressed
   Shook all her trembling bankes amaine;
Then madly at the eygre's breast
   Flung uppe her weltering walls again.
Then bankes came downe with ruin and rout—
Then beaten foam flew round about—
Then all the mighty floods were out.

So farre, so fast the eygre drave,
   The heart had hardly time to beat,
Before a shallow seething wave
   Sobbed in the grasses at oure feet:
The feet had hardly time to flee
Before it brake against the knee,
And all the world was in the sea.

Upon the roofe we sate that night,
   The noise of bells went sweeping by;
I marked the lofty beacon light
   Stream from the church tower, red and high—
A lurid mark and dread to see;
And awsome bells they were to mee,
That in the dark rang "Enderby."

They rang the sailor lads to guide
   From roofe to roofe who fearless rowed;
And I—my sonne was at my side,
   And yet the ruddy beacon glowed;
And yet he moaned beneath his breath,
"O come in life, or come in death!
O lost! my love, Elizabeth."

And didst thou visit him no more?
   Thou didst, thou didst, my daughter deare;
The waters laid thee at his doore,
   Ere yet the early dawn was clear.
Thy pretty bairns in fast embrace,
The lifted sun shone on thy face,
Downe drifted to thy dwelling-place.

That flow strewed wrecks about the grass,
   That ebbe swept out the flocks to sea;
A fatal ebbe and flow, alas!
   To manye more than myne and mee:
But each will mourn his own (she saith),
And sweeter woman ne'er drew breath
Than my sonne's wife Elizabeth.

I shall never hear her more
By the reedy Lindis shore,
"Cusha! Cusha! Cusha!" calling,
Ere the early dews be falling;
I shall never hear her song,
"Cusha! Cusha!" all along
Where the sunny Lindis floweth,
   Goeth, floweth;
From the meads where melick groweth,
When the water winding down,
Onward floweth to the town.

I shall never see her more
Where the reeds and rushes quiver,
   Shiver, quiver;
Stand beside the sobbing river,
Sobbing, throbbing, in its falling
To the sandy lonesome shore;
I shall never hear her calling,
Leave your meadow grasses mellow,
   Mellow, mellow;
Quit your cowslips, cowslips yellow;

Come uppe Whitefoot, come uppe Lightfoot;
Quit your pipes of parsley hollow,
  Hollow, hollow;
Come uppe Lightfoot, rise and follow;
  Lightfoot, Whitefoot,
From your clovers lift the head;
Come uppe Jetty, follow, follow,
Jetty, to the milking shed.

The "romantique spellinges" and bucolic detail of this work, tacked on rather like the imitation oak beams of an English suburban villa, helped to set a style that finally blew itself out with the mock folk songs and newspaper pastorals of the Georgian poets.

The capricious tides were responsible for a number of tragic nineteenth-century ends; one remembers Mary's fate while calling the cattle home in the Reverend Charles Kingsley's "The Sands of Dee."

J E A N I N G E L O W (1820–1897) was born at Boston in Lincolnshire; sadly, most of her verse is now considered reminiscent of the local fen scenery, long and flat. Unlike most Victorian poetesses who had the precocious habit of publishing their works in their mid-teens, Miss Ingelow delayed her first volume until she was thirty. She was mistress of the anapaestic measures and wrote many lengthy poems which gained high popular esteem, particularly in America. Also a novelist and writer of children's stories, she mixed with such literary notabilities as Tennyson, Ruskin, Browning, and Christina Rossetti.

Guild's Signal

BRET HARTE

Two low whistles, quaint and clear,
That was the signal the engineer—
    That was the signal that Guild, 'tis said—
Gave to his wife at Providence,
As through the sleeping town, and thence,
            Out in the night,
            On to the light,
Down past the farms, lying white, he sped!

As a husband's greeting, scant, no doubt,
Yet to the woman looking out,
    Watching and waiting, no serenade,
Love song, or midnight roundelay
Said what that whistle seemed to say:
            "To my trust true,
            So love to you!
Working or waiting, good-night!" it said.

Brisk young bagmen, tourists fine,
Old commuters along the line,
    Brakemen and porters glanced ahead,
Smiled as the signal, sharp, intense,
Pierced through the shadows of Providence:
            "Nothing amiss—
            Nothing!—it is
Only Guild calling his wife," they said.

Summer and winter the old refrain
Rang o'er the billows of ripening grain,
    Pierced through the budding boughs o'erhead:
Flew down the track where the red leaves burned
Like living coals from the engine spurned;
            Sang as it flew:
            "To our trust true,
First of all, duty. Good-night!" it said.

And then one night it was heard no more
From Stonington over Rhode Island shore,
    And the folk in Providence smiled and said,
As they turned in their beds, "The engineer
Has once forgotten his midnight cheer."
        One only knew,
        To his trust true,
Guild lay under his engine dead.

William Guild was the engineer of a train which plunged into Meadow Brook, on the line of the Stonington and Providence Railroad. It was his custom, as often as he passed his home, to whistle an "All's well" to his wife. He was found, after the disaster, dead, with his hand on the throttle-valve of his locomotive. The poet spares us the harrowing details of the wreck: "Conductor Bradley," which follows, is more explicit. Like "Guild's Signal" it is based on an actual occurrence.

FRANCIS BRET HARTE (1836–1902) lost his father in childhood but was a precocious boy, publishing his first poem at the age of eleven. He left the East for California, where he taught, then worked as a miner, in a printing office, and as a pony-express agent for Wells Fargo (it is said), finally entering journalism. With a sinecure position in a branch of the U.S. Mint to support him, Harte gradually won world-wide favor in the profession of letters with his humorous sketches and verses. He became in the process the complete fashionable writer and something of a dandy. He was largely responsible for the romantic and picturesque myth of the Wild West. Famous, he quitted the West Coast for a literary life on the East, was appointed a U.S. consul in Germany and then Scotland, in his latter years settling near London.

Conductor Bradley

J O H N   G R E E N L E A F   W H I T T I E R

Conductor Bradley (always may his name
Be said with reverence!), as the swift doom came,
Smitten to death, a crushed and mangled frame,

Sank with the brake he grasped just where he stood
To do the utmost that a brave man could,
And die, if needful, as a true man should.

Men stooped above him; women dropped their tears
On that poor wreck beyond all hopes or fears,
Lost in the strength and glory of his years.

What heard they? Lo! the ghastly lips of pain,
Dead to all thought save duty's, moved again:
"Put out the signals for the other train!"

No nobler utterance, since the world began,
From lips of saint or martyr ever ran,
Electric, through the sympathies of man.

Ah me! how poor and noteless seem to this
The sick-bed dramas of self-consciousness,
Our sensual fears of pain and hopes of bliss!

Oh, grand, supreme endeavour! Not in vain
That last brave act of failing tongue and brain!
Freighted with life, the downward-rushing train

Following the wrecked one, as wave follows wave,
Obeyed the warning which the dead lips gave.
Others he saved—himself he could not save.

Nay, the lost life *was* saved. He is not dead
Who in his record still the earth shall tread,
With God's clear aureole shining round his head.

We bow, as in the dust, with all our pride
Of virtue dwarfed the noble deed beside.
God give us grace to live as Bradley died!

JOHN GREENLEAF WHITTIER (1807–1892), New En-
gland's Quaker poet, did not allow scant schooling and few books other than the
Bible and Robert Burns to cramp his imagination, for he was publishing verse at
the age of eighteen. The editor of the Newburyport *Free Press* accepted an early
poem, gave the young author a home in his own family, and enabled him to pay
for his schooling by making slippers. He edited a number of journals, took up
the cause of antislavery, but was compelled by frail health to retire to Amesbury
and then Danvers, Massachusetts. There he lived and died a bachelor, enjoying
the companionship of his devoted sister Elizabeth, true to his noble creed of "plain
living and high thinking."

All Quiet Along the Potomac

ETHEL LYNN BEERS

"All quiet along the Potomac," they say,
　"Except now and then a stray picket
Is shot, as he walks on his beat to and fro,
　By a rifleman hid in the thicket.
'Tis nothing—a private or two now and then
　Will not count in the news of the battle;
Not an officer lost—only one of the men,
　Moaning out, all alone, the death-rattle."

All quiet along the Potomac tonight,
　Where the soldiers lie peacefully dreaming;
Their tents in the rays of the clear autumn moon,
　Or the light of the watch-fire, are gleaming.
A tremulous sigh of the gentle night-wind
　Through the forest leaves softly is creeping;
While stars up above, with their glittering eyes,
　Keep guard, for the army is sleeping.

There's only the sound of the lone sentry's tread,
　As he tramps from the rock to the fountain,
And thinks of the two in the low trundle-bed
　Far away in the cot on the mountain.
His musket falls slack; his face, dark and grim,
　Grows gentle with memories tender,
As he mutters a prayer for the children asleep,
　For their mother; may Heaven defend her!

The moon seems to shine just as brightly as then,
　That night, when the love yet unspoken
Leaped up to his lips—when low-murmured vows
　Were pledged to be ever unbroken.
Then drawing his sleeve roughly over his eyes,
　He dashes off tears that are welling,
And gathers his gun closer up to its place,
　As if to keep down the heart-swelling.

He passes the fountain, the blasted pine-tree,
  The footstep is lagging and weary;
Yet onward he goes, through the broad belt of light,
  Toward the shade of the forest so dreary.
Hark! was it the night-wind that rustled the leaves?
  Was it moonlight so wondrously flashing?
It looked like a rifle . . . "Ha! Mary, good-bye!"
  The red life-blood is ebbing and plashing.

All quiet along the Potomac tonight;
  No sound save the rush of the river;
While soft falls the dew on the face of the dead—
  The picket's off duty forever!

"Ethel Lynn Beers" is the pen-name of *E T H E L I N D A   E L I O T
B E E R S* (1827–1879), who was descended from the Indian missionary
John Eliot. This celebrated poem of the Civil War, first published as "The
Picket Guard" in 1861, is now her sole claim to fame.

The Green Eye of the Yellow God

J. MILTON HAYES

There's a one-eyed yellow idol to the north of Khatmandu,
There's a little marble cross below the town;
There's a broken-hearted woman tends the grave of Mad Carew,
And the Yellow God forever gazes down.

He was known as "Mad Carew" by the subs at Khatmandu,
He was hotter than they felt inclined to tell;
But for all his foolish pranks, he was worshipped in the ranks,
And the Colonel's daughter smiled on him as well.

He had loved her all along, with a passion of the strong,
The fact that she loved him was plain to all.
She was nearly twenty-one and arrangements had begun
To celebrate her birthday with a ball.

He wrote to ask what present she would like from Mad Carew;
They met next day as he dismissed a squad;
And jestingly she told him then that nothing else would do
But the green eye of the little Yellow God.

On the night before the dance, Mad Carew seemed in a trance,
And they chaffed him as they puffed at their cigars;
But for once he failed to smile, and he sat alone awhile,
Then went out into the night beneath the stars.

He returned before the dawn, with his shirt and tunic torn,
And a gash across his temple dripping red;
He was patched up right away, and he slept through all the day,
And the Colonel's daughter watched beside his bed.

He woke at last and asked if they could send his tunic through;
She brought it, and he thanked her with a nod;
He bade her search the pocket saying, "That's from Mad Carew,"
And she found the little green eye of the god.

She upbraided poor Carew in the way that women do,
Though both her eyes were strangely hot and wet;
But she wouldn't take the stone and Mad Carew was left alone
With the jewel that he'd chanced his life to get.

When the ball was at its height, on that still and tropic night,
She thought of him and hastened to his room;
As she crossed the barrack square she could hear the dreamy air
Of a waltz tune softly stealing thro' the gloom.

His door was open wide, with silver moonlight shining through;
The place was wet and slipp'ry where she trod;
An ugly knife lay buried in the heart of Mad Carew,
'Twas the "Vengeance of the Little Yellow God."

There's a one-eyed yellow idol to the north of Khatmandu,
There's a little marble cross below the town;
There's a broken-hearted woman tends the grave of Mad Carew,
And the Yellow God forever gazes down.

The late Bransby Williams, grand old man of the English music-hall, imper-
sonator of Scrooge, made Edwardian marrows freeze with this recitation. It
appeared in print in 1911 as No. 62 of Reynolds's Musical Monogues, with music
by Cuthbert Clarke. In *My Brother Evelyn and Other Profiles*, Alec Waugh
records how Milton Hayes, a North Country actor, wrote "The Green Eye" in
five hours, pitching it exactly at the susceptibilities of a theatre audience.

Casey at the Bat

ERNEST LAWRENCE THAYER

The outlook wasn't brilliant for the Mudville nine that day:
The score stood four to two with but one inning more to play.
And then when Cooney died at first, and Barrows did the same,
A sickly silence fell upon the patrons of the game.

A straggling few got up to go in deep despair. The rest
Clung to that hope which springs eternal in the human breast;
They thought if only Casey could but get a whack at that—
We'd put up even money now with Casey at the bat.

But Flynn preceded Casey, as did also Jimmy Blake,
And the former was a lulu and the latter was a cake;
So upon that stricken multitude grim melancholy sat,
For there seemed but little chance of Casey's getting to the bat.

But Flynn let drive a single, to the wonderment of all,
And Blake, the much despis-ed, tore the cover off the ball;
And when the dust had lifted, and the men saw what had occurred,
There was Jimmy safe at second and Flynn a-hugging third.

Then from 5,000 throats and more there rose a lusty yell;
It rumbled through the valley, it rattled in the dell;
It knocked upon the mountain and recoiled upon the flat,
For Casey, mighty Casey, was advancing to the bat.

There was ease in Casey's manner as he stepped into his place;
There was pride in Casey's bearing and a smile on Casey's face.
And when, responding to the cheers, he lightly doffed his hat,
No stranger in the crowd could doubt 'twas Casey at the bat.

Ten thousand eyes were on him as he rubbed his hands with dirt;
Five thousand tongues applauded when he wiped them on his shirt.
Then while the writhing pitcher ground the ball into his hip,
Defiance gleamed in Casey's eye, a sneer curled Casey's lip.

And now the leather-covered sphere came hurtling through the air,
And Casey stood a-watching it in haughty grandeur there.
Close by the sturdy batsman the ball unheeded sped—
"That ain't my style," said Casey. "Strike one," the umpire said.

From the benches black with people, there went up a muffled roar,
Like the beating of the storm-waves on a stern and distant shore.
"Kill him! Kill the umpire!" shouted some one on the stand;
And it's likely they'd have killed him had not Casey raised his hand.

With a smile of Christian charity great Casey's visage shone;
He stilled the rising tumult; he bade the game go on;
He signaled to the pitcher, and once more the spheroid flew;
But Casey still ignored it, and the umpire said, "Strike two."

"Fraud!" cried the maddened thousands, and echo answered fraud;
But one scornful look from Casey and the audience was awed.
They saw his face grow stern and cold, they saw his muscles strain,
And they knew that Casey wouldn't let that ball go by again.

The sneer is gone from Casey's lip, his teeth are clenched in hate;
He pounds with cruel violence his bat upon the plate.
And now the pitcher holds the ball, and now he lets it go,
And now the air is shattered by the force of Casey's blow.

Oh, somewhere in this favored land the sun is shining bright;
The band is playing somewhere, and somewhere hearts are light,
And somewhere men are laughing, and somewhere children shout;
But there is no joy in Mudville—mighty Casey has struck out.

America's most celebrated comic poem, the national anthem of her national
sport, was rescued from its obscure place in the San Francisco *Examiner* of
June 3, 1888, and adopted as a recitation by a young entertainer, William
DeWolf Hopper. He became famous, and so did the most popular piece in his
repertoire: he calculated that he had delivered it over ten thousand times. Various
would-be authors claimed it as theirs—some demanding royalties from Hopper. It
has been transmogrified into a popular song, a couple of silent movies, two

cartoons by Walt Disney, and an operetta, *The Mighty Casey*, in 1953 by the composer William Schuman with libretto by Jeremy Gury. The full story of "Casey" is told by Martin Gardner in *The Annotated Casey at the Bat*.

ERNEST LAWRENCE THAYER (1863–1940), born in Lawrence, Massachusetts, majored in philosophy at Harvard, where he studied under William James and became a passionate spectator at baseball games. One of his less conventional Harvard friends was William Randolph Hearst, who invited him to write for the San Francisco *Examiner*. "Casey at the Bat" earned him five dollars. Later he acknowledged his masterpiece of bathos only with considerable embarrassment: he thought it no better than other ephemera that he contributed to newspapers. For many years he managed his family's woolen mills at Worcester—and squirmed every time "Casey" was mentioned.

8

The Bivouac of Life

It flooded the crimson twilight
Like the close of an Angel's Psalm.

—"A Lost Chord"

"Hullo!"

S. W. FOSS

W'en you see a man in woe,
Walk right up an' say, "Hullo!"
Say "Hullo!" an' "How d'ye do?"
"How's the world a-usin' you?"
Slap the fellow on his back;
Bring your han' down with a whack!
Waltz right up, an' don't go slow;
Grin an' shake an' say, "Hullo!"

Is he clothed in rags? Oh, sho!
Walk right up an' say, "Hullo!"
Rags is but a cotton roll
Jest for wrappin' up a soul;
An' a soul is worth a true
Hale an' hearty "How d'ye do?"
Don't wait for the crowd to go;
Walk right up an' say "Hullo!"

W'en big vessels meet, they say,
They saloot an' sail away.
Jest the same are you an' me—
Lonesome ships upon a sea;
Each one sailin' his own jog
For a port beyond the fog.
Let yer speakin' trumpet blow,
Lift yer horn an' cry "Hullo!"

Say "Hullo!" an' "How d'ye do?"
Other folks are good as you.
W'en ye leave yer house of clay,
Wanderin' in the Far-Away;
W'en you travel through the strange
Country t'other side the range;
Then the souls you've cheered will know
Who ye be, an' say "Hullo!"

SAM WALTER FOSS (1858–1911) was born at Candia, New Hampshire, and graduated from Brown University. Editor of the Boston *Yankee Blade*, he also contributed light verse and other writings to various papers. Much of his poetry has the unmistakable blend of friendliness and genial self-satisfaction of the self-made American that set English hackles bristling and drove the sensitive Henry James, Jr., to Europe. It is exuberantly present in another piece by S. W. Foss, "The Rattle of the Dollar," the first verse of which runs as follows:

> The air it tastes like nectar oozed from Heaven's own laboratory,
> And the sunshine falls like ointment on the forehead of a king,
> When a man feels in his pocket, flushed with full financial glory,
> And he hears the nickels rattle, and he hears the quarters ring.
> Though the winter storms assault his path, and drift his way, and blow,
> In his heart he feels the sunshine of an endless summer-time;
> For he listens to the music of the money in his pocket—

To the rattle of the dollar, and the jingle of the dime.
  The famous violinists,
  And the fiddlers and the cornettists,
  And the mighty organ-players
  Of every age and clime,
  Make a slow and droning music,
  Full of discord and of jangle,
  When you match it with the rattle—
With the rattle of the dollar, and the jingle of the dime.

The rest of this inspiring work, which promises "a billion bulging pockets" to "the millions and the masses," leaves no doubt at all in the reader's mind as to the high seriousness of the poet's belief in a future literally golden.

A Psalm of Life
What the Heart of the Young Man said to the Psalmist

HENRY WADSWORTH LONGFELLOW

Tell me not in mournful numbers,
Life is but an empty dream!
For the soul is dead that slumbers,
And things are not what they
seem.

Life is real! Life is earnest!
And the grave is not its goal;
Dust thou art, to dust returnest,
Was not spoken of the soul.

Not enjoyment, and not sorrow,
Is our destined end or way;
But to act, that each tomorrow,
Find us farther than today.

Art is long, and Time is fleeting,
And our hearts though stout and
brave,
Still, like muffled drums are beating
Funeral marches to the grave.

In the world's broad field of battle,
In the bivouac of Life,

Be not like dumb, driven cattle!
Be a hero in the strife!

Trust no Future, howe'er pleasant!
Let the dead Past bury its dead!
Act,—act in the living Present!
Heart within, and God o'erhead!

Lives of great men all remind us
We can make our lives sublime;
And, departing, leave behind us
Footprints in the sands of time;

Footprints, that perhaps another,
Sailing o'er earth's solemn main,
A forlorn and shipwreck'd brother,
Seeing, shall take heart again.

Let us, then, be up and doing,
With a heart for any fate;
Still achieving, still pursuing,
Learn to labour and to wait.

A persistent strain in nineteenth-century poetry is that of simple moral exhortation. "A Psalm of Life," as much as "Hullo!" "Trust in God and Do the Right," and "Speak Gently," is an indication of the Victorian conception of such virtues as fortitude, dignity, charity, and honesty as almost tangible articles to be acquired and attached to one's character. Longfellow may be a greater poet, but his thought is not far from Martin Farquhar Tupper:

> Never give up! Though the grape shot may rattle,
> Or the full thundercloud over you burst;

Stand like a rock and the storm and the battle
Little shall harm you, though doing their worst.

Never give up! If adversity presses,
Providence wisely has mingled the cup;
And the best counsel, in all your distresses,
Is the stout watchword of "Never give up!"

or from W. E. Hickson:

'Tis a lesson you should heed
Try, try again.
If at first you don't succeed
Try, try again,

and as much in the moralizing mainstream as is Henry Burton:

Have you had a kindness shown?
Pass it on!
'Twas not given for thee alone,
Pass it on!
Let it travel down the years,
Let it wipe another's tears
Till in Heaven the deed appears—
Pass it on!

A note on Longfellow may be found on page 39.

Woodman, Spare That Tree!

G. P. MORRIS

Woodman, spare that tree!
Touch not a single bough!
In youth it shelter'd me,
And I'll protect it now.
'Twas my forefather's hand
That placed it near his cot;
There, woodman, let it stand,
Thy axe shall harm it not!

That old familiar tree,
Whose glory and renown
Are spread o'er land and sea—
And wouldst thou hew it down?
Woodman, forbear thy stroke!
Cut not its earth-bound ties;
Oh, spare that aged Oak
Now tow'ring to the skies!

When but an idle boy,
I sought its grateful shade;
In all their gushing joy
Here, too, my sisters play'd.
My Mother kiss'd me here;
My Father press'd my hand—
Forgive this foolish tear:
But let that old Oak stand!

My heart-strings round thee cling
Close as thy bark, old friend!
There shall the wild-bird sing,
And still thy branches bend.
Old tree! the storm still brave!
Then, woodman, leave the spot;
While I've a hand to save,
Thy axe shall harm it not.

Campaigners for the preservation of trees and forests have made considerable use of this famous plea. Its original title was "The Oak." Ogden Nash's parody, "The Calf," is equally affecting, if somewhat more materialistic:

> Pray, butcher, spare yon tender calf!
> Accept my plea on his behalf;
> He's but a babe, too young by far
> To perish in the abattoir.
> Oh, cruel butcher, let him feed
> And gambol on the verdant mead;
> Let clover tops and grassy banks
> Fill out those childish ribs and flanks.
> Then may we, at some future meal,
> Pitch into beef, instead of veal.

There is a note on George Pope Morris on page 186.

The Old Oaken Bucket

SAMUEL WOODWORTH

How dear to this heart are the scenes of my childhood,
When fond recollection presents them to view!—
The orchard, the meadow, the deep-tangled wildwood,
And every loved spot which my infancy knew!
The wide-spreading pond, and the mill that stood by it;
The bridge, and the rock where the cataract fell;
The cot of my father, the dairy-house nigh it;
And e'en the rude bucket that hung in the well.
The old oaken bucket, the iron-bound bucket,
The moss-covered bucket, which hung in the well.

That moss-covered vessel I hailed as a treasure;
For often at noon, when returned from the field,
I found it the source of an exquisite pleasure—
The purest and sweetest that Nature can yield.
How ardent I seized it, with hands that were glowing,
And quick to the white-pebbled bottom it fell!
Then soon, with the emblem of truth overflowing,
And dripping with coolness, it rose from the well—
The old oaken bucket, the iron-bound bucket.
The moss-covered bucket arose from the well.

How sweet from the green, mossy brim to receive it,
As, poised on the curb, it inclined to my lips!
Not a full, blushing goblet could tempt me to leave it,
The brightest that beauty or revelry sips.
And now, far removed from the loved habitation,
The tear of regret will intrusively swell,
As Fancy reverts to my father's plantation,
And sighs for the bucket that hangs in the well—
The old oaken bucket, the iron-bound bucket,
The moss-covered bucket that hangs in the well!

The genesis of this well-loved Gem is recorded by Henry Frederick Reddall in his collection, *Songs That Never Die*, of 1894. Woodworth "was in the habit of dropping into a noted drinking saloon kept by one Mallory. One day, after drinking a glass of brandy and water, he smacked his lips and declared that Mallory's brandy was superior to any drink he had ever tasted.

" 'No,' said Mallory, 'you are mistaken. There was a drink which, in the estimation of us both, far surpassed this.'

" 'What was that?' incredulously asked Woodworth.

" 'The fresh water we used to drink from the old oaken bucket that hung in the well after returning from the fields on a sultry day.'

" 'Very true,' assented Woodworth, teardrops glistening in his eyes. Retiring to his printing office he seated himself at his desk and began to write." In half an hour the inspiring work was complete.

Among the inevitable parodies is one by an anonymous hand, "The Old Oaken Bucket (As censored by the Board of Health)," which warns of the dangers of enteric fever and ends thus:

> And I gag at the thought of that horrible well,
> And the old oaken bucket, the fungus-grown bucket—
> In fact, the slop bucket—that hung in the well.

S A M U E L W O O D W O R T H (1785–1842), who came from Scituate, Massachusetts, was successful as a poet, playwright, printer, journalist, editor, and co-founder of the *New York Mirror* with G. P. Morris (see page 186). "The Old Oaken Bucket," which appears in his *Poems, Odes, Songs, and Other Metrical Effusions*, is the only one of his many works to have held the popular fancy.

Trust in God and Do the Right

NORMAN MACLEOD

Courage, brother! do not stumble,
   Though thy path is dark as night;
There's a star to guide the humble—
   Trust in God and do the right.

Let the road be long and dreary,
   And its ending out of sight;
Foot it bravely—strong or weary—
   Trust in God and do the right.

Perish policy and cunning,
   Perish all that fears the light;
Whether losing, whether winning,
   Trust in God and do the right.

Trust no party, church, or faction,
   Trust no leader in the fight;
But in every word and action
   Trust in God and do the right.

Trust no forms of guilty passion—
   Fiends can look like angels bright;
Trust no custom, school, or fashion—
   Trust in God and do the right.

Some will hate thee, some will love thee;
   Some will flatter, some will slight;
Cease from man and look above thee—
   Trust in God and do the right.

Firmest rule, and safest guiding,
   Inward peace and inward light;
Star upon our path abiding—
   Trust in God and do the right.

NORMAN MACLEOD, D.D. (1812–1872) was the son of a Scottish clergyman with some reputation as a popular preacher. Greatly beloved by his congregations, he became more and more involved with doctrinal disputes and the amelioration of the sad conditions of the Deserving Poor, establishing the first congregational penny-bank in Scotland and temperance refreshment rooms for workingmen. He edited *Good Words,* in which "Trust in God" and many other of his works first appeared, toured Egypt, Palestine, and India, and engaged in fierce controversy when he sternly refuted the suggestion that the Jewish Sabbath may be equated with the Lord's Day. In 1857 he received the signal honour of being appointed chaplain to Her Majesty the Queen, who condescended to express warm approbation of his sermons in *Leaves from the Journal of our Life in the Highlands* and also to commemorate him in two beautiful stained-glass windows donated to Crathie church.

Speak Gently

DAVID BATES

Speak gently! It is better far
  To rule by love than fear;
Speak gently; let no harsh words mar
  The good we might do here!

Speak gently! Love doth whisper low
  The vow that true hearts bind;
And gently Friendship's accents flow;
  Affection's voice is kind.

Speak gently to the little child!
  Its love be sure to gain;
Teach it in accents soft and mild;
  It may not long remain.

Speak gently to the young, for they
  Will have enough to bear;
Pass through this life as best they may,
  'Tis full of anxious care!

Speak gently to the aged one,
  Grieve not the care-worn heart;
Whose sands of life are nearly run,
  Let such in peace depart!

Speak gently, kindly, to the poor;
  Let no harsh tone be heard;
They have enough they must endure,
  Without an unkind word!

Speak gently to the erring; know
  They may have toiled in vain;
Perchance unkindness made them so:
  Oh, win them back again!

Speak gently! He who gave his life
To bend man's stubborn will,
When elements were in fierce strife,
Said to them, "Peace, be still."

Speak gently! 'tis a little thing
Dropped in the heart's deep well;
The good, the joy, that it may bring,
Eternity shall tell.

This is another of the improving verses parodied in *Alice's Adventures in Wonderland*:

Speak roughly to your little boy,
And beat him when he sneezes:
He only does it to annoy,
Because he knows it teases.

CHORUS: Wow! wow! wow!

D A V I D   B A T E S is a rather shadowy figure, and the information that follows comes from Martin Gardner's delightful *The Annotated Alice*. The poem, attributed by some to G. W. Langford, was nailed down to the Philadelphia bard David Bates by John M. Shaw, in *The Parodies of Lewis Carroll and Their Originals*, 1960. The text appears in *The Eolian*, a book of verse that Bates published in 1849, and the poet's son claims in the preface to his father's *Poetical Works* that "Speak Gently" should be included in the *oeuvre*.

Betsey and I Are Out

WILL CARLETON

Draw up the papers, lawyer, and make 'em good and stout;
For things at home are crossways, and Betsey and I are out.
We, who have worked together so long as man and wife,
Must pull in single harness for the rest of our nat'ral life.

"What is the matter?" say you. I swan it's hard to tell!
Most of the years behind us we've passed by very well!
I have no other woman, she has no other man—
Only we've lived together as long as we ever can.

So I have talked with Betsey, and Betsey has talked with me,
And so we've agreed together that we can't never agree;
Not that we've catched each other in any terrible crime;
We've been a-gathering this for years, a little at a time.

There was a stock of temper we both had for a start,
Although we never suspected 'twould take us two apart;
I had my various failings, bred in the flesh and bone;
And Betsey, like all good women, had a temper of her own.

The first thing I remember whereon we disagreed
Was something concerning heaven—a difference in our creed;
We arg'ed the thing at breakfast, we arg'ed the thing at tea,
And the more we arg'ed the question, the more we didn't agree.

And the next that I remember was when we lost a cow;
She had kicked the bucket for certain, the question was only—How?
I held my own opinion, and Betsey another had;
And when we were done a-talkin', we both of us was mad.

And the next that I remember, it started in a joke;
But full for a week it lasted, and neither of us spoke.
And the next was when I scolded because she broke a bowl;
And she said I was mean and stingy, and hadn't any soul.

And so that bowl kept pourin' dissensions in our cup;
And so that blamed cow-creature was always a-comin' up;
And so that heaven we arg'ed no nearer to us got,
But it gave us a taste of something a thousand times as hot.

And so the thing kept workin', and all the self-same way;
Always somethin' to arg'e, and somethin' sharp to say;
And down on us came the neighbors, a couple dozen strong,
And lent their kindest service for to help the thing along.

And there has been days together—and many a weary week—
We was both of us cross and sulky, and both too proud to speak;
And I have been thinkin' and thinkin', the whole of the winter and fall,
If I can't live kind with a woman, why, then, I won't at all.

And so I have talked with Betsey, and Betsey has talked with me,
And we have agreed together that we can't never agree;
And what is hers shall be hers, and what is mine shall be mine;
And I'll put it in the agreement, and take it to her to sign.

Write on the paper, lawyer—the very first paragraph—
Of all the farm and livestock that she shall have her half;
For she has helped to earn it, through many a weary day,
And it's nothing more than justice that Betsey has her pay.

Give her the house and homestead—a man can thrive and roam;
But women are skeery critters, unless they have a home;
And I have always determined, and never failed to say,
That Betsey should never want a home if I was taken away.

There is a little hard money that's drawin' tol'rable pay:
A couple of hundred dollars laid by for a rainy day;
Safe in the hands of good men, and easy to get at;
Put in another clause there, and give her half of that.

Yes, I see you smile, sir, at my givin' her so much;
Yes, divorce is cheap, sir, but I take no stock in such!
True and fair I married her, when she was blithe and young;
And Betsey was al'ays good to me, exceptin' with her tongue.

Once, when I was young as you, and not so smart, perhaps,
For she mittened a lawyer, and several other chaps;
And all of them was flustered, and fairly taken down,
And I for a time was counted the luckiest man in town.

Once when I had a fever—I won't forget it soon—
I was hot as a basted turkey and crazy as a loon;
Never an hour went by me when she was out of sight—
She nursed me true and tender, and stuck to me day and night.

If ever a house was tidy, and ever a kitchen clean,
Her house and kitchen was as tidy as any I ever seen;
And I don't complain of Betsey, or any of her acts,
Excepting when we've quarreled, and told each other facts.

So draw up the paper, lawyer, and I'll go home tonight,
And read the agreement to her, and see if it's all right;
And then, in the mornin', I'll sell to a tradin' man I know,
And kiss the child that was left to us, and out in the world I'll go.

And one thing put in the paper, that first to me didn't occur;
That when I am dead at last she'll bring me back to her;
And lay me under the maples I planted years ago,
When she and I was happy before we quarreled so.

And when she dies I wish that she would be laid by me,
And, lyin' together in silence, perhaps we will agree;
And, if ever we meet in heaven, I wouldn't think it queer
If we loved each other the better because we quarreled here.

A note on Will Carleton appears on page 190.

The Old Man's Comforts and How He Gained Them

ROBERT SOUTHEY

"You are old, Father William," the young man cried,
"The few locks which are left you are grey;
You are hale, Father William, a hearty old man;
Now tell me the reason, I pray."

"In the days of my youth," Father William replied,
"I remember'd that youth would fly fast,
And abus'd not my health and my vigour at first,
That I never might need them at last."

"You are old, Father William," the young man cried,
"And pleasures with youth pass away.
And yet you lament not the days that are gone;
Now tell me the reason, I pray."

"In the days of my youth," Father William replied,
"I remember'd that youth could not last;
I thought of the future, whatever I did,
That I never might grieve for the past."

"You are old, Father William," the young man cried,
"And life must be hast'ning away;
You are cheerful and love to converse upon death;
Now tell me the reason, I pray."

"I am cheerful, young man," Father William replied,
"Let the cause thy attention engage:
In the days of my youth I remember'd my God!
And He hath not forgotten my age."

Lewis Carroll's superb burlesque in *Alice in Wonderland* is even longer than the
original and has banished it almost to oblivion. Not only is the parody classic nonsense verse in its own right, it also catches Southey's worthy didacticism brilliantly:

"You are old, Father William," the young man said,
   "And your hair has become very white;
And yet you incessantly stand on your head—
   Do you think, at your age, it is right?"

"In my youth," Father William replied to his son,
   "I feared it might injure the brain;
But now that I'm perfectly sure I have none,
   Why, I do it again and again."

And so on.

A note on Robert Southey is to be found on page 44.

Where Is Your Boy Tonight?

AUTHOR UNKNOWN

Life is teeming with evil snares,
  The gates of sin are wide,
The rosy fingers of pleasure wave,
And beckon the young inside.
Man of the world with open purse,
  Seeking your own delight,
Pause ere reason is wholly gone—
  Where is your boy tonight?

Sirens are singing on every hand,
  Luring the ear of youth,
Gilded falsehood with silver notes
  Drowneth the voice of truth.
Dainty ladies in costly robes,
  Your parlours gleam with light,
Fate and beauty your senses steep—
  Where is your boy tonight?

Tempting whispers of royal spoil
  Flatter the youthful soul
Eagerly entering into life,
  Restive of all control.
Needs are many, and duties stern

Crowd on the weary sight;
Father, buried in business cares,—
  Where is your boy tonight?

Pitfalls lurk in the flowery way,
  Vice has a golden gate:
Who shall guide the unwary feet
  Into the highway straight?
Patient worker with willing hand,
  Keep the home hearth bright;
Tired mother, with tender eyes—
  Where is your boy tonight?

Turn his feet from the evil paths
  Ere they have entered in;
Keep him unspotted while yet ye
    may!
  Earth is so stained with sin;
Ere he has learned to follow wrong,
  Teach him to love the right;
Watch ere watching is wholly vain—
  Where is your boy tonight?

Similar concern for the whereabouts of a prodigal inspired the Reverend R.
Lowry. He wrote the words and music (to be performed "With Tenderness")
of No. 303 in Ira D. Sankey's *Sacred Songs and Solos:*

Where Is My Boy Tonight?

Where is my wand'ring boy tonight—
  The boy of my tend'rest care,
The boy that was once my joy and light,
  The child of my love and prayer?

[*269*]

Chorus: Oh, where is my boy tonight?
Oh, where is my boy tonight?
My heart o'erflows, for I love him, he knows!
Oh, *where* is my boy tonight?

Once he was pure as morning dew,
As he knelt at his mother's knee;
No face was so bright, no heart more true,
And none was so sweet as he.

Oh, where is my boy, etc.

Oh, could I see you now, my boy,
As fair as in olden time,
When prattle and smile made a home a joy,
And life was a merry chime!

Oh, where is my boy, etc.

Go for my wandering boy tonight;
Go, search for him where you will:
But bring him to me with all his blight,
And tell him I love him still.

Oh, where is my boy, etc.

The Mother's Sacrifice

MRS. SIGOURNEY

"What shall I render thee, Father supreme,
For Thy rich gifts, and this the best of all?"
Said a young mother, as she fondly watched
Her sleeping babe. There was an answering voice
That night in dreams:—
    "Thou hast a little bud
Wrapt in thy breast, and fed with dews of love:
Give me that bud. 'Twill be a flower in heaven."
But there was silence. Yea, a hush so deep,
Breathless, and terror stricken, that the lip
Blanched in its trance.
    "Thou hast a little harp—
How sweetly it would swell the angel's hymn:
Give me that harp." There burst a shuddering sob,
As if the bosom by some hidden sword
Were cleft in twain.
    Morn came. A blight had struck
The crimson velvet of the unfolding bud;
The harp-strings rang a thrilling strain and broke—
And that young mother lay upon the earth,
In childless agony.
    Again the voice
That stirred her vision:—"He who asked of thee
Loveth a cheerful giver." So she raised
Her gushing eyes, and, ere the tear-drop dried
Upon its fringes, smiled—and that meek smile,
Like Abraham's faith, was counted righteousness.

LYDIA HOWARD SIGOURNEY, *née* HUNTLEY (1791–1865), "The Sweet Singer of Hartford" (Connecticut), was first inspired by the Muse at the tender age of eight. Her husband disapproved of her publishing poetry, but when he ran into financial difficulties found that her genius had its useful side, after all. *The Reader's Encyclopedia of American Literature* observes that death was her favourite subject: "She burst into elegy as easily as a hired mourner bursts into tears, and a contemporary wit called her memorial verses 'death's second terror.'" Mrs. Sigourney was celebrated not only as a poetess: she was an advocate of the higher education of women and established a select school for young ladies at Hartford.

Rock Me to Sleep, Mother

ELIZABETH AKERS ALLEN

Backward, turn backward, O Time, in your flight,
Make me a child again just for tonight!
Mother, come back from the echoless shore,
Take me again to your heart as of yore;
Kiss from my forehead the furrows of care,
Smooth the few silver threads out of my hair;
Over my slumbers your loving watch keep;—
Rock me to sleep, mother,—rock me to sleep!

Backward, flow backward, O tide of the years!
I am so weary of toil and of tears,—
Toil without recompense, tears all in vain,—
Take them, and give me my childhood again!
I have grown weary of dust and decay,—
Weary of flinging my soul-wealth away;
Weary of sowing for others to reap;—
Rock me to sleep, mother,—rock me to sleep!

Tired of the hollow, the base, the untrue,
Mother, O mother, my heart calls for you!
Many a summer the grass has grown green,
Blossomed and faded, our faces between:
Yet, with strong yearning and passionate pain,
Long I tonight for your presence again.
Come from the silence so long and so deep;—
Rock me to sleep, mother,—rock me to sleep!

Over my heart, in the days that are flown,
No love like mother-love ever has shone;
No other worship abides and endures,—
Faithful, unselfish, and patient like yours:
None like a mother can charm away pain
From the sick soul and the world-weary brain.
Slumber's soft calms o'er my heavy lids creep;—
Rock me to sleep, mother,—rock me to sleep!

Come, let your brown hair, just lighted with gold,
Fall on your shoulders again as of old;
Let it drop over my forehead tonight,
Shading my faint eyes away from the light;
For with its sunny-edged shadows once more
Haply will throng the sweet visions of yore;
Lovingly, softly, its bright billows sweep;—
Rock me to sleep, mother,—rock me to sleep!

Mother, dear mother, the years have been long
Since I last listened your lullaby song:
Sing, then, and unto my soul it shall seem
Womanhood's years have been only a dream.
Clasped to your heart in a loving embrace,
With your light lashes just sweeping my face,
Never hereafter to wake or to weep;—
Rock me to sleep, mother,—rock me to sleep!

ELIZABETH ANN (CHASE) (AKERS) ALLEN
(1832–1911), born in Strong, Maine, was a poetess whose compositions appeared under a variety of names, that of Elizabeth Akers (her second husband was a sculptor, Paul Akers), that of Elizabeth Akers Allen (she married in 1865 an E. M. Allen), and her pen-name "Florence Percy." In addition, this moving and famous Gem was claimed by several would-be authors, among them Alexander M. W. Ball. All, however, is now clear. Mrs. Allen wrote novels, worked on newspapers in Portland, and gained especial favour for her tender verses.

Not Lost, but Gone Before

HON. MRS. NORTON

How mournful seems, in broken dreams,
   The memory of the day,
When icy Death has sealed the breath
   Of some dear form of clay.

When pale, unmoved, the face we loved,
   The face we thought so fair,
And the hand lies cold, whose fervent hold
   Once charmed away despair.

Oh, what could heal the grief we feel
   For hopes that come no more,
Had we ne'er heard the Scripture word,
   "Not lost, but gone before"?

Oh, sadly, yet with vain regret,
   The widowed heart must yearn,
And mothers weep their babes asleep
   In the sunlight's vain return.

The brother's heart shall rue to part
   From the one through childhood known;
And the orphan's tears lament for years
   A friend and father gone.

For death and life, with ceaseless strife,
   Beat wild on this world's shore;
And all our calm is in that balm,—
   "Not lost, but gone before."

Oh, world wherein nor death, nor sin,
   Nor weary warfare dwells:
Their blessed home we parted from
   With sobs and sad farewells;

Where eyes awake, for whose dear sake
Our own with tears grow dim,
And faint accords of dying words
Aye change for heaven's sweet hymn;

Oh, there at last, life's trials past,
We'll meet our loved once more,
Whose feet have trod the path to God—
"Not lost, but gone before."

A short biography of the Hon. Mrs. Norton appears on page 69.

A Lost Chord

ADELAIDE ANNE PROCTER

Seated one day at the Organ,
  I was weary and ill at ease,
And my fingers wandered idly
  Over the noisy keys.

I do not know what I was playing,
  Or what I was dreaming then;
But I struck one chord of music,
  Like the sound of a great Amen.

It flooded the crimson twilight
  Like the close of an Angel's Psalm,
And it lay on my fevered spirit
  With a touch of infinite calm.

It quieted pain and sorrow,
  Like love overcoming strife;
It seemed the harmonious echo
  From our discordant life.

It linked all perplexèd meanings
  Into one perfect peace,
And trembled away in silence
  As if it were loth to cease.

I have sought but I seek it vainly,
  That one lost chord divine,
Which came from the soul of the
    Organ,
  And entered into mine.

It may be that Death's bright angel
  Will speak in that chord again,—
It may be that only in Heaven
  I shall hear that grand Amen.

In myriad parlours, on countless concert platforms linger the strains of the musical version of this beloved Gem. Exponents have ranged from the great Caruso to, in more recent times and using a somewhat different text, Jimmy Durante, claiming to be "The Guy who found the Lost Chord." Among the many irreverent parodies, there is one by D. B. Wyndham Lewis:

> Seated one day at the organ
>   I jumped as if I'd been shot,
> For the Dean was upon me, snarling
>   "Stainer—*and make it hot.*"
>
> All week I swung Stainer and Barnby,
>   Bach, Gounod, and Bunnett in A;
> I said, "Gosh, the old bus is a wonder!"
>   The Dean, with a nod, said "Okay."

ADELAIDE ANNE PROCTER (1825–1864) was born in Bedford Square, London, into a poetical family, for her amiable father, Bryan Waller Procter, when he was not busy as a solicitor and commissioner in lunacy, composed songs and dramas under the pseudonym of Barry Cornwall. Miss Procter was a golden-tressed, gentle child whose lispings in verse were fervently encouraged by her doting parents. Her poems appeared pseudonymously in various magazines and she interested herself in the social betterment of women. In a letter, Thackeray asked her, "Why are your verses so very, very sad? I have been reading them this morning till the sky has got a crape over it." Always delicate in health, she finally perished from consumption.

Solitude

ELLA WHEELER WILCOX

Laugh, and the world laughs with you;
Weep, and you weep alone;
For the sad old earth must borrow its mirth,
But has trouble enough of its own.
Sing, and the hills will answer;
Sigh, it is lost on the air;
The echoes bound to a joyful sound,
But shrink from voicing care.

Rejoice, and men will seek you;
Grieve, and they turn and go;
They want full measure of all your pleasure,
But they do not need your woe.
Be glad, and your friends are many;
Be sad, and you lose them all,—
There are none to decline your nectared wine,
But alone you must drink life's gall.

Feast, and your halls are crowded;
Fast, and the world goes by.
Succeed and give, and it helps you live,
But no man can help you die.
For there is room in the halls of pleasure
For a large and lordly train,
But one by one we must all file on
Through the narrow aisles of pain.

ELLA WHEELER WILCOX (1850–1919) "is a power and a
pleasure in the land," said the *Saturday Review*. ". . . She gives to a vast public
the sort of literature they honestly require." Born in Johnstown Center, Wisconsin, this most purple of poetesses showed in tender years the direction of her
future career, writing a sentimental novel at the age of ten and publishing her
first poem a few years later. She studied for a while at the University of

Wisconsin, wrote for newspapers, and had her first sensational success with *Poems of Passion.* In 1876 it was reckoned extremely daring, with such offers as:

> Here is my body; bruise it if you will.
> —"Individuality"

and scenes of unbridled emotion:

> She touches my cheek, and I quiver—
> I tremble with exquisite pains;
> She sighs—like an overcharged river
> My blood rushes on through my veins;
> She smiles—and in mad-tiger fashion,
> As a she-tiger fondles its own,
> I clasp her with fierceness and passion,
> And kiss her with shudder and groan.
> —"Delilah"

alarming and thrilling her mesmerized readers with erotic detail:

> And between the verses for interlude,
> I kissed your throat, and your shoulders nude.
> —"The Duet"

Some of her many later volumes were *Poems of Pleasure, Poems of Power, Poems of Cheer, Poems of Experience,* and *New Thought Pastels.* A soulmate of England's own Marie Corelli (whose novels, her publisher reports, sell tens of thousands annually to an enthusiastic new public in the West Indies and West Africa), she was described by Lloyd Morris in *Postscript to Yesterday* as follows: "A stately figure, Mrs. Wilcox was softly enveloped by plumes, chiffons, and Oriental metaphysics. Her life was blameless, but her imagination simmered. Over the land millions of women throbbed to her verses."

If—

If you can keep your head when all about you
   Are losing theirs and blaming it on you,
If you can trust yourself when all men doubt you,
   But make allowance for their doubting too;
If you can wait and not be tired by waiting,
   Or being lied about, don't deal in lies,
Or being hated don't give way to hating,
   And yet don't look too good, nor talk too wise:

If you can dream—and not make dreams your master;
   If you can think—and not make thoughts your aim,
If you can meet with Triumph and Disaster
   And treat these two impostors just the same;
If you can bear to hear the truth you've spoken
   Twisted by knaves to make a trap for fools,
Or watch the things you gave your life to, broken,
   And stoop and build 'em up with worn-out tools:

If you can make one heap of all your winnings
   And risk it on one turn of pitch-and-toss,
And lose, and start again at your beginnings
   And never breathe a word about your loss;
If you can force your heart and nerve and sinew
   To serve your turn long after they are gone,
And so hold on when there is nothing in you
   Except the Will which says to them: "Hold on!"

If you can talk with crowds and keep your virtue,
   Or walk with Kings—nor lose the common touch,
If neither foes nor loving friends can hurt you,
   If all men count with you, but none too much;
If you can fill the unforgiving minute
   With sixty seconds' worth of distance run,
Yours is the Earth and everything that's in it,
   And—which is more—you'll be a Man, my son!

As exhortation to British lads to show what is now called without apology guts, "If—" is firmly in the tradition of Newbolt's "Vitaï Lampada" and the poets of *Boy's Own Paper* and other children's magazines that had their golden age at the close of the nineteenth century.

R U D Y A R D   K I P L I N G (1865–1936) was born in Bombay, the son of a sculptor, received a brisk but sympathetic education at the United Services College, Westward Ho!, and spent his young manhood as a reporter in India, seeing the imperial creed in action. This was the period when Britain, like Rome over a thousand years before, was finding that the trouble with a far-flung Empire was policing the far-flung frontiers. The current euphoric patriotism was exhibited in songs like the Great Macdermott's "We don't want to fight, but by Jingo if we do," and Kipling obliged a growing public with such poems as "The English Flag." As a writer, he was to combine those apparently antithetical elements, pugnacity and sensitivity, to such a degree that he will continue to provide employment for literary commentators for many years to come.

9

Heart of Oak

Let thy noble motto be,
"GOD—the COUNTRY—LIBERTY!"

—"The Young American"

Love of Country

SIR WALTER SCOTT

Breathes there the man, with soul so dead,
Who never to himself has said,
   This is my own, my native land!
Whose heart hath ne'er within him burn'd,
As home his footsteps he hath turn'd,
   From wandering on a foreign strand!
If such there breathe, go, mark him well;
For him no minstrel raptures swell;
High though his titles, proud his name,
Boundless his wealth as wish can claim;
Despite those titles, power, and pelf,
The wretch, concentred all in self,
Living, shall forfeit fair renown,
And, doubly dying, shall go down
To the vile dust, from whence he sprung,
Unwept, unhonour'd, and unsung.

   O Caledonia! stern and wild,
Meet nurse for a poetic child!
Land of brown heath and shaggy wood,
Land of the mountain and the flood,
Land of my sires! what mortal hand
Can e'er untie the filial band
That knits me to thy rugged strand!
Still, as I view each well-known scene,
Think what is now, and what hath been,
Seems as, to me, of all bereft,
Sole friends thy woods and streams were left;
And thus I love them better still,
Even in extremity of ill.
By Yarrow's streams still let me stray,

Though none should guide my feeble way;
Still feel the breeze down Ettrick break,
Although it chill my wither'd cheek;
Still lay my head by Teviot Stone,
Though there, forgotten and alone,
The bard may draw his parting groan.

There is a note on Sir Walter Scott on page 86.

The Landing of the Pilgrim Fathers in New England

MRS. HEMANS

"Look now abroad! Another race has filled
  Those populous borders—wide the wood recedes,
And towns shoot up, and fertile realms are tilled;
  The land is full of harvest and green meads."

—Bryant

The breaking waves dashed high
  On a stern and rock-bound coast,
And the woods against a stormy sky
  Their giant branches tossed;

And the heavy night hung dark
  The hills and waters o'er,
When a band of exiles moored their bark
  On the wild New England shore.

Not as the conqueror comes,
  They, the true-hearted, came;
Not with the roll of the stirring drums,
  And the trumpet that sings of fame;
Not as the flying come,
  In silence and in fear;—
They shook the depths of the desert gloom
  With their hymns of lofty cheer.

Amidst the storm they sang,
  And the stars heard and the sea;
And the sounding aisles of the dim woods rang
  To the anthem of the free!

The ocean eagle soared
  From his nest by the white wave's foam;

And the rocking pines of the forest roared—
This was their welcome home!

There were men with hoary hair
Amidst that pilgrim band;—
Why had *they* come to wither there,
Away from their childhood's land?

There was woman's fearless eye
Lit by her deep love's truth;
There was manhood's brow serenely high,
And the fiery heart of youth.

What sought they thus afar?
Bright jewels of the mine?
The wealth of seas, the spoils of war?—
They sought a faith's pure shrine!

Ay, call it holy ground,
The soil where first they trod.
They have left unstained what there they found—
Freedom to worship God.

Traditionally, this poem was recited in the family circle at Thanksgiving.
There is a note on the poetess on page 156.

The Homes of England

MRS. HEMANS

"Where's the coward that would not dare
To fight for such a land?"   —*Marmion*

The stately homes of England!
How beautiful they stand,
Amidst their tall ancestral trees,
O'er all the pleasant land!
The deer across the greensward bound
Through shade and sunny gleam,
And the swan glides past them with the sound
Of some rejoicing stream.

The merry homes of England!
Around their hearths by night,
What gladsome looks of household love
Meet in the ruddy light!
There woman's voice flows forth in song,
Or childhood's tale is told,
Or lips move tunefully along
Some glorious page of old.

The blessed homes of England!
How softly on their bowers
Is laid the holy quietness
That breathes from Sabbath hours!
Solemn, yet sweet, the church-bell's chime
Floats through their woods at morn;
All other sounds, in that still time,
Of breeze and leaf are born.

The cottage homes of England!
By thousands on her plains
They are smiling o'er the silvery brooks,

And round the hamlet fanes.
Through glowing orchards forth they peep
  Each from its nook of leaves,
And fearless there the lowly sleep,
  As the bird beneath their eaves.

The free, fair homes of England!
  Long, long, in hut and hall,
May hearts of native proof be reared
  To guard each hallowed wall!
And green forever be the groves,
  And bright the flowery sod,
Where first the child's glad spirit loves
  Its country and its God!

Nowadays, the line "The stately homes of England" recalls first of all Noël
Coward's tribute to an impoverished but ingenious aristocracy.
  A short biography of Felicia Dorothea Hemans is to be found on page 156.

The Young American

ALEXANDER H. EVERETT

Scion of a noble stock!
Hands of iron—hearts of oak—
Follow with unflinching tread
Where the noble fathers led.

Craft and subtle treachery,
Gallant youth! are not for thee:
Follow thou in word and deeds
Where the God within thee leads.

Honesty with steady eye,
Truth and pure simplicity,
Love that gently winneth hearts,
These shall be thy only arts—

Prudent in the council-train,
Dauntless on the battle-plain,
Ready at the country's need
For her glorious cause to bleed.

Where the dews of night distill
Upon Vernon's holy hill;
Where above it, gleaming far,
Freedom lights her guiding star—

Thither turn the steady eye,
Flashing with a purpose high;
Thither with devotion meet
Often turn the pilgrim feet.

Let thy noble motto be,
"GOD—the COUNTRY—LIBERTY!"
Planted on Religion's rock,
Thou shalt stand in every shock.

Laugh at danger, far or near;
Spurn at baseness—spurn at fear;
Still, with persevering might,
Speak the truth, and do the right.

So shall Peace, a charming guest,
Dove-like in thy bosom rest;
So shall Honor's steady blaze
Beam upon thy closing days.

Happy if celestial favor
Smile upon the high endeavor:
Happy if it be thy call
In the holy cause to fall.

ALEXANDER HILL EVERETT (1790–1847), born in Boston, Massachusetts, was a literary man and diplomat of some standing. He served as minister in Spain, where he appointed Washington Irving to the post of attaché to the Madrid legation; he published books and essays, translated Theocritus and Goethe, and was among the first Western scholars to study the Orient.

The Englishman

ELIZA COOK

There's a land bears a well-known name,
  Though it is but a little spot;
I say 'tis first on the scroll of Fame,
  And who shall say it is not?
Of the deathless ones who shine and live
  In Arms, in Arts, or Song;
The brightest the whole wide world can give,
  To that little land belong.
'Tis the star of earth, deny it who can,
The island home of an Englishman.

There's a flag that waves o'er every sea,
  No matter when or where;
And to treat that flag as aught but the free
  Is more than the strongest dare.
For the lion-spirits that tread the deck
  Have carried the palm of the brave;
And that flag *may* sink with a shot-torn wreck,
  But never float over a slave;
Its honour is stainless, deny it who can;
And this is the flag of an Englishman.

There's a heart that leaps with burning glow,
  The wronged and the weak to defend;
And it strikes as soon for a trampled foe,
  As it does for a soul-bound friend.
It nurtures a deep and honest love;
  It glows with faith and pride;
And yearns with the fondness of a dove,
  To the light of its own fireside.
'Tis a rich, rough gem, deny it who can;
And this is the heart of an Englishman.

The Briton may traverse the pole or the zone,
And boldly claim his right;
For he calls such a vast domain his own,
That the sun never sets on his might.
Let the haughty stranger seek to know
The place of his home and birth;
And a flush will pour from cheek to brow,
While he tells of his native earth.
For a glorious charter, deny it who can,
Is breathed in the words, "I'm an Englishman."

The sounding brass of patriotic verse tends to trumpet somewhat repetitively, and the examples collected here are only representative movements from the imperial symphony. Most are as uncomplicated and exclusive as Herman Charles Merivale's "Ready, Ay, Ready":

Old England's sons are English yet,
Old England's hearts are strong;
And still she wears her coronet
Aflame with sword and song.
As in their pride our fathers died,
If need be, so die we;
So wield we still, gainsay who will,
The sceptre of the sea.
England, stand fast; let hand and heart be steady;
Be thy first word thy last: Ready, ay, ready!

American fanfares carry a similar strain. In "England's Message to America," however, Martin Farquhar Tupper extends a friendly, if condescending, hand:

Ho! brother, I'm a Britisher, a chip of heart of oak,
That wouldn't warp, or swerve, or stir, from what I thought or spoke;
And you—a blunt and honest man, straightforward, kind, and true—
I tell you, Brother Jonathan, that you're a Briton too.

The young nation appeared properly grateful. At least one American bard, Washington Alston, acknowledged the debt in "America to Great Britain." His poem begins:

All hail! thou noble land,
Our father's native soil!

and concludes with a feeling of fine magnanimity:

> While the manners, while the arts,
>   That mold a nation's soul,
> Still cling around our hearts,
>   Between let ocean roll,
> Our joint communion breaking with the sun:
>   Yet, still, from either beach
>   The voice of blood shall reach,
>   More audible than speech,
>   "We are one!"

Now, a century later, where debts are concerned the emphasis is strongly in the other direction. There seems, however, to be no recent poetry upon the subject.

A note on Eliza Cook may be found on page 184.

Columbus

JOAQUIN MILLER

Behind him lay the gray Azores,
  Behind the Gates of Hercules;
Before him not the ghost of shores,
  Before him only shoreless seas.
The good mate said: "Now must we pray,
  For lo! the very stars are gone.
Brave Admiral, speak, what shall I say?"
  "Why, say, 'Sail on! sail on! and on!'"

"My men grow mutinous day by day;
  My men grow ghastly wan and weak."
The stout mate thought of home: a spray
  Of salt wave washed his swarthy cheek.
"What shall I say, brave Admiral, say,
  If we sight naught but seas at dawn?"
"Why, you shall say at break of day,
  'Sail on! sail on! sail on! and on!'"

They sailed and sailed, as winds might blow,
  Until at last the blanched mate said:
"Why, now not even God would know
  Should I and all my men fall dead.
These very winds forget their way,
  For God from these dread seas is gone.
Now speak, brave Admiral, speak and say"—
  He said: "Sail on! sail on! and on!"

They sailed. They sailed. Then spake the mate:
  "This mad sea shows his teeth tonight.
He curls his lip, he lies in wait,
  With lifted teeth as if to bite!
Brave Admiral, say but one good word:
  What shall we do when hope is gone?"
The words leapt like a leaping sword:
  "Sail on! sail on! sail on! and on!"

Then, pale and worn, he kept his deck,
  And peered through darkness. Ah, that night
Of all dark nights! And then a speck—
  A light! A light! A light! A light!
It grew, a starlit flag unfurled!
  It grew to be Time's burst of dawn.
He gained a world; he gave that world
  Its grandest lesson: "On! sail on!"

"Joaquin Miller" is the pseudonym of C I N C I N N A T U S H I N E R
M I L L E R (1837–1913), who, when a boy of fifteen, joined the Oregon
Trail westward. He enjoyed a highly colored youth in the goldfields and
among the Indians of the West Coast, but he became a lawyer, then a journalist. He wrote a defence of Joaquin Murrieta, the Mexican bandit, from
whom he took his pen-name. A visit to Europe was a wild success: his un-
conventional behavior and dress swept fashionable London off its feet, and
he even became betrothed to (but did not marry) a baronet's daughter. His
many, somewhat extravagant poems gave him a reputation as spokesman for
the West, but it is for "Columbus" that he is best known in American schools.

The American Flag

JOSEPH RODMAN DRAKE

When Freedom from her mountain height
   Unfurled her standard to the air,
She tore the azure robe of night,
   And set the stars of glory there.
She mingled with its gorgeous dyes
The milky baldric of the skies,
And striped its pure celestial white
With streakings of the morning light;
Then from his mansion in the sun
She called her eagle bearer down.
And gave into his mighty hand
The symbol of her chosen land.

Majestic monarch of the cloud,
   Who rear'st aloft thy regal form,
To hear the tempest trumpings loud
And see the lightning lances driven,
   When strive the warriors of the storm,
And rolls the thunder-drum of heaven,
Child of the sun! to thee 't is given
   To guard the banner of the free,
To hover in the sulphur smoke,
To ward away the battle stroke,
And bid its blendings shine afar,
Like rainbows on the cloud of war,
   The harbingers of victory!

Flag of the brave! thy folds shall fly,
The sign of hope and triumph high,
When speaks the signal trumpet tone,
And the long line comes gleaming on.
Ere yet the life-blood, warm and wet,
Has dimmed the glistening bayonet,
Each soldier eye shall brightly turn

To where thy sky-born glories burn,
And, as his springing steps advance,
Catch war and vengeance from the glance.

And when the cannon-mouthings loud
Heave in wild wreaths the battle shroud,
And gory sabres rise and fall
Like shoots of flame on midnight's pall,
    Then shall thy meteor glances glow,
And cowering foes shall shrink beneath
    Each gallant arm that strikes below
That lovely messenger of death.

Flag of the seas! on ocean wave
Thy stars shall glitter o'er the brave;
When death, careering on the gale,
Sweeps darkly round the bellied sail,
And frighted waves rush wildly back
Before the broadside's reeling rack,
Each dying wanderer of the sea
Shall look at once to heaven and thee,
And smile to see thy splendors fly
In triumph o'er his closing eye.

Flag of the free heart's hope and home!
    By angel hands to valour given;
Thy stars have lit the welkin dome,
    And all thy hues were born in heaven.
Forever float that standard sheet!
    Where breathes the foe but falls before us,
With Freedom's soil beneath our feet,
    And Freedom's banner streaming o'er us.

Perhaps the most stirring and defiant work ever penned, with its allegorical personages and grand poetical diction, this classic has been intoned by generations of American school children. It was first published in the New York *Evening Post* in 1819. The last four lines are said to have been added by Fitz-Greene Halleck.

JOSEPH RODMAN DRAKE (1795-1820) is known as "the American Keats." Orphaned when still very young, he had to fight against poverty and, like Keats, studied medicine. An advantageous marriage with the daughter of a marine architect enabled him to visit Europe. In association with his friend Halleck, he composed a series of witty poems, "The Croakers," and he also wrote "The Culprit Fay," a fairy poem set on the Hudson River, but his promise was tragically cut short by consumption.

Barbara Frietchie

JOHN GREENLEAF WHITTIER

Up from the meadows rich with corn,
Clear in the cool September morn,

The clustered spires of Frederick stand
Green-walled by the hills of Maryland.

Round and about them orchards sweep,
Apple and peach tree fruited deep,

Fair as a garden of the Lord
To the eyes of the famished rebel horde;

On that pleasant morn of the early fall
When Lee marched over the mountain wall,

Over the mountains winding down,
Horse and foot into Frederick town.

Forty flags with their silver stars,
Forty flags with their crimson bars,

Flapped in the morning wind: the sun
Of noon looked down, and saw not one.

Up rose old Barbara Frietchie then,
Bowed with her fourscore years and ten;

Bravest of all in Frederick town,
She took up the flag the men hauled down;

In her attic window the staff she set,
To show that one heart was loyal yet.

Up the street came the rebel tread,
Stonewall Jackson riding ahead.

Under his slouched hat left and right
He glanced; the old flag met his sight.

"Halt!"—the dust-brown ranks stood fast.
"Fire!"—out blazed the rifle-blast.

It shivered the window, pane and sash;
It rent the banner with seam and gash.

Quick, as it fell, from the broken staff
Dame Barbara snatched the silken scarf;

She leaned far out on the window-sill,
And shook it forth with a royal will.

"Shoot, if you must, this old grey head,
But spare your country's flag!" she said.

A shade of sadness, a blush of shame,
Over the face of the leader came;

The nobler nature within him stirred
To life at that woman's deed and word:

"Who touches a hair of yon grey head
Dies like a dog! March on!" he said.

All day long through Frederick street
Sounded the tread of marching feet:

All day long that free flag tost
Over the heads of the rebel host.

Ever its torn folds rose and fell
On the loyal winds that loved it well;

And through the hill-gaps sunset light
Shone over it with a warm good-night.

It is sad to see another legend demolished: when "Stonewall" Jackson occupied Frederick in September 1862 it was not the ninety-six-year-old Mrs. Frietchie who displayed the Union flag in defiance of the Confederate troops, but the "comparatively young" Mrs. Mary A. Quantrell. The officers raised their hats as they marched by, "To you, madam, and not to your flag!" A week later, when Federal soldiers passed through the town, Barbara Frietchie followed Mary Quantrell's example.

On page 243 there is a biographical note on J. G. Whittier.

The Private of the Buffs

Last night, among his fellow roughs
   He jested, quaffed, and swore;
A drunken private of the Buffs,
   Who never looked before.
Today, beneath the foeman's frown,
   He stands in Elgin's place,
Ambassador from Britain's crown,
   And type of all her race.

Poor, reckless, rude, low-born, untaught,
   Bewildered, and alone,
A heart, with English instinct fraught,
   He yet can call his own.
Ay, tear his body limb from limb,
   Bring cord, or axe, or flame,
He only knows, that not through *him*
   Shall England come to shame.

For Kentish hop-fields round him seem'd,
   Like dreams, to come and go;
Bright leagues of cherry-blossom gleam'd,
   One sheet of living snow;
The smoke, above his father's door,
   In gray soft eddyings hung;
Must he then watch it rise no more,
   Doom'd by himself, so young?

Yes, honour calls! with strength like steel
   He puts the vision by.
Let dusky Indians whine and kneel,
   An English lad must die.
And thus, with eyes that would not shrink,
   With knee to man unbent,
Unfaltering on its dreadful brink,
   To his red grave he went.

Vain, mightiest fleets of iron framed;
Vain, those all-shattering guns;
Unless proud England keep, untamed,
The strong heart of her sons.
So let his name through Europe ring—
A man of mean estate,
Who died, as firm as Sparta's king,
Because his soul was great.

To this fine tribute to English scorn for lesser breeds, the poet appended this extract from *The Times* of 1860: "Some Sikhs and a private of the Buffs (the East Kent Regiment), having remained behind with the grog-carts, fell into the hands of the Chinese. On the next morning they were brought before the authorities and commanded to perform the *kotow*. The Sikhs obeyed; but Moyse, the English soldier, declaring that he would not prostrate himself before any Chinaman alive, was immediately knocked on the head, and his body thrown on a dunghill." The Elgin of line 6 is the eighth Lord Elgin, ambassador to China at the time of the war between that country and Britain.

The spirit of Private Moyse lives on: in May 1967, Red Guards tried to compel Peter Hewitt, Officer of the Peking Office of the British Chargé d'Affaires, to bow to a portrait of Mao Tse-tung, Chairman of the Chinese Communist Party. He refused, and, luckier than Moyse, was set free unharmed.

SIR FRANCIS HASTINGS CHARLES DOYLE, second baronet (1810–1888), came of military stock and most of his male relatives seem to have been colonels at the very least. He went to Eton and Oxford, where, the *D.N.B.* reports, "his intercourse with Gladstone became very intimate." Called to the bar, he later received the appointment of receiver-general of customs. To compensate perhaps for remaining a civilian, he wrote stirring military ballads: "The Red Thread of Honour" was translated into Pushtoo and "became a favourite among the villagers on the north-western frontier of India." To crown his literary ambitions, he was elected professor of poetry at Oxford in 1867.

"Rake" Windermere
LEONARD POUNDS

Disgrace he'd brought on an ancient name;
a smirch on an honoured crest.
He'd blotted the page of glorious fame
that his family once possessed.
Eton he'd left beneath a cloud,
and left in the greatest haste.
He'd proceeded whilst there in revels loud,
life's choicest hours to waste.
Sent down from Oxford next was he,
the result of orgies wild.
He'd filled the cup of vice with glee,
and a noble stock defiled.
A nickname he'd earned by his acts of shame,
'mong comrades of many a bout.
From the broken shell of his own true name
"Rake" Windermere stepped out.
As a fitting end to an angry scene,
he had quitted the family home.
With a tearless eye and a smile serene,
he had started the world to roam.
Still lower he'd sunk than e'er before,
and never a vice he'd shun,
till even his roystering friends of yore
forsook him one by one.
He'd drifted at length with a tourist band
to the land of the war-like Moor.
And there on the dreary desert sand
had disaster attacked the tour.
Approached by a tribe of bandit brand,
the party had turned and fled;
but first a shot, fired by some foolish hand,
had pierced a Moorish head.
Besieged for a week on a mound of stone,
and with water getting low,

the bandit chief had appeared alone
and said: "Thou art free to go,
if thou first deliverest up to me
of thy number any one,
so that True Believer's blood may be
avenged ere tomorrow's sun."
Each looked at each as he rode away.
Grim silence reigned supreme.
The sun went down, and the moon held sway,
flooding all with silver stream.
Then a muffled form crept down the mound,
with a wistful glance about.
Then with a head erect, but without a sound,
"Rake" Windermere stepped out.

"Rake" Windermere was obviously an elder cousin of "Beau" Geste, who, as
P. C. Wren recorded, also redeemed his folly on the burning sands of the
Sahara.

Like "The Green Eye of the Yellow God," this is a Musical Monologue,
originally published by Reynolds in 1914 with music by Herbert Townsend.

Death-Doomed

WILL CARLETON

They're taking me to the gallows, mother—they mean to hang me high;
They're going to gather round me there, and watch me till I die;
All earthly joy has vanished now, and gone each mortal hope—
They'll draw a cap across my eyes, and round my neck a rope;
The crazy mob will shout and groan—the priest will read a prayer,
The drop will fall beneath my feet and leave me in the air.
They think I murdered Allen Bayne; for so the judge has said,
And they'll hang me to the gallows, mother—hang me till I'm dead!

The grass that grows in yonder meadow, the lambs that skip and play,
The pebbled brook behind the orchard, that laughs upon its way,
The flowers that bloom in the dear old garden, the birds that sing and fly,
Are clear and pure of human blood—and, mother, so am I!
My father's grave on yonder hill—his name without a stain—
I ne'er had malice in my heart, or murdered Allen Bayne!
But twelve good men have found me guilty, for so the judge has said,
And they'll hang me to the gallows, mother—hang me till I'm dead!

The air is fresh and bracing, mother; the sun shines bright and high;
It is a pleasant day to live—a gloomy one to die!
It is a bright and glorious day the joys of earth to grasp—
It is a sad and wretched one to strangle, choke, and gasp!
But let them damp my lofty spirit, or cow me if they can,
They send me like a rogue to death—I'll meet it like a man;
For I never murdered Allen Bayne! but so the judge has said,
And they'll hang me to the gallows, mother—hang me till I'm dead!

Poor little sister 'Bell will weep, and kiss me as I lie!
But kiss her twice and thrice for me, and tell her not to cry;
Tell her to weave a bright, gay garland, and crown me as of yore,
Then plant a lily on my grave, and think of me no more,
And tell that maiden whose love I sought, that I was faithful yet;
But I must lie in a felon's grave, and she had best forget.
My memory is stained forever; for so the judge has said,
And they'll hang me to the gallows, mother—hang me till I'm dead!

Lay me not down by my father's side; for once, I mind, he said
No child that had stained his spotless name should share his mortal bed.
Old friends would look beyond his grave, to my dishonored one,
And hide the virtues of the sire behind the recreant son.
And I can fancy, if there my corse its fettered limbs should lay,
His frowning skull and crumbling bones would shrink from me away;
But I swear to God I'm innocent, and never blood have shed!
And they'll hang me to the gallows, mother—hang me till I'm dead!

Lay me in my coffin, mother, as you've sometimes seen me rest:
One of my arms beneath my head, the other on my breast.
Place my Bible upon my heart—nay, mother, do not weep—
And kiss me as in happier days you kissed me when asleep.
And for the rest—for form or rite—but little do I reck;
But cover up that cursèd stain—*the black mark on my neck!*
And pray to God for His great mercy on my devoted head;
For they'll hang me to the gallows, mother—hang me till I'm dead!

But hark! I hear a mighty murmur among the jostling crowd!
A cry!—a shout!—a roar of voices!—it echoes long and loud!
There dashes a horseman with foaming steed and tightly gathered rein;
He sits erect!—he waves his hand!—good heaven! 'tis Allen Bayne!
The lost is found, the dead alive, my safety is achieved!
For he waves his hand again, and shouts, "The prisoner is reprieved!"
Now, mother, praise the God you love, and raise your drooping head;
For the murderous gallows, black and grim, is cheated of its dead!

Phew! Will Carleton's recitation must have been doubly effective when the action of law in the West was known to be swift and draconian. This piece belongs, of course, to the same family as "Curfew Must Not Ring Tonight" and innumerable Hollywood movies. The outcome was not always so happy: one popular parlour ballad was entitled "The Pardon Came Too Late."

A note on the author is to be found on page 190.

England's Heart

MARTIN FARQUHAR TUPPER

England's heart! Oh never fear
The sturdy good old stock;
Nothing's false or hollow here,
But solid as a rock:
England's heart is sound enough,
And safe in its old place,
Honest, loyal, blithe and bluff,
And open as her face!

England's heart! With beating
    nerves
It rallies for the throne,—
And, like Luther, well preserves
The knee for God alone!
England's heart is sound enough,
Unshaken and serene,
Like her oak-trees, true and tough,
And old—but glad and green!

England's heart! All Europe hurl'd
To ruin, strife and death,
Sees yet one Zoar in all the world
The Goshen of the earth!
England's heart is sound enough,—
And—though the skies be dark,
Though winds be loud, and waves
    be rough—
Safe as Noah's ark!

England's heart!—ay, God be
    praised,
That thus in patriot pride,
An English cheer can yet be raised
Above the stormy tide:
Safe enough and sound enough,
It thrills the heart to feel
A man's a bit of English stuff,
True from head to heel!

MARTIN FARQUHAR TUPPER (1810–1889), the son of a
medical man, beat Gladstone into second place for Dr. Burton's theological
essay prize at Oxford. Called to the Bar, he never practised, as he had also been
called to the service of the Muses. A million copies of his *Proverbial Philosophy*
were sold in America, but only a quarter of that number in his native Britain.
This collection of metrical effusions has a unique style, the flavour of which can
be conveyed only by quotation. Here is an extract from "Of Marriage":

When thou choosest a wife, think not only of thyself,
But of those God may give thee of her, that they reproach thee not for thy
    being:
See that he hath given her health, lest thou lose her early and weep:
See that she springeth of a wholesome stock, that thy little ones perish not
    before thee:

For many a fair skin hath covered a mining disease,
And many a laughing cheek been bright with a glare of madness.

Unhappily, this sincere and worthy author, despite Fellowship of the Royal Society, despite a gold medal from the King of Prussia, despite a D.C.L. from Oxford, despite the encouragement given to the volunteer movement by his *War Ballads* and *Rifle Ballads,* despite a public testimonial, despite tokens of admiration from Her Majesty the Queen, was treated with scant respect by the press, to a degree amounting, he considered, to persecution. Perhaps the critics were only paying him back in his own coin for what he said about them in "Of Zoilism" in *Proverbial Philosophy:*

Pens are poignards in their hands; an inkstand the fountain of detraction.
The critic, taking refuge in reviling, as an idler method than reviewing,
Filleth the public ear, for gain, with flashy slanders.
But the crowds that laugh and listen, while they like such humours,
Only despise that cankerous tongue, and take the victim's part: . . .
But our unjust judges in literature hunt down men, not books,
Filled with bitter personality, sarcastic and foulspoken.

The Press

AUTHOR UNKNOWN

The Press—the Press—the glorious Press,
    It makes the nations free?
Before it tyrants prostrate fall
    And proud oppressors flee!
In what a state of wretchedness
    Without it should we be;
And can we then too highly prize
    The source of liberty?

The Press—the Press—the glorious Press,
    It dissipates our gloom!
And sheds a ray of happiness
    O'er victims of the tomb:
See, darkness from his ebon throne
    Has fled to realms of night,
And o'er the world is now diffused
    A flood of heavenly light.

The Press—the Press—the glorious Press,
    What thanks are due to those,
Who all attempts to quench its beams,
    Triumphantly oppose;
To them belongs the wreathe of fame!
    The garland of renown!
The honour of a deathless name!
    A never-fading crown!

The Press—the Press—the glorious Press,
    Blessings by it abound!
It changes man, and makes him great,
    Wherever man is found.
The idols of the heathen land,
    And superstition's sway
And sceptres from the tyrant's hand,
    Through it are cast away.

The Press—the Press—the glorious Press,
 It makes the world anew;
And it will bring millennium on,
 And give us then to view
The end of war, and lasting peace,
 When sheathed shall be the sword;
And men shall call this hampered earth
 The "Garden of the Lord."

The noble profession of journalism as seen by nineteenth-century bards seems very different from Pope's Grub Street. This anonymous piece is typical of a massed poetical chorus. G. W. Cutter sang:

Soul of the world! the Press! the Press,
 What wonders hast thou wrought?
Thou rainbow realm of mental bliss;
 Thou starry sky of thought!

and Allan Davenport asked:

What greater gift to man could genius give?
What greater favour could mankind receive?

The answer, of course, is the daily newspaper; and J. C. Prince, who introduces young Genius discovering iron ore and moulding it into an engine that he christens the Press, concludes in a fine flush of enthusiasm:

They were made to exhort us, to teach us, to bless,
Those invincible brothers, the Pen and the Press.

The Good Time Coming

CHARLES MACKAY

There's a good time coming, boys,
　A good time coming;
We may not live to see the day,
But earth shall glisten in the ray
　Of the good time coming.
Cannon-balls may aid the truth,
　But thought's a weapon stronger;
We'll win a battle by its aid—
　Wait a little longer.

There's a good time coming, boys,
　A good time coming;
The pen shall supersede the sword,
And right, not might, shall be the lord,
　In the good time coming.
Worth, not birth, shall rule mankind,
　And be acknowledged stronger;
The proper impulse has been given—
　Wait a little longer.

There's a good time coming, boys,
　A good time coming;
War in all men's eyes shall be
A monster of iniquity
　In the good time coming.
Nations shall not quarrel then,
　To prove which is the stronger,
Nor slaughter men for glory's sake—
　Wait a little longer.

There's a good time coming, boys,
　A good time coming.
Hateful rivalries of creed
Shall not make their martyrs bleed

In the good time coming.
Religion shall be shorn of pride,
    And flourish all the stronger:
And Charity shall trim her lamp—
    Wait a little longer.

There's a good time coming, boys,
    A good time coming.
And a poor man's family,
Shall not be his misery
    In the good time coming;
Every child shall be a help,
    To make his right arm stronger;
The happier he, the more he has—
    Wait a little longer.

There's a good time coming, boys,
    A good time coming:
Little children shall not toil,
Under, or above, the soil,
    In the good time coming.
But shall play in healthful fields
    Till limbs and mind grow stronger;
And every one shall read and write—
    Wait a little longer.

There's a good time coming, boys,
    A good time coming:
The people shall be temperate,
And shall love instead of hate,
    In the good time coming.
They shall use, and not abuse,
    And make all virtue stronger;
The reformation has begun—
    Wait a little longer.

There's a good time coming, boys,
    A good time coming:

Let us aid it all we can,
Every woman, every man,
The good time coming.
Smallest helps, if rightly given,
Make the impulse stronger;
'Twill be strong enough one day,
Wait a little longer.

This brave and very touching work confirms, in concluding this anthology, the unshakeable nineteenth-century faith in the benign workings of Providence, in the certainty of Progress. The prophecies of the fifth and sixth stanzas have largely come to pass in America and Britain; we must continue to wait for the rest, although the Meritocracy promised in the second stanza is almost upon us.

CHARLES MACKAY, LL.D. (1814–1889), was born in Perth and educated at the Caledonian Asylum in London and a school in Brussels. After posts as secretary and tutor, he worked on various periodicals in Scotland, moving to the *Illustrated London News*, of which he became editor, and later reported the American Civil War for *The Times*. Towards the end of his life he developed an eccentric passion for the study of Celtic philology. From his youth he composed lively songs, "The Good Time Coming" having a circulation of nearly half a million, and others such as "Cheer, Boys, Cheer" and "There's a Land, a dear Land" becoming almost as popular. He edited *A Thousand and One Gems of English Poetry*, including (at his publisher's insistence, he hastened to point out) twelve by Charles Mackay.

Index

Index

of poets, titles, and first lines

Where the title is the same as the first line of a poem, only the former is included. A page number in italics indicates an excerpt in the Preface or in the Notes.

[*321*]